MRP II
Standard System

MRP II
Standard System

A Handbook for Manufacturing Software Survival

Darryl V. Landvater
and Christopher D. Gray

THE OLIVER WIGHT COMPANIES

Oliver Wight Publications, Inc.
5 Oliver Wight Drive
Essex Junction, VT 05452

Library of Congress Catalog Card Number: 88-050485

Copyright © 1989 by Oliver Wight Publications, Inc.

ISBN: 0-939246-12-0

Manufactured in the United States of America
by the Maple-Vail Book Manufacturing Group.

3 4 5 6 7 8 9 10

Contents

History of the Standard System and Acknowledgments   *ix*
Structure and Limitations to the Standard System   *xiii*
How to Use This Book and the Accompanying Workbook   *xix*

PART I
INTRODUCTION   1

Chapter 1   *Standard System Overview*   *3*

Chapter 2   *Basic Architectural Issues*   *20*

PART II
MANAGEMENT'S HANDLE ON THE BUSINESS   25

Chapter 3   *Sales and Operations Planning*   *27*

Chapter 4   *Master Production Scheduling*   *38*

Chapter 5   *Demand Management*   *58*

PART III
MATERIAL REQUIREMENTS PLANNING   67

Chapter 6   *The Netting and Exception Checking Logic of MRP II*   *69*

Chapter 7   *Order Planning and Explosion*   *75*

Chapter 8   *Entry into the Planning Sequence for Processing*   *83*

Chapter 9   *Firm Planned Orders*   *86*

Chapter 10   *Pegging*   *89*

Chapter 11   *Human Engineering*   *92*

PART IV
SUBSYSTEMS TO MATERIAL REQUIREMENTS PLANNING   101

Chapter 12   *Bill of Material Subsystem*   *103*

Chapter 13   *Inventory Transaction Subsystem*   *111*

Chapter 14   *Scheduled Receipts Subsystem*   *119*

Chapter 15   *Firm Planned Order Subsystem*   *127*

PART V
EXECUTING THE MATERIAL PLAN   **131**

Chapter 16   *Routing Subsystem*   *133*

Chapter 17   *Shop Scheduling and Dispatching*   *136*

Chapter 18   *Vendor Scheduling and Related Purchasing Activities*   *144*

PART VI
CAPACITY PLANNING AND CONTROL   **151**

Chapter 19   *Capacity Requirements Planning*   *153*

Chapter 20   *Input/Output Control*   *162*

PART VII
DISTRIBUTION AND MULTIPLANT PLANNING   **167**

Chapter 21   *Distribution Resource Planning*   *169*

PART VIII
INTEGRATION WITH OTHER FUNCTIONS   **175**

Chapter 22   *Tool Planning and Control*   *177*

Chapter 23   *Financial Planning Interfaces*   *181*

Chapter 24   *Simulation*   *189*

Chapter 25   *Performance Measurements*   *192*

PART IX
DESIGN AIDS AND GENERAL SPECIFICATIONS   **199**

Chapter 26   *Master Production Scheduling Module*   *201*

Chapter 27   *Demand Management Module*   *211*

Chapter 28   *Material Requirements Planning*   *222*

Chapter 29   *Shop Scheduling and Dispatching Module*   *230*

Chapter 30   *Capacity Requirements Planning*   *237*

Chapter 31   *Input/Output Control*   *244*

Chapter 32   *Vendor Scheduling and Negotiation*   *247*

APPENDICES

Appendix 1   *Two-Level Master Production Scheduling*   *251*

Appendix 2   *Bucketless and Bucketed Systems*   *257*

Appendix 3	*Material Planning Logic That Does Not Make the Rescheduling Assumption*	*260*
Appendix 4	*Automatic Rescheduling*	*261*
Appendix 5	*Safety Stock and Safety Time*	*263*
Appendix 6	*Dynamic Ordering Quantities*	*267*
Appendix 7	*Offset Gross Requirements Dates*	*269*
Appendix 8	*Sequencing Items for Replanning*	*271*
Appendix 9	*Firm Planned Orders*	*273*
Appendix 10	*Full Pegging*	*275*
Appendix 11	*Vertical Versus Horizontal MRP Displays*	*276*
Appendix 12	*Report Summary*	*279*
Appendix 13	*Modular Bills of Material*	*300*
Appendix 14	*Low-Level Code Logic*	*302*
Appendix 15	*Disassembly, Sorting, and Chemical Processes*	*303*
Appendix 16	*Deleting Planned Orders at the Time of Order Release*	*311*
Appendix 17	*Alternative Method for Final Assembly Scheduling*	*313*
Appendix 18	*Updating Component Requirements in Firm Planned Order Maintenance*	*316*

History of the Standard System and Acknowledgments

HISTORY

In 1975, Manufacturing Software Systems (later Oliver Wight Software Research) was formed to produce a kind of "consumer reports" on manufacturing software, specifically MRP (Material Requirements Planning) and MRP II (Manufacturing Resource Planning) software. More and more clients were asking for help in reviewing software—either software that they developed themselves or software that they planned to get from a computer manufacturer or software house.

Even for someone who worked with manufacturing systems all the time, evaluating commercial software was a challenging assignment. Confusions in terminology made it difficult to communicate with the vendors effectively. After reviewing the software, there was the uneasy feeling that the client might run into some surprises that were not apparent.

Imagine the frustration the client companies felt. Most were getting into MRP for the first time, and consequently weren't well-equipped to do the evaluation themselves. In general, they found it expensive and time-consuming; many of the studies tended to be superficial comparisons that consume a great deal of time, money, and effort from their most talented people.

Those in the business of helping people implement and operate MRP and MRP II systems were in a position to help. We were able to do an evaluation in greater depth and from the vantage point of considerable experience. In addition, because of our experience with companies using MRP II effectively, we had already broken the learning curve on what needed to be part of a workable system.

The first thing we did was to define what a Standard System should be, in our opinion. Our opinions on this subject, of course, are based on working with more successful MRP II installations than any other consultants in this country. In fact, there is not a lot of room for opinion on what will work and what won't since this type of system must accurately model the realities of a manufacturing environment.

After defining a standard system, various packages were compared to it. Over the years, significant progress was made in developing software that had basic MRP functionality. Today, among the ten or fifteen most popular packages, there are few real functional differences. As the number of popular packages increased, the cost of maintaining off-the-shelf evaluations escalated, and therefore it became more sensible to handle software evaluations as part of a consulting approach. Today, that software research and software consulting is done by consultants in Oliver Wight Companies, although many clients do their own software evaluations.

Since 1975, we've kept the Standard System up-to-date to help people looking at newer software packages, considering upgrading their existing systems, and trying to eliminate the surprises in commercial MRP II software. It is still the best tool available for breaking the learning curve on MRP II software and helping to identify the major pitfalls in a system.

The Standard System has been rewritten four times since 1975. In 1979, it was rewritten twice—primarily for advances in master production scheduling approaches. In 1983, it was rewritten again for MRP II, with new material added on production planning (sales and operations planning), tooling, financial planning interfaces, simulation, and performance measurements. Each rewrite was based on our experience in working with actual companies, solving actual problems, and operating MRP II at high levels of performance.

The Basis for the Standard System

The new MRP II Standard System evolved out of the research for the original versions, a Just-in-Time conference sponsored by the Oliver Wight Companies in September 1985, subsequent visits to a number of companies with excellent control systems that were simultaneously pursuing Just-in-Time methods, and research on sales and operations planning methods that came from the development of a PC-based sales and operations planning system for some client companies in 1986 and 1987.

The MRP II Standard System is an excellent explanation of a complete and comprehensive software package for MRP II and the modifications needed to support Just-in-Time. It is a collection of functions that have emerged over the years as a result of implementing and running MRP II systems, both with and without Just-in-Time methods. These functions have come to be recognized as the ingredients of a working and successful MRP II system.

ACKNOWLEDGMENTS

We owe our thanks to many people for making the MRP II Standard System possible. In particular we'd like to remember Oliver Wight, whose inspiration, experience, and leadership made the first Standard System possible, and thank Walter Goddard, who has contributed both on technical matters and on methods of presentation from the first Standard System in 1976 through to this edition. Walter is one of the top professionals in his field and his contribution has been invaluable.

There are many others who have contributed, including the reviewers, John Dougherty, Dick Ling, Bill Sandras, Pete Skurla, Bob Stahl, and all of the Oliver Wight Associates. Also, perhaps most significant are the companies who've been the real-world laboratory for MRP and MRP II since 1961, and whose experiences defined the functions of the MRP II Standard System. Our thanks to all of them for sharing their experiences, and our best wishes for continued success.

Darryl Landvater
Williston, VT

Christopher Gray
Newfields, NH

Structure and Limitations to the Standard System

The Standard System is a simple set of functional specifications, as well as the explanation of the assumptions and the experience that lead to the need for these functions.

The Standard System has logical groupings of functions that include the following areas:

1. Sales and Operations Planning.

2. Demand Management.

3. Master Production Scheduling.

4. Material Requirements Planning.

5. Bill of Material Subsystem.

6. Inventory Transaction Subsystem.

7. Scheduled Receipts Subsystem.

8. Shop Floor Control.

9. Capacity Requirements Planning.

10. Input/Output Control.

11. Purchasing.

12. Distribution Resource Planning.

13. Tooling.

14. Financial Planning Interfaces.

15. Simulation.

16. Performance Measurement.

The explanation of the Standard System is organized in parts and chapters. Parts divide the Standard System into broad, logically organized groupings of systems or functions. Each part is divided into chapters, each of which describes a specific and narrow set of functionality. For example, Part II Management's Handle on the Business, covers the up front, high-level planning activities that are an essential part of an MRP II system. These activities—Sales and Operations Planning, Demand Management, Master Production Scheduling—are then described in detail in three separate chapters.

Areas and explanations that are technical, involved, or require a great deal of detail are handled in appendices. This is a way to keep the text of the Standard System as easy-to-read and well-paced as possible.

One part of the Standard System is reserved for a highly technical discussion of the systems and data processing effort required to develop specific software functions. Part IX, Design Aids and General Specifications, includes near-program level specifications for software modules, including:

1. Demand Management.

2. Master Production Scheduling.

3. Material Requirements Planning.

4. Shop Scheduling and Dispatching.

5. Capacity Requirements Planning.

6. Input/Output Control.

7. Purchasing.

CLEAR AND SIMPLE VERSUS CLOUDY AND COMPLEX

Although the Standard System is a complete set of functions, it is not an ideal system with all the possible functions that could exist. Instead, the Standard System describes the simplest set of tools needed to make MRP II work. The Standard System is simple because simple is what works, and it is comprehensive because it covers all the areas that are needed for MRP II.

The definition of what constitutes a standard system is not at all arbitrary. An MRP II system is a simulation of the logistics of a manufacturing company; it must faithfully simulate what actually happens on the factory floor, in purchasing, in distribution, and in the stockroom, or it will not work. The experience of implementing and operating effective systems demonstrates that the fundamentals of planning, scheduling, and coordinating all the different functions within a manufacturing business are the same from company to company. This experience confirms that a standard set of tools exists to solve these problems of planning and scheduling. These standard tools apply as well to a company making brassieres as it does to companies making jet engines.

So the MRP II Standard System explains the subject clearly and in simple terms. Sadly, computers, software, and data processing in general are often concealed by a smoke screen of technical jargon and a sea of acronyms. The emphasis needs to be in another area. Clearly what is needed is a simple explanation of this necessary technical part of an MRP II system. Such an explanation follows.

LIMITS TO THE STANDARD SYSTEM

When the Standard System was developed, the functions of the software were separated into several different categories. Some functions are required and must work properly to accurately simulate the logistics of manufacturing. Other functions are optional: MRP systems have been made to work without them. Still other functions are needed for specific industries (for example, pharmaceutical-lot traceability and military-contract accounting), as are other business systems like standard cost, general ledger, accounts payable, payroll, etc.

Some functions are mandatory for a system to be called MRP II. Some of the early "MRP" systems did not provide a rescheduling capability and consequently failed to accurately simulate the logistics of manufacturing. In practice, material in a manufacturing company is rescheduled, usually through an informal shortage list or hot list system. Any inventory system that does not include the capability to reschedule material cannot truly be considered MRP or MRP II since it will only function as an order launcher and will not replace the informal shortage list system. A rescheduling capability is mandatory in an MRP II system.

Other functions or characteristics of an MRP II system are optional. The system can be a periodic regeneration system or a net change type of system. Either one can be made to work. One has certain advantages from the user's point of view, but both are workable. This and other technical subjects will be covered later in more detail in the body of the Standard System.

Some additional functions may be needed for certain industries. For example, lot traceability, which is required by law for pharmaceutical companies, would not be necessary for a manufacturer of washing machines. Functions for specific industries do not change the fundamental logic of MRP II. MRP II simulates reality, and these optional functions extract information, reformat it, or report it in different forms. Since the optional functions are not needed for all companies, they are not included in the Standard System.

Interfacing business systems, like the software for general accounting, order entry, etc., present an interesting additional problem in defining the Standard System. For example, a good argument can be made that a cost system is an integral part of MRP II since cost information is needed for the financial planning interfaces. In addition, the standard cost for an item is based on certain assumptions regarding production volumes. These production volumes are part of an MRP II system. A similar argument can be made about a general ledger system. The general ledger system in manufacturing companies includes an inventory account. This inventory account should reflect the value of inventory in the stockroom and be recorded in MRP II.

Eventually, the question becomes, "What's not part of MRP II?" Almost every business system is logically part of MRP II or should be interfaced to the system. For the purposes of this explanation, the line had to be drawn somewhere. Consequently, *the explanation of the Standard System is limited to the planning and scheduling functions that form the core around which a complete MRP II system can be built. Without these planning and scheduling functions it is impossible to do MRP II.*

DESIGN PHILOSOPHIES

There are a number of features that are a part of a good software package, but which are not specific functions. These are the design philosophies that have been embodied in the software. A designer who does not understand these philosophies will produce a package with limitations or fundamental flaws. Evidence that a software package does not recognize these design philosophies should be taken as a warning that the software may have hidden flaws or limitations. The most important of these philosophies are the following:

Simulation of Reality

An MRP II system has only one purpose: to accurately simulate the realities of a manufacturing environment. A software package that does not attempt to accurately simulate reality will lose the primary objective of the system.

Consequently, the Standard System is not based on opinions of what "might work" or "should work." The only places where there can even be much opinion revolves around what people will accept. We have consistently emphasized people accountability in making a system work. This is where most systems, even those that are technically sound, too often fail.

Simplicity

All truly great things are simple, and MRP II systems are no exception. A software package needs a full set of functions. Any additional features in the system are both unnecessary and undesirable. They generally make the operation of the system overly complicated, and in doing so, destroy its native and inherent simplicity.

Responsibility

Systems do not make things happen, people do. Most things are accomplished because someone is directly responsible for a task or decision. A software package should be designed to support the responsibility requirements for the day-to-day operation of the system. It should not obscure, impede, or try to assume these responsibilities. The people using the system should have direct operating control over the things for which they will be held accountable. Doing something because the computer said to do it is a lame and unjustifiable excuse. A good software system should recognize the need to present what is happening to the people using the system. It should always provide the information for someone to explain why he or she has taken some kind of action and why that action makes sense.

Standardization

Standardization is general applicability. A system that adheres to the standards and conventions will be one that has fewer problems in implementation and operation. Standardization lays the groundwork for effective communications and problem solving. It allows the hard fought lessons of the past to be brought forward to today and into the future.

Noningenuity

People have the ingenuity to solve the day-to-day operational problems when given a statement of the problem and a clear cut directive to solve it. A good system will point out the problems without attempting to devise a solution. By the time the logic and parameters are designed into a system for solving the endless numbers of situations and occurrences, the system becomes too complicated and cumbersome. Even the designers are likely to wonder if the system will ever work. Instead, the system should allow the people using it to find a solution and then be able to implement the solution within the existing framework of the system.

What makes a package simple or complex? In whose eyes does a function provide for accountability or destroy it? Each issue can be seen as judgmental or subjective, and yet experience yields an objective basis for such determination. Each point in the Standard System describes, from the point of view of our experience, what is simple versus complex, what maintains accountability and what doesn't, and so on.

How to Use This Book and the Accompanying Workbook

IMPORTANCE OF MOVING QUICKLY THROUGH THE DESIGN PHASE

Many people believe that spending more time evaluating software pays off later by reducing the time needed for implementing the system. Sadly, the opposite seems to be true. The companies that spend the most time evaluating software seem to be the last ones to get the desired results. An extended search to find a perfect MRP software package tends to divert people from the real issues of MRP: management and people, transform what might have been a normal implementation into the installation of a series of computer modules (bills of material, inventory, scheduled receipts, etc.), and often produce a technically correct piece of software that never becomes a system. Rather than the effective management controls that they expected, companies who stretch out the search process tend to get a set of expensive computer programs that are never used effectively.

Furthermore, the return on investment from implementing an effective MRP II system is about $100,000 per month in a $60 million company. In other words, the cost of managing a company of this size without MRP II is about $100,000 per month. So a software search that extends beyond the time needed to make an informed decision adds $100,000 per month to the cost of the software.

Any time there is an extended delay in implementing MRP II, the likelihood increases that the system will never produce its full results. Experience suggests a correlation between extended implementation schedules and substandard results. So the emphasis needs to be on making an informed decision quickly, and moving into implementation without delay.

FUNCTIONAL EVALUATION OF SOFTWARE

The real issue in evaluating software functionality is to identify what must be done to the software to make it work as an MRP II system. This issue can be addressed effectively through a six-step evaluation process:

1. Clearly define the objectives. The objective of the software evaluation process is not to find the ''best'' software. The real objectives are:

A. To find a workable system and get the project team to feel ownership and accountability for making the system work.

B. To eliminate the surprises from the implementation. By evaluating the logic of the software, a company can identify the modifications required with sufficient time to prepare for them.

C. To effectively compare different packages with different functionality and significantly different prices.

D. To include a statement in the software contract that defines expectations regarding the software functionality.

For a thorough discussion of these issues, read *The Right Choice: A Complete Guide to Evaluating, Selecting, and Installing MRP II Software* by Christopher D. Gray, Oliver Wight Limited Publications.

2. Agree upon a standard for comparison. The MRP II Standard System is the core set of functions that must be present in a piece of software to be a generalized MRP II system. However, not all functions in the Standard System are required to run all types of businesses. For example, a company making products to stock will probably not need logic for two-level master scheduling (Chapter 4) or final assembly scheduling (Chapter 14). A company without distribution centers, branch warehouses, or interplant shipments shouldn't worry about whether the software includes Distribution Resource Planning (Chapter 21). In other words, the Standard System should be tailored to eliminate the points that are inappropriate for a particular type of business or industry.

Conversely, a company may be looking for software that goes beyond the scope of the Standard System or which must include functions that are specific to certain types of industries. For example, order entry is a vital function in any company, but is not included in the MRP II Standard System. Companies in the pharmaceutical business require lot traceability logic to satisfy the FDA. Defense contractors typically require specialized reporting to satisfy the accounting rules in the Federal Acquisition Regulations and Defense Acquisition Regulations. In such cases where additional functions are required to manage a particular type of business, those functions need to be identified and included in the standard being used for comparison. At least the same level of detail contained in the Standard System should be provided to describe the logic of these specialized functions.

The Workbook that accompanies the MRP II Standard System summarizes the key functions in a generalized MRP II system, and provides a structured and organized method for evaluating a piece of commercial software or an existing system. Over 270 individual points are contained in the workbook. These individual points should be tailored into a description of the functions needed to operate MRP II within a specific company. Some points can be eliminated. Others can be marked as "nice to have," but something that could be lived without. Additional worksheets should be prepared for any specialized functions that need to be part of the software.

3. Review documentation. The next phase is a review of the system documentation. The level of this documentation varies since many of the smaller software vendors have only limited documentation, while some of the larger vendors are able to supply well over 1,000 pages. In most cases, between 200 and 500 pages of documentation are used for each package. Normally this documentation is proprietary and is handled under a nondisclosure agreement.

The objective of the documentation review is to identify the following:

A. The functions of the system that work normally and along the lines of the explanation in the Standard System.

B. The capabilities that roughly correspond to functions included in the Standard System, but that seem to have logic problems.

C. System options that must be used in a particular way to operate MRP II in a normal manner.

D. Functions that are part of the software that are inconsistent with operating a Class A MRP II system and that shouldn't be used at all.

E. Functions that are missing from the system and that have to be added.

Notes describing the specific logic used in each feature are the primary output of the documentation review process. The worksheets from the MRP II Standard System Workbook can be used to provide a structured format for writing a description of each section of logic in the system. For many people it is also helpful to describe interrelationships between files, describe edit rules on transactions, and list major data elements used in the system. In addition, functions that are part of the system but don't work properly should be identified for discussion with the vendor. Global options in the system (for example, control file options) should also be identified.

Many people also find it helpful to make notes on the work sheets and to attach selected pages of documentation, sample transaction formats, and display or report formats from the documentation. Doing so makes it easy to reconstruct how the logic of the system works and why a particular question or concern has arisen.

For each function listed in the workbook, sections are provided to describe the logic of the software package as well as the analysis of the function and whether it works correctly. In cases where a function does not work properly, sections are provided to document the workarounds, or the modifications needed to correct the software.

The final result of this reading and note-taking process is a fairly detailed understanding of how the software is designed to operate, the potential complexity of the software, and possible problems that have to be resolved. Blank worksheets are evidence that major functions are either not part of the system or are going to be difficult to implement because of the lack of documentation.

4. Interview vendor. A one day (or in some cases two or more days) interview with the software vendor normally follows the documentation review process.

Usually there are two people from the vendor in this interview: one has management responsibility for the software, and the other is technically knowledgeable in the system.

The interview covers the contents of the software as it compares to the tailored Standard System. Each of the points in the Standard System is covered, and the notes from the documentation review are used to move the discussion along as quickly as possible. The notes and documentation assembled from the documentation review will assist in directing the conversation to those areas that are potential problems; in effect, they help verify those areas that work properly and zero-in on the needed changes or missing functions.

Some portion of the day should be reserved for a demonstration of the system. Such a demonstration should verify, at a high level, that the software actually exists, reveal the on-line functionality and human engineering of the system, and produce a level of comfort on the software.

In cases where functions do not work properly or where a function simply does not exist, there should be a discussion of the size of the effort to fix the problem, who has to make the change, and what the effect will be on the software warranty.

Users or potential users can work with the software supplier to define the changes and then schedule and track them. The Workbook includes sections for schedule dates and assignments of responsibility. In this way it serves as a scheduling and project management tool for keeping the software changes on schedule.

5. Review sample or test output. An important step following the vendor meeting is a sample or test output review. Although it is normally not possible to test every function of the software package, it is possible to verify some of the basic numbers and to understand which reports various individuals will be using (for example, how many reports display the following information to a planner: basic descriptive information, the time-phased display, pegging, supporting details to scheduled receipts and firm planned orders, and exception messages).

6. Seek comments from other users. In the final phase of evaluating the functionality of the software, a responsible buyer should contact some users of the system as a way to gain some assurance that the software works without problems. Most well-informed software purchasers make it a point to visit at least one user of the software package and to talk by phone with several more references. Generally, the software vendor should be expected to provide the names of the companies for the user reference.

Some suggested questions for the user reaction:

Stage of implementation. What software modules are being used, and for how long? The objective is to determine whether the functions in the software have been exercised.

Functionality. Do the functions explained in the system documentation and by the vendor work? The objective is to determine whether the system documentation and the vendor accurately understand and have accurately explained the functions in the system.

Bugs. Did the users of the system experience significant bugs in working with the system? Notice that the word "significant" is used here. Experience seems to indicate that all systems have bugs. A small bug that does not disrupt operations, however, is a different matter from one that halts progress and slows down the implementation.

Vendor support. How do the users of the system rate the support provided by the vendor?

Users. Do the people using the system like it? What features or changes would make them feel better about it?

Other. Are there any comments about the system that would be of interest to people considering the system, such as the documentation, maintenance, run time, and other important aspects.

PERIPHERAL ACTIVITIES

Some additional areas should also be covered in the software evaluation process:

1. An analysis of the cost/benefit relationships should be made. A judgment between a package with a limited set of functions at a low cost, and another package with a more complete set of functions, but at a higher cost, needs to be made.

2. An analysis of computer run and response times is required. A company purchasing software needs assurances that the software will actually handle the transaction activity and file sizes required for their product lines. The efficiencies of the software can be measured in benchmark tests, assessed by interviews with users of the software with similar volumes, or estimated through a mathematical model. In order to be most valid, the run and response time estimates should be done using the specific configuration of computer and the company's actual data files. However, in most instances this is impractical so that companies use one of the other methods.

3. An analysis of other interfacing business packages offered by the vendor may be required. One vendor might have interfacing applications that are a part of a larger system architecture. Another vendor, having no other packages, could create an interface problem between systems, or force a company to write the other application software themselves. It may make sense to evaluate these applications and any potential problems prior to making a major commitment to the MRP II software.

4. An analysis of the vendor's financial strength makes a lot of sense. Whether the vendor is likely to remain in the business of developing and marketing manufacturing software is an important question to a potential purchaser.

5. An assessment of the vendor's people who are responsible for helping a company implement the system should be part of the evaluation effort. In most cases, companies will want to review the Class A and Class B experience of the vendor's support people, as well as their industry-specific knowledge and technical expertise.

USE OF OUTSIDE RESOURCES IN SOFTWARE EVALUATION AND SELECTION

A qualified consultant can help move a company through the software evaluation and selection process quickly. Typical areas of assistance include:

1. Laying out a complete educational process to understand MRP II and how it will be applied within the company.

2. Understanding the MRP II software functions required to make the system work properly. Tailoring the standard to the proper functionality.

3. Identifying the software alternatives available, including new software packages and upgrading the existing system.

4. Evaluating one or more packages in detail against the MRP II Standard System.

The Oliver Wight Companies provide these software services. For more information, call 802/878-8161 or 800/343-0625.

PART I

Introduction

Chapter 1

Standard System Overview

UNIVERSAL MANUFACTURING EQUATION

Like double entry bookkeeping in accounting, a standard logic exists for planning, scheduling, controlling, and coordinating manufacturing activities. This standard logic is a simulation of the universal manufacturing equation: What are we going to make? What does it take to make it? What do we have? What do we have to get? These are questions that have to be answered by any manufacturing organization, regardless of size, product, engineering content, or manufacturing process.

A scheduling system must answer the question, "What do we really need and when?" by projecting the needs for material, capacity, cash, storage space, engineering time, etc., based on the company's business and production plans. The Standard System shown in Figure 1 includes functions for:

• Business Planning.

• Sales and Operations Planning.

• Master Production Scheduling.

• Material Requirements Planning.

• Capacity Requirements Planning.

• Executing the Capacity Plan.

• Executing the Material Plan.

• Feedback.

Business planning defines the business mission of the company; its markets, profit objectives, and financial resources. It states, in dollars, what the company expects to sell, what it plans to produce, the amount of money that will be invested in research and development, and the amount of profit that it plans.

The sales and operations plan states (typically in units by product family) how

Figure 1
MRPII: Manufacturing Resource Planning
"Closed Loop System"

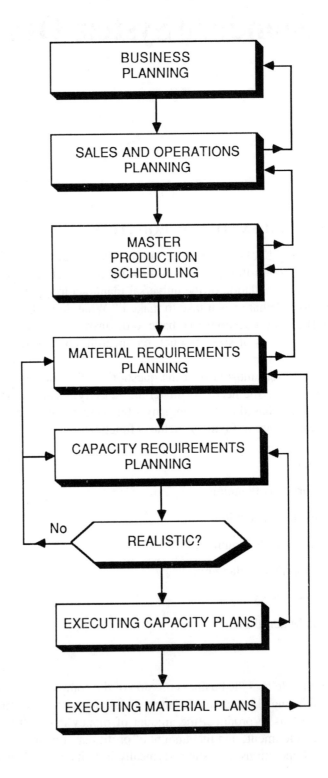

the business plan will be achieved. The sales plan states planned rates of sales; the production plan states planned rates of output. These planned rates are typically by major product family, and have the effect of regulating all other schedules in the system.

The master production schedule is the statement of production for specific end items and product options. The master production schedules for items within a family of products is constrained by the production plan for the family: the total of the master production schedules must equal the production plan.

Material Requirements Planning breaks down the master production schedule into individual schedules for purchasing, fabricating, and assembling all component items. The individual schedules are sometimes called the priority plans for manufacturing and purchasing.

Capacity Requirements Planning translates MRP's schedules into capacity requirements for each work center, labor resource, tool, etc.

The execution systems for material planning and capacity planning provide the tools to control material and capacity. MRP plans priorities; shop sheduling and vendor scheduling control priorities. Capacity Requirements Planning plans capacities; input/output control controls capacities.

Feedback from vendors, planners, foremen, and others communicates problems in executing the plan, and provides the method for "closing the loop" on the system. Feedback is necessary when the plans cannot be executed and must be revised.

The Standard System description is a detailed and accurate explanation of these manufacturing logistics. An overview of the mechanics covered in the Standard System is provided below with permission from Oliver Wight Limited Publications.

THE MECHANICS OF MRP II

Section 1
The Closed Loop System

The logic of the closed loop MRP system is extremely simple. It's in every cookbook. The "bill of material" says, "Turkey stuffing takes one egg, seasoning, bread crumbs, etc." The routing says, "Put the egg and the seasoning in a blender." The blender is the work center. The master schedule is Thanksgiving.

But, in manufacturing, there is a lot more volume and a lot more change. There isn't just one product. There are many. The lead times aren't as short as going to the corner store. The work centers are busy rather than waiting for work—because some of them cost a third of a million dollars or more—and it simply is not wise economically to let them sit idle and to have excess capacity. In addition, the sales department will undoubtedly change the date of Thanksgiving several times before it actually arrives! And this isn't through perversity. This is because the customers want and need some things earlier or later.

The volume of activity in manufacturing is monumentally high; something is happening all the time. And change is the norm, not the exception.

But the point is that the *logic* of MRP is very straightforward indeed. Figure 2 shows the closed loop system.

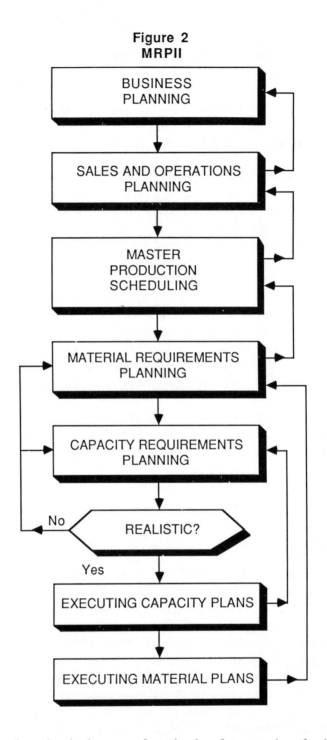

Figure 2
MRPII

The production plan is the *rate* of production for a product family typically expressed in units like, "We want to produce 1100 Model 30 pumps per week." The production plan is made by taking into account current inventory, deciding whether inventory needs to go up or down during the planning period, projecting the sales forecast, and determining the rate of production required to maintain, raise, or lower the inventory level. For a make-to-order product, as opposed to a

Figure 3
Sales and Operations Plan

Month Ending		Sales (thousands)	Production (thousands)	Inventory (thousands)
3/31	Plan			
	Actual			60
4/30	Plan	30	35	65
	Actual	25	36	71
6/30	Plan	30	35	75
	Actual			

make-to-stock product, the "order backlog" rather than the inventory is the starting point for the production plan.

Figure 3 shows a typical production plan. Figure 4 shows a business plan which is simply an extension of the production plan into dollars. The complete business plan in a manufacturing company will include research and development and other expenses not directly related to production and purchases. But the core of

Figure 4
Business Plan

Month Ending		Sales (thousands)	Production (thousands)	Inventory (thousands)
3/31	Plan			
	Actual			6000
4/30	Plan	3,000	3,500	6,500
	Actual	2,500	3,600	7,100
5/31	Plan	3,000	3,500	7,000
	Actual	3,800	3,200	6,500
6/30	Plan	3,000	3,500	7,500
	Actual	3,200	3,700	7,000
12/31	Plan	3,000	3,500	10,500
	Actual			

any business plan in a manufacturing enterprise is the production plan. With MRP II, the production plan and business plan are interdependent and, as the production plan is updated, it is extended into dollars to show it in the common denominator of business—money.

The closed loop MRP system then takes a master schedule (''What are we going to make?''), ''explodes'' this through the bill of material (''What does it take to make it?''), and compares this with the inventory on hand and on order (''What do we have?'') to determine material requirements (''What do we have to get?'').

This fundamental material requirements planning logic is shown in Figure 5. Figure 6 shows the bill of material. For this example, a small gasoline engine for a moped is the product being manufactured. The bill of material shown in Figure 6 is what's known as an ''indented bill of material.'' This simply means that the highest level items in the bill of material are shown farthest left. For example, the piston asssembly components are ''indented'' to the right to indicate that they go into that assembly. Therefore, in this example, they are at ''level 2.''

A bill of material ''in reverse'' is called a ''where-used'' list. It would say, for example, that the locating pins go into the crankcase half-left, which goes into the engine.

Figure 7 shows a master schedule for engines. In a make-to-stock company, the master schedule would be very similar, but it would take into account the inventory on hand.

Section 2
Material Requirements Planning

Figure 8 shows the material requirements plan for the crankcase half-left and also for the locator pin that goes into the crankcase half-left. The projected gross requirements come from the master schedule plus any service parts requirements. ''Scheduled receipts'' are the orders that are already in production or out with the vendors. The projected available balance takes the on-hand figure, subtracts requirements from it, and adds scheduled receipts to it. (In Figure 8, the starting on-hand balance is 120 for the crankcase half-left.) This calculation projects future inventory balances to indicate when material needs to be ordered or rescheduled.

The material on hand and on order subtracted from the gross requirements yields ''net requirements'' (sixty in week eight for the crankcase half-left in Figure 9). This is the amount that is actually needed to cover requirements. When the net requirements are converted to lot sizes and backed off over the lead time, they are called ''planned order releases.''

The ''planned order releases'' at one level in the product structure—in this case 200 ''crankcase half-left''—become the projected gross requirements at the lower level. The 200-unit planned order release in period four for the crankcase half-left becomes a projected gross requirement of 400 locator pins in period four since there are two locator pins per crankcase half-left.

Most MRP systems also include what is called ''pegged requirements.'' This is simply a way to trace where the requirements came from. For example, the

Figure 5
MRP Logic

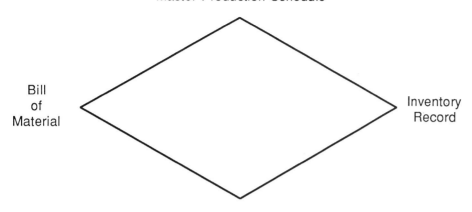

Master Production Schedule

Bill of Material

Inventory Record

Material Requirements Plan

Figure 6
Moped Engine Bill of Material

Part Number	
87502	Cylinder Head
94411	Crankshaft
94097	Piston Assembly
91776	Piston
84340	Wristpin
81111	Connecting Rod—Top Half
27418	Connecting Rod—Bottom Half
81743	Piston Rings Compression (2)
96652	Piston Ring Oil
20418	Bearing Halves (2)
59263	Lock Bolts (2)
43304	Crankcase Half Right
28079	Crankcase Half Left
80021	Locator Pins (2)

Figure 7
Master Production Schedule

ENGINES

	Week							
	1	2	3	4	5	6	7	8
Master Schedule	80	0	100	0	0	120	0	120
Actual Demand	40	40	30	30	30	40	40	20
Available to Promise	0	0	10	0	0	40	0	100

Figure 8
Material Requirements Plan

CRANKCASE HALF—LEFT

LEAD TIME = 4 WEEKS ORDER QUANTITY = 200	Week							
	1	2	3	4	5	6	7	8
Projected Gross Requirements		80	0	100	0	0	120	0	120
Scheduled Receipts				240					
Proj. Avail. Bal.	120	40	40	180	180	180	60	60	−60
Planned Order Release					200				

LOCATOR PIN (2 Per)

LEAD TIME = 4 WEEKS ORDER QUANTITY = 500	Week							
	1	2	3	4	5	6	7	8
Projected Gross Requirements					400				400*
Scheduled Receipts									
Proj. Avail. Bal.	430	430	430	430	30	30	30	30	−370
Planned Order Release					500				

*Requirements from another crankcase

pegged requirements for the locator pins would indicate that the 400 in period four came from the crankcase half-left and that the 400 in period eight came from another product. Pegged requirements show the quantity, the time period, and the higher level item where the requirements are coming from.

Figure 9 shows the same crankcase half as in Figure 8. Note, however, that now the scheduled receipt is shown in period four. This means that the due date on the shop order or the purchase order is week four. An MRP system would generate a reschedule message for the planner to move the scheduled receipt from week four into week three to cover the requirements in week three.

Note, also, that the fact that the scheduled receipt for the crankcase half needs to be rescheduled does not affect the requirements for locator pins. The locator pins have already been released into production for the crankcase halves that are on order. The "requirements" for locator pins are for planned orders that have *not* been released yet.

The bill of material is the instrument for converting planned order releases at one level into projected gross requirements at a lower level. The bill of material for the crankcase half-left, for example, would show that two locator pins per crankcase half were required.

Figure 9
MRP—Rescheduling

CRANKCASE HALF—LEFT

LEAD TIME = 4 WEEKS ORDER QUANTITY = 200	Week							
	1	2	3	4	5	6	7	8
Projected Gross Requirements		80	0	100	0	0	120	0	120
Scheduled Receipts					240				
Proj. Avail. Bal.	120	40	40	−60	180	180	60	60	−60
Planned Order Release					200				

LOCATOR PIN (2 Per)

LEAD TIME = 4 WEEKS ORDER QUANTITY = 500	Week							
	1	2	3	4	5	6	7	8
Projected Gross Requirements					400				400*
Scheduled Receipts									
Proj. Avail. Bal.	430	430	430	430	30	30	30	30	−370
Planned Order Release					500				

*Requirements from another crankcase

Section 3
Capacity Planning and Scheduling

Capacity planning for the manufacturing facility follows the same general logic as the material requirements planning shown in Figure 5. Figure 10 shows this capacity requirements planning logic. The remaining operations on released shop orders and all of the operations on planned order releases are "exploded" through the routings (like bills of material for operations) and posted against the work centers (like an inventory of capacities). The result is a capacity requirements plan in standard hours by work center showing the number of standard hours required to meet the material requirements plan. This capacity requirements plan shows the capacity that will be required to execute the master schedule, and consequently, the production plan.

It's important to note that everything in a closed loop MRP system is in "lock step." If the capacity to meet the material requirements plan can't be obtained either through a company's own manufacturing facilities, subcontracting, or purchasing material on the outside, obviously the master schedule will have to be

Figure 10
CRP Logic

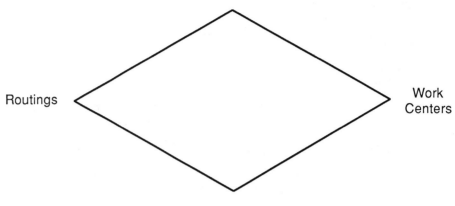

Shop Orders/Planned Order Releases

Routings

Work Centers

Capacity Requirements Plan

changed. But that is the last resort. The objective is to make the master schedule happen.

Operations scheduling involves assigning individual schedule dates to the operations on a shop order using scheduling rules. Scheduling rules would typically be similar to these:

1. Allow two days for inspection. (This is a matter of judgment.)

2. Round the standard hours up to the nearest day.

3. Allow X days for queue time.

4. Release work to stockroom one week prior to first operation.

Scheduling with a regular calendar is extremely awkward. For example, if a job was to be completed on August 31 (see Figure 11) and the last operation—inspection—was scheduled to take two days, the previous operation would have to be completed on August 27, not August 29 (Sunday) or August 28 (Saturday). The scheduler would have to reference the calendar continuously to avoid scheduling work on weekends, holidays, during plant vacation shutdown week, etc. Figure 12 shows a "shop calendar" where only the working days are numbered. This allows the scheduler to do simple arithmetic like "subtract two days from day 412," thus the previous operation is to be completed on day 410. Shop calendars are in very common use in manufacturing companies today, but they do have drawbacks. People don't relate to these calendars as easily as they do to a regular calendar. And, of course, they are awkward in dealing with customers who don't use the same shop calendar. Therefore, the shop calendar dates must, once again, be translated back to regular calendar dates. There is a simple solution to this problem with today's computers. A shop calendar can be put in the computer and the computer can do the scheduling using the shop calendar, but print

Figure 11
Calendar

August						
S	M	T	W	T	F	S
1	2	3	4	5	6	7
8	9	10	11	12	13	14
15	16	17	18	19	20	21
22	23	24	25	26	27	28
29	30	31				

Figure 12
Calendar

August						
S	M	T	W	T	F	S
1	2 391	3 392	4 393	5 394	6 395	7
8	9 396	10 397	11 398	12 399	13 400	14
15	16 401	17 402	18 403	19 404	20 405	21
22	23 406	24 407	25 408	26 409	27 410	28
29	30 411	31 412				

the schedule dates out in regular calendar days. If a company has a shop calendar, there is no reason to discontinue using it if people are used to it. On the other hand, there is no need to introduce the shop calendar today when the computer can do the conversion.

Figure 13 shows a shop order for the locator pin. This will be used as an example of operations scheduling and, in this example, a shop calendar *will* be used in order to make the arithmetic of scheduling clear. The due date is day 412 and that is determined, in the case of the locator pin that goes into the crankcase half-left, from the material requirements plan.

Operations scheduling works back from this need date to put scheduled finish dates on each operation using scheduling rules like those discussed above. Inspection will be allowed two days. Thus, finish turn must be completed on day 410. It is assumed that the work center file indicates that there are two shifts working in work center 1204 (two shifts at eight hours apiece equals sixteen hours), thus the 27.3 hours required for finish turn will take two days. Planned queue time in this example is assumed to be two days ahead of finish turn. Rough turn must be completed four days earlier than the finish turn must be completed, and its scheduled finish date, therefore, is day 406. The standard hours are calculated by multiplying the quantity by the time per piece and, in this case, adding in the setup time. Where machine operators do not set up their own machines, it might make sense to keep this separate.

It is important to recognize that Figure 13 shows the information that would be in the computer. *The finish dates would not appear on the shop paperwork that was released to the factory.* The reason is that material requirements planning would be constantly reviewing the need date to see if it had changed. If, for example, the left crankcase halves are scrapped because of a problem with the castings, and the best possible date to have a new lot of castings for the crankcase halves is day 422, the master schedule would be changed to indicate that. The shop order for the locator pins in the computer would be given a new finish

Figure 13
Shop Order NN. 18447

SHOP ORDER NN. 18447
PART NO. 80021—LOCATOR PIN
QUANT. 500   DUE: 412   RELEASE 395

Oper.	Dept.	Work Center	Description	Setup	Per Piece	Std. Hrs.	Finish
10	08	1322	Cut Off	.5	.010	5.5	402
20	32	1600	Rough Turn	1.5	.030	16.5	406
30	32	1204	Finish Turn	3.3	.048	27.3	410
40	11		Inspect				412

date of 422 and operation thirty would then become 420, operation twenty would become 416, etc.

Capacity requirements will not be posted against the work centers using the routine shown in Figure 10. A capacity plan, as shown in Figure 14, will be the result.

This capacity plan has, of course, been cut apart to show it in the figure. It would include many more shop orders, as well as the planned order releases from MRP, in reality. The locator pins are shown here as a released shop order. (Note: there is no released shop order for locator pins in Figure 9. It would show as a "scheduled receipt" if there were.) One of the great values of MRP is the fact that it projects "planned order releases." These planned order releases are used to:

1. Generate lower-level material requirements.

2. Generate capacity requirements.

3. Determine when lower-level material—both purchased and manufactured— must be rescheduled to earlier or later dates.

This ability to see capacity requirements ahead of time is especially important to good manpower planning. Seeing the capacity requirements coming rather than seeing the backlogs of work out on the factory floor enables factory supervision to do a far better job of leveling production, resulting in less overtime, and less need to hire and lay off people on a short-term basis.

Figure 15 shows a summary of the capacity requirements over an eight-week period. In practice, this would typically be projected over a far longer period. The summary is drawn from the capacity requirements plan illustrated in Figure

Figure 14
Capacity Requirements Plan

Work Center 1600

Part No.	SO No.	Qty.	Week 396-400	Week 401-405	Week 406-410	Week 411-415	Week 416-420
91672	17621	50		3.5			
80021	18447	500			16.5		

Includes Planned Orders

Total Std. Hrs.			294	201	345	210	286

14 which would also extend much further into the future than the five weeks shown. A typical manpower plan would extend three to six months into the future and would be calculated weekly. A "facilities plan" that would be used for determining what new machine tools were needed would be calculated typically once every two to three months and extended three to four years into the future because of the lead time for procuring machine tools.

The most important information for a foreman is the average hours that he must plan to turn out. This production rate is usually calculated as a four-week average because the individual weekly hours are not particularly significant. The variations between these hours are more random than real. Figure 14 shows one reason why this happens. The 16.5 hours for part number 80021, the locator pin, are shown in the week bracketed by days 406 to 410. Referring back to Figure 13, it can be seen that these 16.5 hours are *actually going to be in work center 1600 Tuesday of the previous week!*

Many people have tried to develop elaborate computer load leveling systems because they were alarmed by the weekly variation in the apparent "load" shown in the capacity requirements plan. These variations are random. They are exaggerated by the fact that capacity plans are usually done in weekly time periods, and any foreman can attest to the fact that the hours never materialize exactly the same way they are shown on the plan. The most important thing to know is the average rate of output required so that *manpower* can be planned accordingly.

In Figure 15, the four-week averages are 263 standard hours for the first four weeks and 277 for the second four weeks, or an average of 270 standard hours per week. Now the capacity planner must determine whether that capacity requirement can be met. The first step is to find out what the output from the work center has been over the last few weeks. This is called "demonstrated capacity." (This term was coined by David Garwood and is very useful in describing the present capacity of a work center as opposed to its potential capacity when all shifts are manned, etc.)

It is the job of the capacity planner to then determine whether or not the current

Figure 15
Capacity Requirements Summary
(in Standard Hours)

CAPACITY REQUIREMENTS
SUMMARY (IN STANDARD HOURS)

Week	4-Week Total	4-Week Average	Hours	Week	4-Week Total	4-Week Average	Hours
1	294			5	286		
2	201			6	250		
3	345			7	315		
4	210	1050	263	8	257	1108	277

capacity is sufficient. Or, what needs to be done to get the capacity to meet the plan. Or—as a last resort—to feed back information that the plan cannot be met.

If the plan cannot be met, the master schedule and, perhaps, even the production plans will have to be changed. If, for example, a company has one broach and it is the only one of its type available because it was made specifically for this company, it could well become a bottleneck. If the capacity plan indicates that more hours were required at the broach than could possibly be produced, the master schedule would have to be changed to reflect this.

Once again, however, it's important to emphasize that this is the *last resort*. The job of the capacity planner is to get the capacity that is needed to meet the plan. And that is an important point to emphasize. If there is any problem that exists in practice with capacity planning, it is the fact that people expect the computer to do the capacity planning rather than recognizing that all it can do is generate numbers that will be given to an intelligent, experienced person—the capacity planner—to use in working with other people to fix capacity problems.

Once it is agreed that the capacity requirements can be met, an output control report as shown in Figure 16 is set up. Three weeks have passed since the one in the figure was made, and the actual standard hours produced (shown in the second line of the figure) are falling far short of the required standard hours at work center 1600. The deviation in the first week was twenty hours. In the second week, it was fifty hours—for a cumulative deviation of seventy hours. In the third week, it was eighty hours, giving a total cumulative deviation of 150 hours. This is a true *control* report with a plan and feedback to show where actual output in standard hours compares with the plan. It shows the deviation from the plan. The 150 hour deviation in week three indicates that 150 standard hours of work required to produce material to meet the master schedule has not been completed.

The amount of tolerance around the plan has to be established. If it were determined, for example, that the company could tolerate being one half week behind schedule, the tolerance in Figure 16 would be 135 standard hours. When the deviation exceeds 135 standard hours, that would require immediate attention to

**Figure 16
Output Control**

OUTPUT CONTROL
WORK CENTER 1600
WEEK NO. 4
(IN STD. HRS.)   Today

	Week 1	Week 2	Week 3	Week 4
Planned	270	270	270	270
Actual Std.	250	220	190	
Deviation	−20	−70	−150	

Figure 17
Dispatch List

DISPATCH LIST WORK CENTER NO. 1600				DAY 405
Shop Order No.	Part No.	Qty.	Scheduled Date	Std. Hours
17621	91762	50	401	3.5
18430	98340	500	405	19.2
18707	78212	1100	405	28.6
18447	80021	500	406	16.5
19712	44318	120	409	8.4
			TOTAL HOURS	76.2

increase output through overtime, adding people, etc. Whenever the planned rate in the output control report is changed, the deviation will be reset to zero.

It's a good idea to show input to a work center as well as output. That way, when a work center is behind on output because a feeding work center has not given them the work, it can be detected very quickly since the input report will show the actual input below the planned input. This is called an "input/output report."

The capacity planning and output control reports are concerned with capacity. The dispatch list shown in Figure 17 is concerned with priority.

The dispatch list is generated daily—or as required—and goes out to the shop floor at the beginning of the day. It shows the sequence in which the jobs are to be run according to the scheduled date for the operation in that work center. The movement of jobs from work center to work center is put in to the computer so that each morning the foremen can have an up-to-date schedule that is driven by MRP. If part 80021 had been rescheduled to a new completion date of day 422 as discussed above, its priority would drop on the dispatch list because its scheduled date would now be 416. This would allow part number 44318 to be made earlier. The dispatch list gives the foremen the priority of jobs so that they can pick the proper job to start next. Since the dispatch list is driven by MRP, it tells the foremen the right sequence in which to run the jobs to do the best job of preventing predicted shortages.

Section 4
The MRP Output Reports

The figures in this chapter represent the major reports that are used in a closed loop MRP system. Referring back to Figure 2, the functions of the production plan (Figure 3), the master schedule (Figure 7), the material requirements plan (Figures 8 and 9), and the capacity requirements plan (Figure 14) are illustrated. The output control report (Figure 16) is the means for monitoring output against the plan to be sure that capacity plans are being executed. The dispatch list (Figure 17) is the report for the factory to use in executing the material plans. Vendor scheduling is the way the material requirements plans are executed with the "outside factories."

It is important to emphasize the feedback functions in a closed loop system. For example, if vendors are not going to ship on time, they must send in an anticipated delay report as soon as they recognize that they have a problem. In the past, ship dates were not valid. The typical company had many past due purchase orders with the vendor. With MRP—if it is properly managed—dates will represent real need dates, and, thus, it is important to feed back information as quickly as possible to indicate when these dates cannot be met. This, of course, is also true for the factory, where the anticipated delay report should be a regular part of their feedback to the closed loop system.

A closed loop MRP system is a fairly modern development. Many companies talked about material requirements planning for years and *did* explode bills of material on a computer. But, it was the advent of the modern computer with its great processing speeds and storage capabilities that made modern MRP practical. The ability to break requirements down into weekly, or even daily, time periods rather than showing them in monthly increments, for example, helped MRP to become a scheduling system rather than just another order launching system (even though it is superior to the order point as an ordering system). The ability to plan requirements weekly—or even daily—made MRP a practical scheduling tool. Before 1971, it would be hard to find any closed loop MRP system in existence. Master scheduling was not well understood. Capacity planning and dispatching were tried, but were usually ineffective because the priority planning wasn't valid. Computers of the day couldn't keep schedules up-to-date and the people using them didn't understand how to master schedule properly to do this. Closed loop MRP is truly a product of the computer age.

Chapter 2

Basic Architectural Issues

The logic of MRP II attempts to accurately model the realities of a manufacturing environment. Its sole purpose is to describe within the computer the manufacturing events that are happening now, and as well as those which are planned to occur in the future. As scrap occurs on the factory floor, as the master production schedule is changed, as one component is replaced by another in an engineering change, etc., the MRP II system simulates the events that will and must occur in the future, pointing out the potential problems and pitfalls while there is still enough time to avoid them. Of course, it is not always possible to avoid potential problems, but MRP II tries to identify them at the earliest possible moment.

By simulating events and allowing people to examine them, the system provides a window into the future. Visibility exists into areas that were hidden before. Potential problems stand out. People can look at different alternatives to avoid these problems before they become crises.

With operating MRP II logic, a tool exists to begin planning. Without it, running a manufacturing plant is like driving a car by following the white line through a hole in the floor: you can see where you are, but knowing that doesn't help with the driving. You really need to see where you are going.

Four general architectural features are fundamental to an operating MRP II system. These are:

1. The method by which a resource plan (material requirements plan, capacity requirements plan, etc.) is recalculated.

2. The way in which manufacturing events are stored for replanning.

3. The method of describing working and nonworking days for the resource planning calculations.

4. The length of the planning horizon.

NET CHANGE AND REGENERATIVE PLANNING SYSTEMS

Two methods exist for recomputing a resource plan. One method is called a regeneration (or a regenerative calculation); the other is called net change. A regeneration destroys the old resource plan and completely recalculates a new plan. In a regenerative material requirements planning system, for example, the old plan is discarded each time planning is run. A new plan is developed using the status of the on-hand balance, allocations, master production schedule, and scheduled receipts at the time of the regeneration.

Regenerative systems are said to be "status driven." In other words, the replanning calculations are done on all items that could have exception messages or planned orders regardless of whether there has been a change since the last replanning calculation.

Regenerative systems are typically run weekly. Companies trying to run a regeneration less frequently than weekly (say every other week or monthly) find that too many changes occur between the regenerations to make the plan valid for longer than a week. Because of master schedule changes, engineering changes, scrap, etc. in a typical company, there tend to be problems getting the full benefits from MRP when the system is run less frequently than weekly. Companies trying to run a regeneration more frequently than weekly (say every day or three times a week) often have serious computer run time problems. Consequently the regenerations are typically limited to weekends.

Net change systems are said to be "change driven." Replanning is done on items that have had a change that might have affected the existing plan or the exception messages.

Net change planning recalculates only those portions of the plan that need to be replanned. If there has been no activity and the plan for an item is still valid, it is not recalculated. In a net change material requirements planning system, replanning is based on changes that have occurred since the last replanning run. These changes may include changes to the on-hand balance, gross requirements coming from higher levels, allocations, changes due to unanticipated scrap, changes in ordering rules and lead times, etc.

Normally, a net change system can be run as frequently as the users desire. Since fewer items are being replanned during each planning run, the number of runs can increase. For example, in some situations, a net change MRP system may be run every hour—more commonly, the MRP planning calculation is run every day, or several times a week.

Two distinct types of net change MRP systems exist today:

1. Batch net change.

2. Continuous net change.

Batch net change systems accumulate a listing of items that should be replanned. As transactions occur that may affect the plan for an item, the system marks the item as one to be replanned in the net change replanning run. Later, all items marked for replanning are processed in a batch net change processing run. During this processing, additional items may be marked for replanning because of changes to requirements that resulted from revisions to parent items.

Continuous net change systems replan without delay. As a transaction occurs that should cause net change replanning, the transaction is processed and immediately afterward the net change planning calculation is called for the item and it is replanned. The old plan is immediately accessed, old exception messages deleted, a new plan developed, and any new exception messages queued for the proper planners.

Most continuous net change systems can also be run as batch net change or regenerative systems, and it is possible to switch back and forth. A net change system can be run as a regenerative system one time and as a net change system the next, or vice versa. However, it is not possible to run a regenerative system as a net change system, or a batch net change system as a continuous system.

Some perspective on net change systems is appropriate here. A net change system has the potential to be more responsive than a regenerative system. Taken to its extreme, a net change system can be completely up-to-date at all times. In regenerative systems today, the speed of computer hardware and the volume of information that has to be processed prevents the system from being up-to-date at all times. In fact, it is hard to envision a time in the future when this will not still be the case.

An MRP II system must accurately represent the events that are occurring now, and predict the events that need to occur in the future. When a transaction occurs and MRP II does not reflect the change or changes in the plan, the system fails, at least for a limited period of time, to accurately portray the proper events.

Consequently, the more up-to-date a system is, the better it is. In general, net change is a more favorable way to recalculate the plan, and a continuous net change calculation is potentially better than a batch net change process. However, there is still a question of degree. How much better is continuous net change than batch net change? How much better is net change than regeneration? People using net change systems are generally convinced that net change is superior to regeneration. The idea of changing to a regenerative system stikes an extremely sour chord. And companies using regenerative systems generally praise the responsiveness of a net change system.

Yet some companies with net change systems print exception messages once a week. Furthermore, there has been virtually no migration from regenerative to net change systems among Class A and B MRP II users. Even fewer Class A or B MRP II users have converted from batch net change to continuous net change. So the questions still remain: "How much better is net change over regeneration?" and "How much better is continuous net change over batch net change?"

In fact, the current experience in the field is not sufficient enough to answer these questions, nor does it appear that an answer will be forthcoming in the near future.

All the methods (regeneration, batch net change, continuous net change) seem to be workable, and each type of system has been made to work effectively. Some of the best users of MRP II systems are using regenerative systems, and there is nothing to prevent a company from being an excellent MRP II user with a regenerative system.

Companies aggressively implementing the methods of Just-in-Time typically prefer net change systems because the plan can be updated daily rather than weekly. However, if the plan can be recomputed more frequently using a regenerative system, then it makes most sense to use the regenerative software.

The real issue is not whether the system is net change or regenerative, but whether the replanning calculations can be run frequently. If the system is regenerative and can run a regeneration each evening, then the system will work fine. Conversely, in a Just-in-Time environment where a net change system can be run no more than once a week, then there may be problems in operating the system effectively.

By convention, if the logic of material requirements planning is net change, then the system is said to be net change. This happens even when the capacity requirements planning, master production scheduling, rough cut capacity planning, and tool planning calculations in the same system are regenerative. Similarly, a system is said to be regenerative if the logic of MRP is regenerative—even though the master production scheduling logic may be net change.

BUCKETED AND BUCKETLESS

Another part of the architecture of an MRP II system is the way the manufacturing events (gross requirements, scheduled receipts, planned orders, etc.) are used in the planning calculations. One method is to define a series of time periods (or "buckets"), usually weekly, extending out into the future: all manufacturing events are summarized into these buckets and all resource planning calculations are done from these buckets. The other method is to store individual manufacturing events as individual records by date: all resource planning calculations would then be done by date rather than in weekly buckets.

In a bucketed material requirements planning system, all scheduled receipts, planned orders, gross requirements, etc. are accumulated into a fixed number of time buckets. These buckets, usually weekly, are then used for netting, exception checking, order planning, and reporting. The system does not attempt to compute precise dates for new planned orders and component requirements, nor is it able to calculate exact need dates for existing scheduled receipts. Planned order due dates, gross requirement dates, and scheduled receipt need dates are determined to the nearest week—specific dates within a week cannot be computed.

In a plan-by-date or "bucketless" MRP system, manufacturing events are stored as individual records by date: the future is not divided up into time buckets. The individual manufacturing events are used for the netting, exception checking, order planning, and reporting. MRP computes precise dates for planned orders, gross requirements, and scheduled receipts.

By convention, a system is referred to as "bucketed" if the material requirements planning logic uses a fixed number of time periods; a system is "bucketless" if the material requirements planning logic uses individual scheduled receipts, planned orders, and gross requirements to compute exceptions and need dates. For example, if the MRP logic is bucketed, but the master production scheduling logic is bucketless, the system is considered bucketed. If the MRP logic is bucketless, but the master scheduling logic and the capacity requirements planning logic is bucketed, the system is typically said to be bucketless, even though there may be some significant disadvantages to having a bucketed master scheduling system feed the material requirements planning logic.

Over the years, both bucketed and bucketless systems have been demonstrated to work. However, today a number of companies are actively implementing Just-in-Time approaches. In these companies, shortened lead times and daily (or more frequent) deliveries cause problems with a bucketed material requirements planning system. Consequently, most companies implementing the methods of Just-in-Time find it necessary to provide replanning in daily or smaller time periods. At some point, most companies involved with Just-in-Time will need bucketless replanning calculations.

Bucketless systems provide a significant advantage over bucketed approaches. Appendix 2 explains the general differences between bucketed and bucketless systems, and lists specific advantages and disadvantages of the different methods.

SHOP CALENDAR

The logic of the system should project what needs to happen and when based on the planned working days for the company. The system should not assume that all companies work fifty-two weeks per year, or that Saturdays and Sundays are always days off, or that Thanksgiving is always a holiday.

Consequently, a shop calendar needs to be part of an MRP II system to specify work days. In a bucketed system, the calendar is typically in weeks: some weeks are identified as work weeks, others as nonwork weeks (shutdown, vacation). In a bucketless system, the calendar is by date: the specific work days, and non-working weekends, shutdown periods, vacations or holidays.

A shop calendar relates working days to regular calendar dates. Only working days are numbered in the shop calendar, and logic in the system exists to convert back and forth from shop calendar dates to regular dates. In effect, a shop calendar provides a way for the system to easily calculate the manufacturing events at different times in the future and then convert those shop dates to regular calendar dates that make sense to people.

PLANNING HORIZON

The planning horizon needs to extend beyond the aggregate material lead time and, in some cases, beyond the lead time needed to make major capacity adjustments. In addition, the planning horizon needs to extend far enough to allow financial simulations and comparison back to the business plan.

For most companies, the planning horizon is at least one year. Some companies need planning horizons that are longer, and may be two, three, or more years in length.

The planning horizon for MRP may be different from the planning horizon for master scheduling or capacity planning. Since material and capacity plans are derived from the master production schedule, it makes most sense to have a master scheduling horizon that is at least as long as the MRP and capacity requirements planning horizons. The master scheduling horizon might be longer in order to drive long-range financial planning and capital budgeting processes. And since the capacity requirements plans are calculated, in part, from the planned orders in MRP, the MRP planning horizon needs to be as long or longer than the capacity requirements planning horizon.

PART II

Management's Handle on the Business

Chapter 3

Sales and Operations Planning

The sales and operations plan serves two essential purposes within an operating MRP II system. First, it is the key linkage between the business and strategic planning process and the detailed planning and execution systems in the company. Second, the approved sales and operations plan is a regulator of all the other plans and schedules: it is the budget that management sets for the master production schedule and, in turn, all the supporting schedules. The sales and operations plan is management's primary input to an MRP II system.

Sales and operations planning is a vital connection between strategic business and financial plans and the master production schedule. It provides the mechanism to reconcile high-level plans, and then communicate the agreed upon company game plan to sales, finance, engineering, research and development, manufacturing, purchasing, etc. An effectively managed sales and operations planning process promises greater visibility, better managed finished goods inventories or customer backlogs, and better customer service.

The sales plan and the production plan, two outputs from this process, drive the detailed planning and scheduling for most of the company. People are involved in developing the high-level plans and reconciling them to create a company game plan. This company game plan, although perhaps not the best marketing plan, or the best manufacturing plan, or the best engineering plan, balances the needs of sales and marketing against the capabilities of the factory to produce. Individual sales plans can be created that are consistent with the factory's ability to produce. Conversely, production plans can be developed to support both long-term sales plans and inventory and backlog targets. In the long term, the marketplace should be the driver and the factory should meet the needs of the marketplace. In the short term however, factory limitations may determine the rates of production.

Human judgment and decision are essential components of both sales and operations planning and master production scheduling. The management of a company is responsible for making the sales and operations plan the best estimation of future rates of production and for making the master production schedule represent the best estimation of what specific items will be produced in the future. The value judgments and decisions needed to effectively handle the process of sales and operations planning (and master scheduling) cannot be made by a computer. The computer can only provide support and information to assist people in producing and managing these important plans and schedules.

Because of the subjective human decision-making required, sales and operations planning cannot be reduced entirely to numbers. The sales and operations planning software explained in this topic provides people with information to use in evaluating different sales and operations planning strategies. The software described here will not automatically produce and approve the sales and operations plan.

The fact that there are few fixed rules or set formulas for sales and operations planning does not imply that it is an unstructured process. On the contrary, most successful companies use similar sales and operations planning formats, use several conventional calculations and comparisons, have comparable policies for managing the sales and operations planning process, and meet frequently to review progress, analyze and evaluate proposed changes to the existing plan.

Two simple formulas exist to help in the setting of production plans and in managing the sales and operations planning process. One formula, for products made-to-stock, controls production based on the current and desired inventory. The other formula, for products made-to-order, controls production based on the current and the desired backlog. Both formulas are similar and can be represented by the simplified calculation:

Production plan = sales plan + the adjustment in backlog or inventory.

Or, in a different way:

Inventory = starting inventory − the sales plan + the production plan.
Backlog = starting backlog + the sales plan − the production plan.

Several options are available to do the simple calculations that are part of sales and operations planning. Some companies use computer programs that are part of the larger MRP II system architecture. Other companies use computer spreadsheet software like Lotus 1-2-3 that runs on a microcomputer. A few companies do these calculations manually. In most cases, companies use a standardized sales and operations planning report format similar to those described in a section that follows, Report Features.

SALES AND OPERATIONS PLANNING PURPOSE

Sales and operations planning involves two related processes:

1. The process of developing and agreeing upon a sales plan for each product family.

2. The process of developing and agreeing upon a rate of production for each product family.

Sales and operations planning is a high-level planning process based on logical product families. The primary objective of the process is to develop rates of production for families, not schedules for individual items. By categorizing items into families, it is possible to limit the groupings that have to be reviewed and approved by top management.

Normally, it is best to limit the number of product families that have to be evaluated and maintained. However, there are several situations where more families are better than fewer families:

1. Where having more families communicates more effectively the requirements of the market place and the limits of the factory. For example, a manufacturer of electrical components made-to-stock has twenty distinct product families that are used in sales and operations planning.

2. Where the natural product line (marketing) families are not the same as the process (manufacturing) families. For example, a manufacturer of lighting fixtures has marketing families that are organized according to application, while the manufacturing process is based on fixture size.

In situations where marketing and manufacturing families are not the same, some translations have to be made. Typically, a computer program is used to convert the product line sales plans into forecasts by process family. Then production plans can be set that are within the constraints of key resources, vendors, etc. These production plans can be translated back, if necessary, to review the impact on the marketing families.

Management is responsible for developing and then executing both the sales plans and the production plans for the company, and they must have direct control over these plans. The computer should not add to, delete from, or change the sales and operations plans developed by people. The computer can critique and evaluate by using some simple rules, and produce recommendations, but people will be held accountable and, therefore, need direct operating control over these high-level plans.

The sales plan includes a forecast of total bookings or total demand for the product family. In the case of a product family that is made-to-stock, the sales plan is the statement of demand for the family. In the case of the product family that is made-to-order, the sales plan is a statement of orders received for the family. In each case, the sales plan represents the company's current and best estimate of customers' future requirements.

The sales plan for the product family must agree with the sum of the individual forecasts for items within the family. In some cases, the sales plan for the family will be developed from the sum of the sales forecasts for individual items within the family. In other cases, the sales plan for the family will be prorated, and sales forecasts for individual items within the family will be developed from the total sales plan. For example, if the sales plan for the family is 1,000, and one item is 10% of the family, the forecast for the item is 100.

Regardless of how the numbers are developed, the sales plan and the sum of the individual sales forecasts must be in agreement. For example, if there are five items in the family and the sum of their individual forecasts equals 1,100, and the sales plan for the family equals 1,000, then one or the other must be revised until they are equal. The reconciliation process is explained in Chapter 5, Demand Management.

An agreed upon rate of production for each product family is the second essential output from the sales and operations planning process. This rate, called the production plan, is the rate of production stated in gross terms. Depending upon the product, the rate may be 2,000 cars a week, fifteen machines a month, or one machine every three months.

The production plan is usually stated as the rate per month for the type of product or a family of products. It is also possible to state the production plan as a daily or weekly rate and convert it to the rate for the production planning period. The production plan is a rate of production and does not include the timing or quantities of individual production lots.

The factors that are used to develop the production plan include the sales plan, vendor and capacity limitations, the current and desired inventory (for a make-to-stock product), and the current and desired backlog (for a make-to-order product). For a family that contained some products made-to-stock and others made-to-order, the production plan would include both the inventory plan and the backlog plan.

The production plan is often set at a rate different from the sales rate. For example, the production plan may be set to build inventory in anticipation of a peak selling season. Or, the production plan may be set to reduce the backlog of customer orders as a way to gain a more competitive lead time. Or, the production plan may be set to increase the backlog on one product line to free resources for other product lines to capture significant market opportunities.

In a make-to-stock situation, the production plan will be set using the beginning inventory and a management decision on the desired ending inventory for the production period. This information, together with the expected shipments coming from planned bookings, customer orders for future delivery, branch warehouse demands, and interplant orders is used to develop a production rate. The resulting production rate must then be checked against any vendor, capacity, or material limitations. If it passes this check, then this production rate is a candidate to be approved as the production plan for the family.

The situation is similar in a make-to-order business. The production plan is usually set using the beginning backlog of customer orders and a management decision on the desired backlog of customer orders at the end of the production period. This backlog information, together with the bookings plan, branch warehouse demands (if any), and interplant orders, is used to develop a production rate for the family. Again the resulting production rate must be checked against any vendor, capacity, or material limitations before it can be approved as a production plan.

Master production schedules for individual items within the family will be developed from the production plan. The broad statement of production must be broken down into a schedule for specific items, dates, and quantities. Working within the constraints of the production plan, the master scheduler will develop the statement of production for individual items and set the timing and quantities of individual production lots.

The production plan and the sum of the master schedules must be in agreement if the production plan is to truly act as a regulator of the master production schedule. The master schedules for specific items within the product family, when totalled, must equal the production plan for the family. If the master production schedule differs significantly from the production plan, then it must be revised until it is equal to the production plan.

REPORT FEATURES

The sales and operations planning report provides a display of the sales plan, the production plan, and the essential comparisons so that the sales and operations planning process can be properly managed. Factors that are part of the sales and planning process that can be represented as numbers should be displayed in this report. These factors include the sales plan, actual sales, the production plan, actual production, current and projected inventory, and the current and projected backlog. Other factors such as management decisions, vendor, capacity, and material limitations are a different, more subjective type of information and are not on the report.

The sales and operations planning report contains both historical information (what has happened in the recent past) and future plans. Performance measurement is an essential part of sales and operations planning. Sales planning performance can be evaluated by comparing the sales plan against actual orders; production planning performance can be evaluated by comparing the production plan against the actual production. Company performance is reflected in the comparison of planned to actual inventory or backlog.

Most companies find it most effective to display at least three periods of historical comparisons. Some companies store and display six to twelve months of history, but three months is typically the minimum amount of history needed to operate an effective sales and operations planning process. In a seasonal business, even more visibility may be needed.

Future operating plans normally go out beyond the current fiscal year. Anytime there are long cumulative lead times, the operating plan will extend beyond the end of the budget year. Near the end of the budget year, the operating plan will extend into the following year. Most companies find that a rolling horizon of one year is the minimum visibility necessary to operate the sales and operations planning process effectively. The planning horizon is "rolling," because as time passes, new periods are added to the end of the horizon to extend it.

The sales and operations planning report can be thought of as having three segments. These segments are listed below with the types of information that may appear in the report:

SALES (DEMAND)

1. Bookings or demand plan.

   A. Anticipated bookings/demand.

   B. Actual bookings/demand.

   C. Comparison of planned to actual.

2. Customer orders promised for shipment.

    A. Customer orders by due date.

PRODUCTION (SUPPLY)

1. Production plan.

    A. Planned production.

    B. Actual production.

    C. Comparison of planned to actual production.

COMPARISONS

1. Inventory.

    A. Planned inventory.

    B. Actual inventory.

    C. Comparison of planned to actual inventory.

2. Backlog.

    A. Planned backlog.

    B. Actual backlog.

    C. Comparison of planned to actual backlog.

The section of the report labeled SALES typically includes two parts:

1. Bookings (orders written).

2. Customer orders by promised ship dates.

Both bookings and customer orders by promised ship dates are essential to the sales planning process and need to be monitored to have effective control over the sales plan. The bookings plan provides the early warning mechanism: by forecasting order bookings and then monitoring the actual orders written, visibility is provided at the earliest possible moment. Trends can be identified early and potentially out-of-control situations recognized while there is still time to take effective action. If bookings are less than anticipated, several alternatives may be available: marketing plans can be revised, promotional programs established, prices changed, new product introductions accelerated, and training for the sales force stepped up. If bookings are greater than anticipated, the impact on manufacturing can be identified in advance so that any necessary trade-offs can be discussed, such as increasing backlogs (or reduced inventory) versus capacity adjustments, working capital required to support additional sales, pricing adjustments, etc. In addition, sales can focus on protecting market position and share during a period of potentially scarce capacity.

The customer orders by promised ship dates yield visibility into future product shipments, financial performance against the current business plan, and anticipated revenue. The customer orders provide good visibility into future shipments as well as a type of early warning signal. For example, if most of the backlog is scheduled far in the future, the company may have problems hitting its shipping goals over the next month or two. By seeing the problem in advance, some alternative plans can be created to maintain shipments at the desired level.

The PRODUCTION section includes the authorized rate of production and, for past periods, actual production against this rate. The production plan is the basis for allocating capacity, and a factor in the computations of inventory levels and order backlogs.

Past performance can be evaluated by some simple comparisions. For example, planned bookings can be compared to actual bookings, planned shipments to actual shipments, and planned production to actual production. This comparison may be done by computing either the period-by-period deviation and the cumulative deviation from some specified starting point. A graphical display of these deviations is often helpful in identifying problem situations.

In addition, the CALCULATIONS section of the sales and operations planning report provides information to evaluate and manage the inventory and backlog for the product family. The INVENTORY display shows past inventory performance as well as the planned stock build-up or depletion in the future. For each past period, the planned inventory can be compared to the actual inventory. For future periods, the planned inventory is calculated based on the production plan and projected shipments:

Planned inventory = on-hand balance + production plan − projected shipments.

The BACKLOG display shows past performance against the backlog plan, as well as the planned backlog in the future. For each past period, the planned backlog can be compared to the actual backlog. For future periods, the planned backlog is calculated from the bookings plan and projected shipments:

Planned backlog = current backlog + planned bookings − projected shipments.

In the case of a family of products made-to-stock, planned shipments and the production plan are the same.

Figures 18 and 19 are examples of a sales and operations planning reports. Figure 18 is a sales and operations planning report for a make-to-stock family. Figure 19 is a sales and operations planning report for a make-to-order family.

CONVERTING PLANS TO MEANINGFUL MEASURES

The sales and operations planning software should provide some method of converting sales plans and production plans from the primary unit of measure to units of measure meaningful to finance, manufacturing, engineering, sales and marketing, etc. The purpose of this type of logic is to convey the needs in terms that are easily communicated and that best fit the specific area. Showing meaningful units may mean displaying sales dollars for marketing, cost dollars for finance, pieces, hours, or tons for manufacturing, etc.

Figure 18
Sales and Operations Report-Make to Stock Products
Push Lawn Mowers

PRODUCT FAMILY: M350
UNIT OF MEASURE: UNITS
CURRENT INVENTORY: 435

CURRENT DATE:
1/2/88

SALES PLAN

Date	9/11/87	10/10/87	11/07/87	12/05/87	1/02//88	1/30/88	2/27/88	3/26/88	4/23/88
Planned Demand	420	450	480	500	550	550	550	550	550
Actual Demand	455	495	500	550					
Deviation	+35	+45	+20	+50					
Cum Deviation	35	80	100	150					
Customer Orders by Due Date	455	495	500	550					
Actual Shipments	455	495	500	550					

PRODUCTION PLAN

Date	9/11/87	10/10/87	11/07/87	12/05/87	1/02//88	1/30/88	2/27/88	3/26/88	4/23/88
Planned Production	500	500	500	500	550	550	550	550	550
Actual Production	450	450	460	470					
Deviation	−50	−50	−40	−30					
Cum Deviation	−50	−100	−140	−170					

INVENTORY PLAN

Date	9/11/87	10/10/87	11/07/87	12/05/87	1/02//88	1/30/88	2/27/88	3/26/88	4/23/88
Planned Inventory	685	735	755	755	435	435	435	435	435
Actual Inventory	600	555	515	435					
Deviation	−85	−180	−240	−320					

COMPARING ACTUAL TO PLAN

The sales and operations planning software should also provide a means to convert scheduled shipments into a revenue projection for comparison to the current business plan. If the numbers from the sales and operations plan disagree with the numbers from the business plan, then one or the other need to be changed.

Figure 19
Sales and Operations Planning Report—Make to Order Products

PRODUCT FAMILY: 0138 LIFT TRUCKS
UNIT OF MEASURE: UNITS
CURRENT BACKLOG: 448

CURRENT DATE:
1/2/88

SALES PLAN   Current

Date	9/11/87	10/10/87	11/07/87	12/05/87	1/02//88	1/30/88	2/27/88	3/26/88	4/23/88
Planned Bookings	300	300	300	300	300	300	300	300	300
Actual Bookings	300	290	305	303					
Deviation	0	−10	+5	+3					
Cum Deviation	0	−10	−5	−2					
Customer Orders by Due Date	300	300	300	300	300	148			
Actual Shipments	300	300	300	300					

PRODUCTION PLAN

Date	9/11/87	10/10/87	11/07/87	12/05/87	1/02//88	1/30/88	2/27/88	3/26/88	4/23/88
Planned Production	300	300	300	300	150	150	150	150	150
Actual Production	300	300	300	300					
Deviation	0	0	0	0					
Cum Deviation	0	0	0	0					

BACKLOG PLAN

Date	9/11/87	10/10/87	11/07/87	12/05/87	1/02//88	1/30/88	2/27/88	3/26/88	4/23/88
Planned Backlog	450	450	450	450	598	748	898	1048	1198
Actual Backlog	450	440	445	448					
Deviation	0	−10	−5	−2					

ROUGH-CUT CAPACITY REQUIREMENTS PLANNING

Effectively managing changes to the production plan and the master production schedule is one of the most challenging and difficult jobs in an MRP system. Decisions must be made by evaluating several intangible or qualitative factors, many times in an emotion charged climate as customers vie for position in production schedules and as the shop is pushed to, and sometimes beyond, its ability to produce.

In these situations, the need for facts is vital. The problems and decisions must be reduced to alternatives with proposals for action. Managing the production plan and master production schedule without the means to evaluate the effects of changes on both material and capacity fails to provide a valid assessment of the alternatives. An incorrect or incomplete assessment of the alternatives is an open invitation to problems in managing the high-level plans and schedules and, consequently, in running MRP.

The only really effective way to handle changes in the production plan and master schedule is to begin by correctly assessing the alternatives and identifying any limitations that must be resolved. Everyone involved must then press for a decision on any commitments that are necessary in order to resolve the limitations that exist.

The intent of rough-cut capacity planning is to convert high-level plans (production plans or master production schedules) into the impact on resources needed to carry out those plans. Rough-cut capacity planning is an approximate type of capacity planning using some representative routings for product families or for items in the master production schedule. Normally, companies validate the sales and operations plan against major resources using rough-cut capacity planning.

In some instances, rough-cut capacity planning can't be done by product family, and has to be run using the items in the master production schedule. This can happen when resource requirements vary significantly based on the mix of items in the master schedule. In this situation, rough-cut capacity planning should be run directly from the master production schedule; it can be an invaluable tool for assessing changes to the master production schedule when the product mix is changing. In addition, in some companies, spare parts account for a significant part of the total business and consequently the total resources. As a result, spare parts demands should be included in rough-cut capacity planning when assessing the effect on master production schedule changes.

The representative routings used in rough-cut capacity planning are a way to relate product families or individual master schedule items to the key resources required to produce them. The representative routings should contain the resource identifier, number of hours, pounds, molds, etc., and the approximate offset in time from the completion date of the production plan or the master production schedule.

The production plan or master production schedule is extended through the representative routings to generate rough-cut capacity requirements by date. These rough-cut capacity requirements are summarized into weekly or monthly periods and displayed as a rough-cut capacity picture.

Rough-cut capacity planning has several limitations. It does not calculate capacity requirements by work center, take completed parts and assemblies into account, and it assumes lot-for-lot ordering in the calculation of resource requirements. In spite of these clear limitations, rough-cut capacity planning does provide a way to assess the capacity requirements created by a sales and operations plan or master production schedule in a rough-cut way. A plan that is grossly overstated or a change to the plan that generates a significant overload on a resource or key piece of equipment will be clear from a rough-cut capacity planning run.

Since rough-cut capacity planning is a type of capacity planning, the report should be identical in format to the capacity requirements planning report, showing the resource number and description, period date, total capacity required in the period, and total capacity available. A sample report is shown in Figure 57 in Appendix 12.

To effectively solve rough-cut capacity planning problems, a way needs to be provided to identify the source of the capacity requirements. The simplest way is to provide a report or display that shows the individual product families (or master schedule orders) causing the rough-cut capacity requirements in each time period. The detail to the rough-cut capacity report is similar to the detailed capacity planning report shown in Appendix 12 in Figure 58.

Chapter 4

Master Production Scheduling

The master production schedule is a statement of production by item. In other words, the master production schedule is a statement of *what* will be produced, *when* it will be produced, and *how much*. All other schedules in MRP are based on the master production schedule.

The master production schedule is developed from the production plan and the detailed sales plans for each item. The broad statement of production and the demands from the marketplace must be broken down into a schedule for specific items, dates, and quantities. The master scheduler takes the total demand for each master schedule item and uses it to develop the master production schedule. Working within the constraints of the production plan, the master scheduler develops the statement of production for specific items. He sets the timing of the production lots and the quantities of these lots. Typically, the master scheduler sets the specific dates and the quantities manually.

The master production schedule is regulated by the production plan. The production plan is the budget that management sets for the master production schedule. Consequently, the master production schedule for the specific items within a family of products, when totalled, must equal the production plan for the family. If the master production schedule differs significantly from the production plan, then it must be revised until it is equal to the production plan.

Even though the production plan regulates how many units can be in the master production schedule, the detailed sales plans indicate which items to make first, second, third, etc. In effect, the master production schedule is prioritized by the detailed sales plans. The sales plan is the anticipated demand for the item and these projected requirements can be netted against inventory and any existing master schedules to determine the items that are needed and the sequence. The different categories of demand that make up the sales plan are explained later in this chapter.

The master production schedule determines all the other schedules in the system. Material Requirements Planning uses this statement of production to calculate all supporting plans. The master production schedule is exploded down to all lower levels in the product structure, and so it has tremendous leverage on the items found there. Errors in the master production schedule have the potential to be magnified many times as they are passed down through the product structure. When this happens, the effectiveness of the entire system is destroyed.

An almost unlimited number of factors go into developing the master production schedule. These factors are combined to produce a master production schedule for specific items. The factors that go into developing a master production schedule can be categorized into seven major groupings:

1. Sales forecast.

2. Production forecast.

3. Customer orders.

4. Branch warehouse demands.

5. Interplant orders.

6. Management decisions.

7. Vendor, capacity, or material limitations.

None of these are the master production schedule itself. They are combined in a process of human judgment and evaluation to produce the master production schedule. The forecast, as one of the factors used to make the master production schedule, can be the sales forecast for the item or it can be a production forecast. A sales forecast is used whenever the master schedule item is forecast individually. For example, a sales forecast might be used for wooden kitchen cabinets. A production forecast is generally used whenever a number of related master production schedules have to be coordinated; the option packages (V-8 and V-6 engines, air-conditioning options, etc.) that are part of an automobile product line are examples of this type of master schedule item. For this kind of product line, the option packages are not individually forecast but are master scheduled based on the master production schedules for the type of product. In other words, the type of product is master scheduled and some forecast percentages are used to help break down the production for the product into the estimated requirements for each of the master schedule items. The estimated requirements are the production forecasts and they are will be explained in more detail later in this chapter.

The forecast alone is not the master production schedule. A forecast is a statement of demand (what is to be removed from the stockroom) and not a statement of production (what is to be manufactured). For any number of reasons, the master production schedule may be set at levels above or below the sales forecast. For example, the master schedule may be set higher than the sales forecast if stock is being built in anticipation of a peak selling period. During the period when stock is being built, the master production schedule is greater than the sales forecast; during the peak season, the master production schedule is less than the sales forecast. For example, cosmetics are produced in anticipation of peak selling seasons like Christmas and Mother's Day.

Customer orders are the second factor used to develop the master production schedule. Regardless of the forecast, actual customer orders never appear exactly as the forecast predicts. This means that the master production schedule may have to be changed to satisfy the customer orders. Sometimes the forecast is close and other times the errors are significant since forecasting is, and will likely continue to be, an imprecise art.

When customer orders deviate from the forecast, the master scheduler may choose to change the master production schedule or he may choose to leave the master production schedule alone. In deciding whether or not to change the master production schedule, the customer orders are used with the forecast, management decisions, branch warehouse demands, interplant orders, and vendor, capacity, or material limitations.

What the master scheduler does when customer orders differ from the forecast depends on how the customer orders deviate. Deviations from the forecast fall into two categories: deviations in the total quantity of customer orders for a family of products, and deviations in the mix of products within a family where the total forecast quantity is nearly correct. If the forecasted mix of products is incorrect, but the total quantity is nearly equal to the total forecasted quantity, the master scheduler will generally shift the production in the master production schedule from one item to another. If the total forecasted quantity is in error, the master scheduler may decide to increase or decrease the quantities in the master production schedule to meet customer service objectives. This is not the same as changing the forecast, which is a marketing responsibility. As mentioned before, a forecast that is significantly in error should be flagged and brought to the attention of the appropriate people.

But promising something to a customer does not necessarily make it happen in the factory. Customer orders are only one of the pieces in the master production scheduling process. Their impact is significant but cannot be considered alone.

Branch warehouse demands and interplant orders are also factors in making up the master schedule. Where they exist, branch warehouse demands and interplant orders are planned orders or unshipped scheduled receipts either from another MRP system or part of the same MRP system. Distribution Resource Planning creates planned orders to supply the branch warehouses. These planned orders are the branch warehouse demands that appear as one of the factors in the master production schedule at the central supply location. When the planned orders are released, allocations are created and used to show branch warehouse demands that the master scheduler still needs to be aware of. MRP in a multiplant company creates planned orders for items needed at one plant and produced at another. These planned orders at the receiving plant produce the interplant orders which appear as one of the factors in the master production schedule at the supplying plant. In a similar way, allocations from unshipped interplant orders are shown as a demand against the master schedule in the supplying plant.

Branch warehouse demands and interplant orders do not exist in all cases. If a company is not supplying a distribution warehouse system or is not part of a multiplant operation, these factors will not exist and need not be of concern in the design of the system.

Management decisions of a nearly unlimited variety go into making up the master production schedule. For example, increasing or decreasing production as a way of providing a stable source of employment, building stock in anticipation of a shutdown, putting on a third shift, beginning to master production schedule an item even though the customer order has not been received (as a way to reduce the delivery time), or deciding among customers by changing the master production schedule when everyone cannot be supplied are all management decisions that have been and are made in master scheduling.

The need for responsible management decisions make it clear why master production scheduling be done by an intelligent human being and not by a computer. The factors and variables involved in these decisions are intangible and require judgments and assessments that cannot be made by a computer. Developing and managing the master production schedule is a difficult and challenging task, that must be done by people.

Another factor in master production scheduling is any vendor, capacity, or material limitations. The master production schedule must not create a load on a work center or a vendor that exceeds what that work center or vendor can achieve. To do so would create a master production schedule that is not attainable. The master production schedule would no longer represent the best estimation of the production in the future, and the material requirements plan would no longer be a simulation of reality. The result would be rapidly deteriorating priorities, and the system would no longer provide accurate and usable information.

Vendor, capacity, or material limitations are handled in the master production schedule by highlighting the problem and seeking resolution; not by simply changing the master production schedule without attempting to solve the problem. A master production schedule that creates an overload on a work center must be identified and all attempts must be made to devise a solution before considering a change to the master production schedule. Extra shifts, subcontracting, and offloading work to another work center are possible solutions. If none of these provide a solution, the master production schedule must be reduced to a level that creates an attainable work load on the critical work center. The same method used for handling capacity problems applies to vendor or material limitations. If a vendor cannot supply components or material at the rate called for in the master production schedule, a solution should be sought that does not require a change to the master production schedule. If no solution can be found, then the master production schedule must be reduced to the level that is determined by the supply of components or material.

RULES—INCLUDING ITEMS INTO THE MASTER PRODUCTION SCHEDULE

Master production scheduling and MRP (material requirements planning) are mutually exclusive. Either an item is controlled by material requirements planning or it is controlled through the master production schedule. It must be one or the other, and cannot be both. MRP makes certain assumptions about the way an item will be handled: planned orders are created, deleted, and changed automatically by the computer; planned orders are exploded and posted as gross requirements to the component parts without human evaluation or approval. Master production scheduling makes other assumptions: master schedule orders are not added, deleted, or changed by the computer without human evaluation and approval; once the master production schedule has been evaluated and approved, then it is exploded and posted as gross requirements to the component parts. The rules for material requirements planning do not suit the process of master production scheduling and vice versa.

Items are master scheduled if they require a high degree of human control. Items are not master scheduled based on some location in the product structure, dollar value, or other fixed requirement. Items are master scheduled because they need a degree of control that only a human being can provide. If this kind of control over an item is needed, then it should be included into the master production schedule. If that control is not needed, then the item can be handled by MRP.

The types of things that would qualify an item for master schedule control would be any of the following:

1. Significant impact on capacity.

2. Significant impact on material.

3. Human evaluation of the need to change.

4. Human evaluation of the ability to change.

Items are candidates to be master scheduled if a small change in the schedule causes a significant problem, either an overload or underload, on a key resource, bottleneck work center, or specialized skill. Significant changes in capacity requirements on these resources can cause serious problems, and human control over the master production schedule is needed to prevent them.

Items are also candidates to be master scheduled if a small change to the schedule causes a serious problem of material availability. Significant changes on material requirements for key materials can create serious problems, and human control over the master production schedule is needed to stabilize the changes.

Human evaluation of the *need to change* means that someone should evaluate whether the master production schedule needs to be changed based on a change in forecast, customer orders, or any of the other factors that go into making the master production schedule. If changes in these factors still require someone to evaluate whether the schedule needs to be changed, then human control over the master production schedule is needed.

Human evaluation of the *ability to change* means that someone should evaluate whether it is possible to change the schedule based on a change in forecast, customer orders, or any of the other factors that go into the master production schedule. If changes in these factors still require someone to evaluate whether it is possible to change the schedule, then human control is needed over the master production schedule.

An item that has no significant impact on either capacity or material, and requires no human evaluation of the need to change or the ability to change the master production schedule, should not be in the master schedule regardless of whether it is an end item. For example, a purchased item sold as a finished good and covered by a blanket order should not be in the master production schedule. The item has no impact on capacity and, in this case, has little impact on material.

A change in forecast for this item does not require an evaluation of whether the delivery schedule for the item should or can be changed since a blanket order was negotiated with the vendor with the understanding that changes in dates and quantities will be allowed on short notice. This item should not be in the master production schedule even though it is an end item and a number of other end items are in the master schedule. There is no need for close human control of this item; the item can be planned by MRP rather than being master scheduled. The forecast can be used as gross requirements and the normal netting, exception checking, and order planning logic of MRP can be used to control the item.

Another item may have a significant impact on capacity or material and therefore need a greater degree of human control. Someone would have to evaluate any changes to the master production schedule to determine the effects on capacity and material, and to determine whether the change could be made and whether the change would be attainable. The degree of human control required is much greater for this item and consequently the item should be in the master production schedule.

Another way to visualize the process master production scheduling is to think of reaching into the product structure for a product or product family to find the items that give the greatest leverage and control over the other items. The master production schedule takes hold of these items and, by controlling them, yields the greatest leverage and control.

EXAMPLES—SOME MASTER SCHEDULE ITEMS

Any number of different types of items can be master scheduled. The items being master scheduled made-to-stock or made-to-order. They may be end items actually sold to customers, modules (logical groupings of parts) which are combined to make a product, or subassemblies that are combined to make a product.

Some of the different types of items that can be in the master production schedule include:

1. Make-to-order items with a long lead time. These are items in which the lead time to the customer is greater than or equal to the cumulative lead time to manufacture the item.

2. Make-to-order items with a short lead time. These are items in which the lead time to the customer is less than the cumulative lead time to manufacture the item.

3. Make-to-order items where the final product configuration is assembled from a number of options; either modules (logical groupings of parts), or subassemblies. In this case the modules or subassemblies would be master scheduled.

4. Make-to-stock items. These are end items which are shipped from stock.

A custom built turbine is an example of a make-to-order item with a long lead time. The turbine is unique: designed and built to customer specifications. The cumulative lead time to design and build the turbine is one and a half years. The customer has been promised delivery in two years since there is an existing backlog of work that prevents the turbine from being promised to the customer in a year and a half.

A laboratory scale is an example of a make-to-order item with a short lead time. The total cumulative lead time to make this scale is eight months. The market for these scales dictates that delivery be made in four weeks.

An automobile is an example of a make-to-order item where the final configuration of the product is assembled from a number of options. Modules (logical groupings of parts) exist for V-8 engines, AM-FM radios, and accessory trim packages. These modules may be actual subassemblies that can be stocked and then put into the automobile, or may be logical groupings of parts that are actually assembled in a number of different subassemblies. A V-8 engine would be an example of a module which is a physical assembly. An accessory trim package is an example of a logical grouping of parts which is not a physical assembly. When the automobile is built, parts of the accessory trim package are included when the door is assembled, the frame is built, and the interior is completed.

In this type of product, the master production schedule is different from the final assembly schedule. The master production schedule is stated in terms of the logical groupings of parts. When the time comes to actually build the product, a final assembly schedule is created. The final assembly schedule calls for all the parts needed to build the car and shows the assembly operations required. This is stated in terms of the final automobile assembly. This is not the same as the master production schedule which is stated only in terms of the modules. The purpose of the final assembly schedule is to put a picking list and a work authorization onto the final assembly floor for use in building the final product.

Silverware is an example of a make-to-stock item. The total cumulative lead time to make this silverware is six months. The market dictates that delivery be made off the shelf.

Regardless of the type of item, the same factors explained previously are used to develop the master production schedule. These factors are:

1. Sales forecast.

2. Production forecast.

3. Customer orders.

4. Branch warehouse demands.

5. Interplant orders.

6. Management decisions.

7. Vendor, capacity, or material limitations.

All of these factors do not always exist for all items in the master production schedule. A forecast may not exist for an item which is a long lead time make-to-order item. A make-to-stock item may have no visible backlog of customer orders. Branch warehouse demands and interplant orders may not exist. No management decisions may be in effect to alter the master production schedule, and no vendor or capacity limitations may exist for a master schedule item.

Regardless of whether all these factors exist for each item in the master production schedule, the master production scheduling software must provide for them. A long lead time make-to-order item may become a short lead time make-to-order item due to economic conditions or marketing strategy. A make-to-stock item may have large customer orders placed for future delivery. A branch warehouse distribution system may be started or a multiplant operation may be started. A management decision or a vendor, capacity, or material limitation may appear for an item that previously had no such decision or limitation.

MASTER PRODUCTION SCHEDULE ORDER

The master scheduler is responsible for the accuracy of the master production schedule and he must therefore have direct control over it. The computer cannot be allowed to add to, delete from, or change in any way the master production schedule developed by the master scheduler. The master scheduler's statement of production is used directly. The system must allow the master scheduler to state a master production schedule and then have that master schedule used without any change.

A master schedule order is used to state the master production schedule. A master schedule order is a statement of production that is not changed in any way by the computer. Master schedule orders are functionally equivalent to firm planned orders. In some systems, master schedule orders exist as distinct and separate types of orders in the system. In other systems, firm planned orders are used as master schedule orders. Either method is workable: master schedule orders and firm planned orders are functionally the same. Generally the use of either a master schedule order or a firm planned order is based on technical considerations that make one or the other a better choice for a particular set of software and the software designer's choice.

Master scheduling software normally provides some method for reducing the work load on the master scheduler in creating new master schedule orders. Typical methods include:

1. Planning master schedule orders and displaying them as exception messages.

2. Time fence logic that creates new master schedule orders for dates outside the master scheduling horizon.

3. Specialized transactions to authorize planned master schedule orders individually or in groups.

One helpful function in the master scheduling software is logic to plan master schedule orders and show these to the master scheduler in the form of exception messages. However, these planned master schedule orders are not passed on to MRP. The planned master schedule orders are used as information for the benefit of the master scheduler in evaluating and authorizing the orders that should be added to the master production schedule. Only when the master scheduler has specifically authorized the planned master schedule orders and made them a part of the master production schedule are they passed on to MRP.

A few master scheduling systems include time fence logic that controls the timing of the suggested master schedule orders. A so-called planning time fence splits the master scheduling horizon into two parts: in time periods prior to the time fence, only the master scheduler can add, change, or delete master schedule orders for an item. In these time periods, the computer will not create orders that should be added to the master production schedule. In the time periods later than the planning time fence, the system uses logic similar to that of MRP to create, change, and delete master schedule orders.

The orders outside the planning fence may be passed to MRP, or they may take the form of exception or action messages. In cases where the orders are passed automatically to MRP, the planning time fence is normally set to a date after the master scheduling horizon to preserve the accountability requirements of the master scheduler.

In the event this is not done and planned master schedule orders are created inside the master scheduling horizon and passed to MRP, some warnings are in order. First, this does not relieve the master scheduler of the responsibility for a valid and realistic master production schedule. In practical terms, this means the master scheduler must review all the planned master schedule orders after they've been created, verify that they are all correct, and reverse any that are incorrect. Second, if the new planned orders have been passed to MRP and are reversed, the master scheduler has the responsibility to communicate this information to the proper people so that actions are not taken on incorrect data. The result is that most people choose not to allow master schedule orders to be automatically created and passed to MRP inside the master scheduling horizon.

Some master scheduling systems contain a specialized transaction for authorizing planned master schedule orders. These systems include a transaction which authorizes groups of master schedule orders that need to be added to the master production schedule. For example, the master scheduler may choose to authorize all the planned master schedule orders between 11/27 and 1/15. Orders outside this range are authorized individually using other transactions, or are not authorized at all.

MASTER PRODUCTION SCHEDULE REPORT

The master production schedule report provides the master scheduler with a display of the information that will assist him to develop and manage the master production schedule. Several of the factors that go into making up the master production schedule can be presented in the form of numbers. These include the sales forecast, production forecast, branch warehouse demands, interplant orders, and customer orders. Since these factors can be presented numerically, they can appear on the master production schedule report.

The other factors: management decisions, and vendor, capacity, or material limitations are a different, more subjective type of information and they are typically handled in the form of a memo. These factors are not typically presented on the master production schedule report.

The master production schedule report can be thought of as having three segments. These segments are listed below with the types of information that can appear on the report:

DEMANDS

1. Sales forecast.

2. Production forecast.

3. Customer orders.

4. Branch warehouse demands.

5. Interplant orders.

PRODUCTION

1. Master production schedule.

CALCULATIONS

1. Projected available balance.

2. Available to promise.

Some of these different lines may not be present. For example, a production forecast or branch warehouse demand may not exist for a particular master schedule item. For another master schedule item, a sales forecast may not exist. In these cases, a category of information that does not exist for a master schedule item should not appear a a line on the report. The master scheduler should only see a line of information in the report if it is meaningful. The best arrangement would be to allow each of these lines to be printed as options. This makes the master production schedule report clearer and easier for the master scheduler to use.

The section of the report labeled DEMANDS lists each of the different types of demands. These are the different types of demands that could occur, and it is possible that an item could have all these different types. A more normal situation would be where an item would have several, but not all, of the different types of demands.

The PRODUCTION section includes the master production schedule. This line is not optional and should be printed for all master schedule items.

The CALCULATIONS section is a way to assist the master scheduler. The computer can do some calculations using the master production schedule and the demands. The purpose of these calculations is to provide the master scheduler with information about the master production schedule.

The projected available balance calculation shows the projected stock build-up or depletion to the master scheduler. This calculation is similar to the projected on-hand balance calculation in MRP. The calculation is also used to generate exception messages for the master scheduler.

The available-to-promise calculation shows where new customer orders can be promised for delivery based on the current master production schedule. The emphasis should be on slotting customer orders for shipment based on the existing master production schedule and not on attempting to change the master production schedule for each customer. A good master production schedule policy recognizes that there is an expense in direct and setup labor, inventory, overhead, and confusion for each change to the master production schedule. Yet changes can and should be made to the schedule. The policy should be to provide an evaluation of the effects and cost of each change prior to the change being made.

The available-to-promise calculation compares the master production schedule to customer orders in either of two ways:

1. By master schedule order.

2. Cumulatively.

In the first method, an available to promise is computed for the first time period and for each time period where there is a master schedule order. This available to promise is a simple comparison: the available-to-promise quantity is the quantity of the master schedule order less any customer orders between the date of the order and the date of the next. In addition, the calculation includes some logic to prevent the available-to-promise quantity from dropping below zero. If the calculated available to promise is negative in a period, the available-to-promise quantity is set to zero and the available to promise in an earlier period reduced by the overpromised amount. This continues back to the first time period.

In the second option, the available to promise is a cumulative calculation. The available to promise for the first period is the on-hand balance plus master schedule orders due in the past or current period less all customer orders due before the end of the first period. For later periods, the available to promise is the prior period available to promise plus any master schedule orders less any customer orders for the period.

Figure 20 is an example of a master production schedule report. This figure contains two report examples. The one at the top of the page is a master production schedule report for a make-to-stock item. At the bottom of the page is a master production schedule report for a make-to-order item.

These sample master production schedule reports show the factors that can be represented numerically and which apply to the sample situations. The demands shown in the example are: the sales forecast, branch warehouse demands (the make-to-stock item), and customer orders. Also shown are the master production schedule and two calculations to assist the master scheduler. These are the projected available balance calculation and the available-to-promise calculation.

The sales forecast is shown by time period. In this case, a customer order has reduced the forecast quantity. Although it would also be possible to show the original forecast, it is generally better to display the unconsumed forecast and the customer orders. Showing the information this way makes it easier to see the total demand in each time period. This total demand is being used for exception checking and for creating planned master schedule orders.

The customer orders are displayed at their ship dates. In the example shown in

Figure 20
Master Production Schedule Reports

MAKE-TO-ORDER ITEM
ON HAND = 0

	Period							
	1/09	1/16	1/23	1/30	2/06	2/13	2/20	2/27
Forecast	0	0	0	0	4	4	3	3
Customer Orders		10		6		0		
Master Schedule		10		10		10		
Projected Available	0	0	0	4	0	6	3	0
Available To Promise		0		4		10		

MAKE-TO-STOCK ITEM
ON HAND = 200
SAFETY STOCK = 100

	Period							
	1/09	1/16	1/23	1/30	2/06	2/13	2/20	2/27
Forecast	70	70	70	70	70	70	70	70
Branch Whse Demands			120			120		
Customer Orders								
Master Schedule		400				400		
Projected Available	130	460	270	200	130	340	270	200

Figure 20, customer orders happen to be promised at the dates that master schedule orders are due to be completed. Customer orders could also be promised at a date later than the completion date of the master schedule order. In these cases, the items would sit for some time before being shipped to customers. This would be done, for example, where several items are being collected for shipment together.

The branch warehouse demands are shown at the date the items are scheduled to ship from the central supply location to the branch warehouses. The scheduled ship dates are the planned order start dates of the planned orders at the branch warehouses. If interplant orders exist, these are also shown at the date the items are scheduled to ship from the supplying plant to the receiving plant.

The master production schedule in Figure 20 is shown as a series of master schedule orders at their receipt dates. The master schedule items are due to be completed on these dates and will be available for shipment to customers. While this is the most common way to show the master schedule, it is also possible to show the master production schedule by release date (due date offset by the lead time).

The projected available balance is calculated using the on-hand balance and the master schedule orders less demands for the period. In this example, the total demand is the sum of the forecast and the customer orders.

The master production schedule report contains master production schedule totals by family. The purpose of these totals is to verify that the master production schedule is in fact a reflection of the production plan. The quantities in the master production schedule, when totaled, must equal the quantities in the production plan (plus or minus some small tolerance). Top management of the company has agreed to a production plan as an overall rate of production; the master scheduler is responsible for working within the constraints of this production plan.

In the normal course of making changes to the master production schedule, it is possible for the master scheduler to make an error so that the master production schedule no longer reflects the production plan. In this case, the totaled master production schedule is not within a specified tolerance of the production plan for the family. For example, the master production scheduler may have moved production on an item from one week to a later week. The master scheduler may have also planned to move production for another item from a later week to an earlier one to compensate for the previous change. If this second change is forgotten or otherwise not made, the master production schedule no longer reflects the production plan.

The method used to audit errors like the one described above is to total the master production schedule quantities and compare them to the production plan. The weekly master production schedule quantities for specific items are totaled into monthly production figures for families of products. These totals can be compared to the quantities in the production plan for agreement.

If the master schedule items in a type of product are modules, the totals will generally make little sense. In the case of an automobile, a total of all frames, engines, radios, and trim packages is not a meaningful number. What is meaningful is the total number of frames, the total number of engines, the total number of radios, and the total number of trim packages. The master scheduler can review these more meaningful numbers and determine whether the master production schedule is a reflection of the production plan.

For this reason, the logic which calculates totals for the master production schedule must also contain logic to provide subtotals. The master scheduler is responsible for assigning an identifier to each of the master schedule items within a subgroup. Subtotals are calculated and displayed in the master production schedule report wherever subgroups or subfamilies have been assigned.

EXCEPTION MESSAGES

The master production schedule software includes some exception reporting to direct the attention of the master scheduler to the items that require his attention.

The purpose of these exception messages is to allow the master scheduler to go directly to the items that require evaluation. In some situations this is essential; for example, in a company where there are several thousand items in the master production schedule, the system should point out the specific items requiring attention. In other situations, there may be fewer items in the master production schedule. Yet even in these situations, exception messages are highly desirable since they relieve the master scheduler of the responsibility for scanning all of the master scheduling information for all the items in the master production schedule.

Seven types of exception messages are part of the master production scheduling system. These are:

1. Reschedule a master schedule order to an earlier date.

2. Reschedule a master schedule order to a later date.

3. Not enough in the master production schedule to cover demands.

4. Master schedule order due for release.

5. Overpromised customer orders.

6. Past due master schedule order.

7. Cancel a master schedule order.

The exception messages to reschedule a master schedule order to a later or earlier date or to cancel a master schedule order indicate that the master schedule is out of agreement with the latest forecast, customer orders, branch warehouse demands, or interplant orders. The master scheduler may choose to change any of the master schedule orders or he may leave them unchanged. These rescheduling and cancel exception messages function like the exception messages in material requirements planning. The exception messages are based on the projected available balance calculation in the master production schedule report.

Having forecast consumption logic in the system helps to prevent exception messages due to minor sales fluctuations. Sales will always go up and down from week to week and the master scheduler should not have to review the situation each time these minor sales fluctuations occur. Allowing the customer orders to reduce the sales forecast over a period of time has the effect of assuming the sales forecast to be correct over that period; consequently rescheduling exception messages are produced only when significant variations occur. However, if abnormal demands are not identified and flagged, the master scheduler may not be alerted to sales that are above or below forecast. When deciding how to set the rules for identifying abnormal demands, it is generally better to err on the side of tolerances that are too tight rather than too loose; in effect, forcing the master scheduler to review marginal cases. The master scheduler does not have to change the master production schedule each time he is alerted to sales that are above or below the forecast.

The exception message for a master schedule order due for release is generated when the master schedule order is ready for release. This exception message is produced by checking the start date of the order against the current date plus a few days or a week. By producing this message a few days before the actual start date of the order, the master scheduler can make a final check of the order quantity and date, check component availability, prepare any documentation or paperwork, etc.

The exception message for not enough in the master production schedule is generated when the master production schedule will not cover the forecast, customer orders, branch warehouse demands, and interplant orders. The master scheduler may choose to add to the master production schedule or he may leave it unchanged. This exception is based on the projected available balance calculation in the master production schedule report.

The exception message for overpromised customer orders is generated whenever more customer orders have been promised than the master production schedule can support. Generally, this indicates that an error has occurred; either in customer order promising, or possibly a change to the master production schedule that was not made. The exception is created whenever the available to promise in the master production schedule report is less than zero.

The exception message for a past due master schedule order is generated when a scheduled receipt for the master schedule item is past due. This is an extremely serious condition since it probably means that the company has been unable to ship the product to the customers or distribution centers to whom it has been promised. This exception message is produced by checking the due date of the order against the current date.

TWO-LEVEL MASTER PRODUCTION SCHEDULING

In some types of products there is an advantage in master production scheduling at two levels. This is useful whenever the master scheduler must coordinate a number of related master production schedules. The automobile explained at the beginning of this topic is an example of a product where the master production schedule is stated in terms of modules. The two levels of master production scheduling would be a master production schedule for automobiles, and also master production schedules for the different modules, like 4-cylinder engines, V-6 engines, AM-FM stereo cassette radios, etc.

The advantage in this method is that it allows the computer to assist the master scheduler in managing and coordinating a number of related master production schedules. In the case of the automobile, the master production schedules for the modules are related because they depend on the production of the cars. It is easy to see how the module master production schedules could get out of line with one another and with the reproduction of cars. Any changes in the master production schedule for automobiles means that the master production schedules for all the modules also have to be changed. Likewise, as customer orders appear for a different mix of modules, the master scheduler may have to consider a change to the master production schedules for some of the modules. As with any type of master production schedule, the computer does not automatically create or approve the master production schedule for the modules. It only assists the master scheduler by providing information that allows him to coordinate a number of related master production schedules.

The way to assist the master scheduler in coordinating these related master production schedules is to pass information from the master production schedule for the type of product to the master production schedules for the modules or other items. This information is called the production forecast and it is one of the factors used to develop the master production schedules for the modules.

The term production forecast is used to describe these numbers because they are calculated using both a master production schedule and a forecast percentage. The master production schedule for the type of product is used and may be different from the demand for the item. Also, a forecast percentage is used to distribute the production over the master schedule items in the type of product. These percentages are a forecast of the mix of items within the type of product. Because the production forecasts are based on the master production schedule for the type of product, they may be different from the forecast or demand for these items if the master production schedule is being set above or below the forecast rate of sales.

One way to calculate a production forecast for a master schedule item is using a planning bill of material. A planning bill of material is a bill of material where the parent item number is the type of product. The component item numbers in the bill of material are the modules or other master schedule items in the type of product. The quantities per assembly in the bill of material are the percentages that each module or other item in the type of product contributes to the production of the product as a whole.

An automobile illustrates a planning bill of material. In this case, the parent item number is the type of product, like a Pontiac Fiero or a Ford Mustang. The planning bill of material lists as components all the other options and features that are available in this type of car. This typically includes the basic car, the engine, the transmission, the radio, etc. The quantities for the options and features are the percentages that each is used in building the cars. For example, the basic car has a quantity of 1.0. The V-6 engine might have a quantity of .85 since 85% of the cars typically have V-6 engines, and so on.

Planning bills of material are not the only method that can be used to pass information in this type of two-level master production scheduling. The objective is to calculate some numbers: the production forecasts. The method that is used to calculate these numbers is not really important as long as they are calculated correctly. Another method for calculating production forecasts would be to use a matrix of numbers that connect the master schedule items in a type of product, and show the percentages that each master schedule item in the type of product contributes to the production of the product as a whole. In most systems, planning bills of material are used to calculate production forecasts. For this reason, whenever an example is illustrated, planning bills of material will be used for the purpose of the explanation but other methods are also workable.

One goal of two-level master production scheduling is to produce the most accurate picture of demand on the product options. This demand, the production forecast, can be calculated in several different ways, regardless of whether a planning bill of material or a matrix of numbers is used. Some calculations of the production forecast are more effective than others.

The simplest calculation to produce a production forecast is to extend the master production schedule for a type of product by the planning bills of material to give the production forecasts for the items in the product. These production forecasts would then be posted to the master schedule items.

While this is the simplest method, it is not the best available. A production forecast, like any forecast, is a guess. A guess should only be used in those situations where it is necessary to guess and not in any situations where better information is available. In a time period where no customer orders have been promised, it is necessary to guess on the entire master production schedule quantity. In a time period where the entire master production schedule quantity has been promised to customers, there is no reason to guess at all. The customers have indicated their preferences and the mix in the master production should match the customer orders, if possible, or the customer orders should be promised in another time period. In a time period where some customers orders have been promised, but some of the production is still available to be promised, it is necessary to guess only on the quantity available to promise customers and it is not necessary or even desirable to guess on the entire master production schedule quantity.

Therefore, a production forecast must be calculated from the uncommitted portion of the master production schedule, not from the entire master production schedule for the type of product.

Normally, the most effective method for developing production forecasts is to compute them using the available to promise for the type of product. The available-to-promise quantity would be extended by the planning bills of material and posted as production forecasts to the master schedule options in the family. The advantage in this method is that is has the effect of improving the ability to guess and consequently to master schedule. As customer orders are promised in a time period, the customer preferences begin to reveal themselves and, in many situations, they will be different from the forecast quantities. The master schedule report will show the customer orders to the master scheduler. This will also revise the production forecast quantities since they are calculated using the available to promise calculation. In effect, this calculation recomputes the available to promise, and as a result, the production forecast for all the options each time a customer order is promised. This has the effect of showing the master scheduler any trends in the customer orders and alerting him so that he can consider a change to the master production schedule to provide for these trends. The emphasis is on making the master scheduler aware of the trend. He does not have to change the master production schedule. Based on this evaluation, the master scheduler may decide to change the master production schedule, or he may choose to leave it as it was.

Figure 21 is an example of a master production schedule report for a product being master production scheduled at two levels using this method. This example shows the extension of the available-to-promise quantity by the planning bills of material. In this sample report, the master schedule item has a quantity per assembly in the planning bill of material of 50%. There are some limited circumstances where calculating a production forecast from the available to promise may not be the best method. This happens when the products being master scheduled are produced in low volumes and where the percentage on the planning bill of material for an option is small. For example, a company manufacturing large mainframe computers may produce only one computer per week and some of the options may only be required in one out of ten computers.

In this situation, there can be some problems with excessive production forecast requirements for the options, and with additional (sometimes unnecessary) exception messages. This is because (in this set of circumstances) the calculation of the production forecasts using the available-to-promise quantities violates a basic principle. The principle is that when an item is forecast over a time period (a month for example), the consumption of that forecast must be done over the same period. For example, if an item is forecast at a certain quantity per month, then all customer orders in that month should reduce that forecast quantity. In the case of low volumes, and low percentages in the planning bill of material, the method of calculating the production forecasts from the available to promise does

Figure 21
Master Production Schedule Reports

TYPE OF PRODUCT

	Period							
	1/09	1/16	1/23	1/30	2/06	2/13	2/20	2/27
Forecast					6	4	10	10
Customer Orders		20		14		6		
Master Schedule		20		20		20		20
Projected Available	0	0	0	6	0	10	0	10
Available To Promise		0		6		14		20

PLANNING BILL OF MATERIAL = 50%
MODULE BEING MASTER SCHEDULED

	Period							
	1/09	1/16	1/23	1/30	2/06	2/13	2/20	2/27
Production Forecast		0		3		7		10
Customer Orders		12		7		5		
Master Schedule		12		12		10		10
Projected Available	0	0	0	2	2	0	0	0
Available To Promise		0		5		5		10

not use the time period between master schedule orders as the time period for both calculating the production forecasts and for consuming the production forecasts. In the case of the computer manufactured once a week with a 10% option, the production forecast for the option is correctly computed over a ten-week period, but is not consumed over a ten-week period. This is incorrect. If a customer order is received for the 10% option, the system should consume the production forecast for the option by reducing it over a ten-week interval, not just in the week the order is promised.

This is a specialized problem. For those companies that actually have a serious problem of this nature, an alternative method exists for calculating and updating the production forecasts. This alternate logic would allow a time period for the calculation of production forecasts and the reduction of these forecasts by actual customer orders as they appear.

In order to be complete, the logic which handles a master production schedule at two levels must have two additional features. The first is to recognize that planning bills of material (like other bills of material) change. An option may be forecast to become more or less popular in the future. For example, the V-6 engine option for a Pontiac Fiero may be forecast to increase in popularity when the 5-speed manual transmission option is available. At the same time, the popularity of the 4-speed manual transmission and the 4-cylinder engine options are expected to fall.

Two methods for handling changing bills of material are explained as part of the bill of material subsystem. These methods, date effectivity and bill of material deviations tied to an order, can be used to handle a future forecast change to the planning bills of material. Both methods should be available in the maintenance system for planning bills of material.

The other feature that is needed is a calculation to reduce rounding errors as the available to promise quantity is extended by the planning bills of material to create the production forecasts. If either the available to promise quantity or the quantity per assembly in the planning bill of material is small, production forecasts may be created in decimal quantities. It is not acceptable to round all the production forecasts either up or down because this could seriously under- or overstate the production forecast and consequently the master production schedule.

Typically the calculation to reduce this rounding error accumulates the decimal part of each production forecast. When the quantity in the accumulator equals one, the production forecast in that time period would be increased by one and the accumulator would be cleared. For example, if the quantity per in the planning bill was .3333 and the available to promise for the type of product was one per period, this logic would generate production forecasts of 1, 0, 0, 1, 0, 0, 1, etc.

LEAD TIME PICTURE

Three methods are available to assess the effects of a change to the master production schedule. These are: rough-cut capacity planning, a lead time picture for a product, and a detailed simulation of proposed changes to the master production schedule. Rough-cut capacity planning was discussed in Chapter 3, Sales and Operations Planning; the lead time picture is discussed here; simulation is covered in Chapter 24.

A lead time picture for a product is a way for the master scheduler to see the accumulated lead times for the items in a product. Using this picture, the master scheduler has a quick guide which he can use to find the critical items which could affect a change to the master production schedule.

Typically the lead time picture is a multi-level bill of material showing the accumulated lead times for the items listed on the bill. If the master scheduler is investigating a change to the master production schedule eight weeks in the future, he could use the lead time picture to pick off the items that may be a problem in implementing the proposed change. The master scheduler can go to the MRP report for these items and see what effect the proposed change to the master production schedule has on the items.

Like rough-cut capacity planning, the lead time picture should not be used for more than what it really is. The lead time picture is just a simple way for the master scheduler to find the critical items affecting a change to the master production schedule. It does not determine whether or not a change to the master production schedule can be made. That can only be determined when the master scheduler reviews the MRP reports for the critical items. Also the lead time picture is concerned only with material. It does not address capacity. Finally, the lead time picture will not be very helpful to the master scheduler if the number of critical items is quite large. This could be caused by a proposed change to the master production schedule which is close to the current date, or it could be caused by a proposed change to an item with several hundred or a thousand components. It would take the master scheduler a long time to evaluate the effects of such a change using the lead time picture. In these cases, a detailed simulation of the proposed change is the best approach.

Chapter 5

Demand Management

Demand management encompasses the areas of forecasting, customer order entry, distribution, and interplant movement of material and as such is an integral part of the high level planning and scheduling process. In a manufacturing company, forecasts and the backlog of customer orders are the starting point for company business plans, the sales and operations planning process, and the master production schedule. The customer orders also may identify future requirements for the final assembly schedule. In a distribution business, demands from physical distribution play a major role in the development of valid production plans and master production schedules.

Demands are one of the inputs to the sales and operations planning and master production scheduling processes. The demands for a product family or item are not the sales and operations plan or the master production schedule itself. Instead, they are combined in a process of human judgment and evaluation to produce a valid sales and operations plan and individual master production schedules.

The purpose of demand management is to develop the most reasonable projection of future requirements, and then update this projection when change is warranted. By properly managing the different demand streams, trivial changes to the sales and operations plan and master schedule can be avoided—and meaningful differences in the marketplace can be recognized at the earliest possible moment so that effective action can be taken.

The demand management capabilities in the system must recognize that forecasting, customer order promising, etc. are a people process, and that the essence of effective demand management is good communication, quick feedback, and properly defined accountabilities. The computer logic that is part of an effective demand management system should support these important activities.

FORECASTING SYSTEM

For most companies, a significant portion of the demand management and high-level planning activities starts with the forecast. Forecasts are a primary input to the business plan, the sales and operations plan, and the master production schedule. The management of a company and the master scheduler must evaluate the forecast along with the other factors that make up the business plan, sales plan, and the master production schedule.

Forecasting, like many business functions, is a management process with specific accountabilities: it also happens that for many companies the computer can provide significant assistance in developing and updating the forecast. In the end, though, people evaluate and approve forecasts and develop sales plans to make the forecast happen. Ultimately, people have to be held accountable for hitting the forecast.

A comprehensive forecasting system should have four basic functions:

1. Several simple forecasting techniques and a method for evaluating these different techniques.

2. A way to take seasonal factors into account.

3. A way to break down and allocate forecasts of families of items by warehouse, configuration, package size, etc.

4. A way to review and approve the forecast before updating the system.

The functions that should be part of a comprehensive forecasting system developed over a number of years of experience working with forecasting systems. For a long time, there were two major misconceptions about forecasting. One misconception was that it was possible to develop a "right number"; that by developing more and more sophisticated and complicated forecasting algorithms it would be possible to compute the right number. The other misconception was that it was possible to develop a single technique that would work to forecast all items.

For many years, most research on forecasting focused on sophisticated mathematical approaches like multiple regression analysis, least squares, correlation analysis, adaptive smoothing, Box Jenkins, etc. This was an attempt to develop a single sophisticated forecasting technique that would generate the right forecast, and which would work for all items.

Unfortunately, with each increase in sophistication came a corresponding decrease in the ability of humans to evaluate and use the forecasts, with little improvement in forecast accuracy.

Most of the effort expended in developing forecasting techniques has been in the area of mathematical optimization. Yet experience shows that if people don't understand why a system produces certain numbers or recommendations, typically because of the complexity of the mathematics used to develop those numbers, then they will not be able to use the system effectively. In most cases, the advances in forecasting techniques have actually made it more difficult to understand and use the forecasts that can be generated.

Today, the trend is waning away from mathematical optimization and moving toward simulating alternatives. Instead of trying to find the single right formula that will generate the one right forecast, companies are using the computer to simulate different forecasting strategies and evaluate their effectiveness. People can then review the different strategies and the recommendations of the forecasting system, choosing the technique that makes the most sense in developing a forecast of future sales.

This approach to forecasting is called focus forecasting (*Focus Forecasting: Computer Techniques for Inventory Control,* Bernard T. Smith, Oliver Wight Limited Publications, Essex Junction, Vermont, 1978). Focus forecasting is a system that can simulate and evaluate a number of different strategies, selecting the forecasting technique that would have proven most effective in forecasting the recent past. The forecasting techniques that are part of a focus forecasting system are typically simple techniques like a moving average or simple strategies like "whatever we sold the last three months is probably what we'll sell the next three months," but they could be sophisticated mathematical approaches. In addition, some companies may also find it important to include models of product life cycles for assistance in forecasting. All these techniques are accommodated by the focus forecasting approach.

Most people using focus forecasting systems end up choosing simple forecasting strategies because they are easy to understand and use. In addition, the benefits from focus forecasting come from using a computer to simulate alternatives, rather than from using it for a single sophisticated technique to develop the "right answer."

Effective forecasting software accommodates both the intrinsic and the extrinsic factors that may make up a forecast. Intrinsic forecasts are based on the past. The most common ways to make these predictions use an average, a moving average, or a weighted moving average. The extrinsic forecasts are based on outside information like marketing information, etc.

The strategies that are part of a forecasting system must provide a way to take seasonal factors into account. This would allow the system to handle regular patterns that repeat at certain times each year. For example, demand for both cigars and cosmetics is highly seasonal. This seasonality can be analyzed and some numbers developed for each time period. These numbers, often called base indices, can then be used to spread the total forecast over the year, quarter, or month in whatever pattern makes sense.

The forecasting system must also provide a way to break down and allocate forecasts for families of items by warehouse, configuration, package size, etc. In a Distribution Resource Planning system, for example, it is necessary to develop sales forecasts by item and distribution center. Many companies choose to develop a nationwide forecast, and break it down into individual item and distribution center forecasts. This breakdown would typically use historical percentages. This same approach can be used to take an overall product family forecast and break it down to specific forecasts by product configuration or package size.

Similarly, the system must provide a method for reconciling the aggregate forecast for a product family with the sum of the individual forecasts by item. Reconciliation of the forecasts might mean adjusting the aggregate forecast in some situations. In other situations, the individual forecasts might be recomputed using a proration of the aggregate forecast.

Finally, and perhaps most importantly, a forecasting system must have a way to review the forecast after it has been generated and before the system is updated. The experience of operating effective forecasting systems shows that the key is to combine simple forecasting techniques with good human judgment. A human being will be responsible for the forecast, and a human being needs to review it before it is updated. A person must have the opportunity to change the forecast before it goes into the system so that he or she can be held accountable for the forecast being used.

ORDER ENTRY SYSTEM

An order entry system is used to add, delete, and change customer orders. If the item ordered by the customer is planned by MRP, the customer order will be presented to the MRP netting and exception checking logic as a demand. If the item is controlled through the master scheduling system, these customer demands will be presented to the master production scheduling netting and exception logic.

The order entry system must be able to create multiple line items on a single customer order. The multiple line items may be for different items on the same date, for different items on different dates, or for the same item on different shipment dates. Each line item represents a demand to MRP or the master scheduling system. One or more shipments may be included on a single customer order.

Five pieces of information are required for each customer order line item. These are the item number, required (promised) date, quantity, customer order number, and customer request date. The item number is used to present the customer order information to MRP and master scheduling. The required date and quantity are used in the netting and exception logic. The customer order number is needed for pegging. The customer request date is the date the customer originally specified for the line item, and may be different from the required date or promised date that is being used in the MRP or master scheduling system. For example, the customer may have asked for the item in week three, but, because of supply problems, it will not be available until week six. In this case, the date the customer is promised is week six, but the request date for the item is week three. The customer request date is needed for an available-to-promise check when the order is entered, and can be helpful for performance measurement, forecasting, and forecast consumption.

Besides having the capability to create customer orders and customer order line items, the order entry system must be able to change and delete existing orders. Once a customer order has been created, the information must be available for change. It must be possible to change the required date and the quantity for each line item. When a customer order is deleted, the system should close the order and remove each of the line items regardless of the order status. When a customer order line item is deleted, the system should remove the line item, and if all line items are completed or closed, mark the order complete.

Paperwork to assist the stockroom or finished goods inventory people may be helpful and can be produced when the customer order is ready for shipment. This computer generated paperwork typically includes picking lists and shipping documents.

Logic for producing hardcopy customer confirmations may be helpful. Confirmations are typically printed immediately following the creation of all the line items.

The order entry process should include an available-to-promise check for each line item on the customer order. As explained in Chapter 4, Master Production Scheduling, by promising customer orders using the available-to-promise calculation new customer orders can be slotted for shipment based on the existing master production schedule.

There are a number of different ways to do an available-to-promise check:

1. In cases where the customer promise is made before the order is entered, the available to promise has to be checked prior to the actual entry.

    A. Done using the master production schedule report or display.

    B. Done using special on-line promising displays to automate the checking and promising process.

2. The available to promise checked as the order is entered, with items not available on the requested date highlighted and shown with both the requested date and the available date for review by a person.

3. Available-to-promise check run after the order is entered with orders not available on the requested date listed on a report or in an on-line display for repromising.

An automated check of the available to promise normally works by comparing the cumulative available to promise on the request date with the quantity required on the customer order. The available to promise for the first period is the on-hand balance plus master schedule orders due in the past or current period less all customer orders due before the end of the first period. For later periods, the available to promise is the prior period available to promise plus any master schedule orders less any customer orders for the period. The customer order quantity is compared to the available-to-promise quantity for the period of the request date. If the available to promise is greater than or equal to the requirement, then the line item can be promised.

If the available to promise is less than that required, then a person has to make a decision about the importance of changing the master production schedule for this single customer order. A good master production schedule policy recognizes that there is an expense in direct and setup labor, inventory, overhead, and confusion for each change to the master production schedule. Yet changes can and should be made to the schedule. The policy should be to provide an evaluation of the effects and cost of each change prior to the change being made.

The order entry system requires some additional capabilities to handle customer orders for products made-to-order from a number of options. This type of product is like the automobile described in the master production scheduling chapter (Chapter 4). For automobiles, modules exist for V-8 and V-6 engines, AM-FM radios, accessory trim packages, etc. These modules may be actual subassemblies that are stocked and then put into the automobile (for example, the V-6 and V-8 engine options), or they may be logical groupings of parts that cannot physically be assembled (like accessory trim packages). The parts associated with this type of module are put together with the parts of other modules to create a number of different subassemblies, like the front and rear door subassemblies.

In this type of product, the customer order is not for a specific finished item number from a product catalog. Instead, the customer order is for a type of product and a series of options. For example, the customer order might be for a silver Buick Skylark automobile with V-6 engine, AM/FM cassette stereo, special trim, etc. The customer order is the only unique product identifier, and it is entered at two levels: for the type of product (Buick Skylark) and modules and options (Buick Skylark common parts module, V-6 engine option, AM/FM cassette option, etc.).

For products made from options, the order entry mechanism should include two additional capabilities:

1. Assistance in selecting the proper modules and options for the product.

2. A check of the available to promise for both the type of product and each option.

The order entry mechanism should provide a menu of available choices for each type of product. For example, the order entry system should prompt for the entry of the type of product; show that an engine option is required, displaying the available choices of engines; show that the transmission option is required, displaying the available choices for transmissions, etc. And, since not all options necessarily work with all other options (for example, in the case of the Buick Skylark, the 5-speed manual transmission option may only be available with the 4-cylinder engine), the system should eliminate the choices that are not valid based on earlier choices. This way, once the order entry person picked a Skylark with 6-cylinder engine, the system would not show the 5-speed transmission as an available option.

For a product made from options, the customer request date is a single date, but product availability is based on the dates of the individual options and modules. Consequently, the order entry mechanism should check the available to promise for the type of product and the available to promise for each product option. If all of the modules and options are not available by the requested date, then the order should be flagged for human review and approval.

METHOD FOR ANALYZING CUSTOMER ORDERS

Not all customer orders are necessarily part of the forecast. Sometimes major orders are received from new customers, and sometimes high-impact orders are forthcoming from new, unanticipated market segments. At other times, changes in the marketplace may be signaled by significant increases (or decreases) in customer order demands.

Unless mechanisms exist to identify abnormal demands (and give them some type of special handling) and to pick up trends in the marketplace, a company may jeopardize its ability to service existing customers that are part of the forecast. Abnormal demands are not part of the forecast, they are in addition to the forecast quantities. Major volume increases indicate that the forecast is being oversold and that the forecast needs to be revised. If the system assumes that these abnormal demands or volume increases replace the forecast, then the total demand for the item will be significantly understated in the system. Not enough of the required items will be built to satisfy the real demands. Eventually, the excitement of the major new accounts may be dampened by the problems that come from being without a product genuinely needed to support the needs of long-term, loyal customers.

Consequently, some method is needed to assist in analyzing incoming customer orders. This has two parts:

1. Computer logic to compare existing customer orders to the forecast for the purpose of identifying demands that may be abnormal, or major shifts in the marketplace.

2. A way to code demands that have been identified as abnormal.

The volume of orders promised in many companies makes identifying abnormal demands manually a challenging, if not impossible, job. For this reason, simple computer logic to compare customer orders, individually and in groups, to forecasts is helpful. This logic can assist in identifing abnormal demands.

Generally, companies set up some simple rules, such as:

1. Individual customer orders that exceed X% of the forecast quantity for the period are potentially abnormal.

2. Total customer orders exceeding Y% of the forecast for a specified period may be abnormal or indicative of an upward business trend that should be reviewed.

3. Customer orders less than Z% of the forecast for a specified period may be indicative of a downward business trend that should be reviewed.

4. Total customer orders through a period (all the orders between the current date and the specified future period) exceeding some specified percentage of the total forecast may be abnormal or indicative of an upward business trend that should be reviewed.

5. Total customer orders through a period (all the orders between the current date and the specified future period) less than some specified percentage of the total forecast may be indicative of a downward business trend that should be reviewed.

6. An unsold forecast quantity that has fallen past due and that exceeds some percentage of the month's forecast may be indicative of a downward trend that requires review.

Customer orders in excess of the limits can be coded as abnormal demands automatically, or listed on an exception report for review by someone who can evaluate the situation. A person would be responsible for reviewing the situation and deciding if additional actions should be taken. This way, early communication with the customer may avert bad commitments and future service problems. In situations where the customer orders are less than the limits, the items should be listed on an exception report for human review.

Abnormal demands should be excluded from the forecast consumption logic that is part of the system (and described below). Abnormal demands should be added to the remaining forecast, other customer orders, etc. to compute total demand against the master schedule. Demands coded as abnormal may need to be excluded from the forecasting process because they represent events not likely to happen again in the future.

FORECAST CONSUMPTION LOGIC

The system should also include a method to reduce the forecast by customer orders that are part of the forecast. The objective of this forecast consumption logic is to most accurately represent the needs of the marketplace based on current projections and actual orders. By consuming the forecast properly it is possible to compute total customer demand for each period, taking into account timing differences between the actual customer orders and the forecast. These timing differences can occur when customer demands match the forecast quantities, but are for different dates than those anticipated.

Forecast consumption logic can be done in either of two places:

1. As customer orders are entered.

2. In a separate calculation that is run periodically.

Either of these two methods is workable. In the first case, the unconsumed forecast is updated as each customer order is entered. The system finds the proper unconsumed forecast quantities and reduces them by the customer order quantity. In the second case, the forecast consumption logic is part of a separate calculation and not part of the order entry process. In other words, the forecast is left unchanged as customer orders are received. In a separate computation, either as part of the master production schedule report or a separate batch run, the customer orders are combined with the original forecast to compute the unconsumed forecast.

In each of these methods, both the original forecast and the unconsumed forecast are stored in the system. The original forecast is needed so that customer orders can be reanalyzed periodically to identify potentially abnormal demands and trends. By storing the unconsumed forecast, the master scheduling and material requirements planning logic is simplified. The unconsumed forecast can be added to the other demands to compute total demand for the item. No forecasts consumption calculations are required in the MRP or master production scheduling logic to combine the original forecast and the customer orders.

In the forecast consumption logic that is part of the system, the forecast should be reduced in the period in which the customer order is requested. If demand exceeds the forecast in the period, the system can reach ahead or back to reduce forecasts in other time periods.

It is also necessary to provide logic to handle forecasts and customer orders that fall past due. It is incorrect to drop off the unconsumed forecast at the end of each week. In most situations, this has the effect of changing the forecast—even though no change was intended or indicated. For example, take the situation where the original forecast for a month was forty, split into four weekly quantities of ten. At the end of week one, only seven have been sold. Should the system drop the unsold three from the forecast? If so, the forecast has now been revised from forty to thirty-seven? Or should the remaining three units accumulate as an unsold forecast, in effect leaving the original forecast of forty for the month without change?

The simplest way to handle this problem is to specify the number of weeks that should be accumulated in the past due time period before being dropped. For example, four weeks could be specified. Unconsumed forecasts would accumulate in the past for a month, and then be dropped automatically. In most situations, an exception report should list the forecasts that were dropped automatically; this way, a person can review the situation and add back a forecast quantity if it was dropped in error.

When the forecast consumption logic is part of a separate batch process in the system, some additional logic is needed in the mechanism that drops unconsumed forecasts. This additional logic recodes any past due customer orders in the system as abnormal demands when the unconsumed forecasts are dropped. This prevents the system from incorrectly consuming the forecast in future time periods with these customer orders.

An effective system includes a calculation of total demand that summarizes the unconsumed forecast, normal and abnormal customer orders, dependent demands, distribution requirements, and interplant orders by date. This total demand is used in developing and managing the sales and operations plan and the master production schedule.

INDEPENDENT DEMAND

The system must also provide a way to enter independent demands into the MRP system. These independent demands are not apart of the master production schedule but are included in MRP.

This method for entering independent demands into the system is used for spare parts as well as items where the need for human control through the master production schedule is not needed. These items have no significant effect on capacity or materials, and no human evaluation is needed to evaluate the need or ability to change the schedule.

Independent demands are entered into MRP as gross requirements. The gross requirements are added to any exploded gross requirements to give the total gross requirements that are used in the logic of MRP. Normal netting, exception checking, and order planning take place.

The same functions for analyzing abnormal demands and handling past due forecasts in the master scheduling system should be available for independent demands entered directly into MRP.

PART III

Material Requirements Planning

Chapter 6

The Netting and Exception Checking Logic of MRP II

MRP netting logic simulates a process similar to physical parts staging to determine shortages. Netting logic calculates what is available to satisfy the requirements for an item by comparing the on-hand balance and scheduled receipts to the projected gross requirements. At the same time, this logic determines whether the scheduled receipts are due to be completed when they are needed. Via the netting logic, MRP can determine whether material is, or will be, available to satisfy the requirements and whether the material will be available at the right time.

NETTING CALCULATION

The netting logic uses the on-hand balance less safety stock as the beginning available balance. Normally, the beginning available balance is reduced by individual gross requirements and allocations until it has been consumed. (In some systems, the beginning available balance is reduced by the total allocated quantity, and then reduced by individual gross requirements until consumed. This method, where allocations are not time phased but instead treated as immediate withdrawals from the stockroom, is workable, although less desirable.) As needed, scheduled receipts (released manufacturing orders and purchase orders) are brought into the calculation and used to satisfy requirements.

For MRP to operate as a proper simulation, the netting logic must make one fundamental assumption, the "rescheduling assumption." The netting logic assumes that an existing scheduled receipt will be rescheduled to an earlier date in order to satisfy requirements before a new order is created and released. For example, in a situation where unsatisfied demands for an item exist next week, and a manufacturing order is on the shop floor due to be completed, netting logic that makes the rescheduling assumption assumes that the order will be expedited.

The rescheduling assumption recognizes that it makes more sense to expedite an existing order than to create an entirely new order and attempt to get through before the existing one. The assumption simply reflects the fact that in the real word which MRP simulates, existing orders are expedited before new orders are placed. Notice that the rescheduling assumption does not assume that the order can in fact be expedited and completed by next week. It simply assumes that if any order can be completed by next week, it will be the one on the shop floor working and not a new order. Notice also that the logic does not change the date of the scheduled receipt. It simply uses the order in a netting calculation. Appendix 3 is a detailed explanation of logic that does not make the rescheduling assumption and the resulting difficulties in the system.

The netting logic always uses the on-hand balance to satisfy gross requirements before passing requirements to the order planning and explosion logic. In effect, the netting logic does not distinguish between normal stocked subassemblies and fabrications, and items that are designated as phantoms, transients, or self-consumed assemblies that are built on an assembly line and immediately consumed in another assembly. Although a phantom item is not normally found in stock, the normal netting logic uses any on-hand balance to satisfy requirements before calling for new sets of components.

Netting logic that handles phantoms, transients, and self-consumed assemblies properly is essential, particularly in cases where a company may have an active Just-in-Time program. In most of these cases, normal subassemblies and fabrications are being converted to phantoms as part of the effort to flatten the bill of material. The system needs to recognize any existing inventory and use it up prior to calling for new components.

In other situations, an overrun on a phantom or scrap on the main assembly may cause a phantom item to be built and put into stock. When this happens, the system should satisfy future requirements with the balance on hand of the phantom item. Once this on-hand balance has been consumed, the system can create requirements for component items.

In still other situations, a component may be scheduled for phase out as part of the engineering change. In this case, the phase out may be dependent upon using up any existing inventory. By coding the component as a phantom and restructuring its bill of material to reflect the components being phased in, the system can satisfy any future requirements with the balance remaining of the component. Once this on-hand balance has been used up, the system will create requirements for the components being phased in.

Any additional logic like ignoring the balance on hand for a phantom and simply "blowing through" to generate component gross requirements, is incorrect.

The netting logic of MRP should include a shrinkage factor (or a yield factor) that can be used to show the effect of scrap on the scheduled receipts and planned orders in the future. The effect of a shrinkage factor is to reduce the scheduled receipt and planned order quantities by the anticipated scrap. This can be done in any of several different ways:

1. As each scheduled receipt is read into the netting calculation, reduce the scheduled receipt quantity by the anticipated shrinkage. Inflate the planned order quantities by the amount of shrinkage expected.

2. After the balance on hand has been consumed, inflate the remaining requirements by the shrinkage factor. This has the same effect as reducing the scheduled receipt and planned order quantities by the anticipated shrinkage.

Chapter 13, the Inventory Transaction Subsystem, refers to an "inspection inventory," which are purchase orders that have been received but not put away into the stockroom. This inventory has to be treated like a scheduled receipt in the netting calculation, which means that it must first be reduced by the shrinkage factor.

RESCHEDULING EXCEPTION MESSAGES

Rescheduling exception messages are calculated in the netting calculation. As each scheduled receipt is brought into the netting calculation, the system compares the due date to the date of the last unsatisfied requirement.

If a scheduled receipt is not due into stock soon enough, a parts shortage will occur. In such a situation, an exception message should be generated to indicate that the order needs to be rescheduled to an earlier date to prevent the shortage.

If a scheduled receipt is due too early, then an equally serious problem will occur: either valuable capacity will be used to produce the wrong item, or the formal priority planning system will cease to identify what is really needed and when. An exception message should be generated for a scheduled receipt that is due into stock earlier than the date the order is needed. This exception message indicates that an order needs to be rescheduled out to a later date.

Sadly, many people feel it is more important to reschedule orders to earlier dates than to reschedule orders to later dates. This feeling is understandable: a shortage appears to be a more serious problem than an order which comes into stock before it is needed.

On the surface, this kind of thinking seems to make sense. However, if orders are moved in to earlier dates, but are not moved out, how is it possible to separate the orders that are needed from the ones that are not required for some time? An order due week five may be needed in week five or it may not, how can anyone tell?

The solution, of course, is to reschedule orders to the dates they are needed. Then the system tells the truth about when an order is needed. Exception messages for rescheduling orders to later dates really are as important as the exception messages for rescheduling orders to earlier dates. Another way to look at is that by rescheduling orders out, it is possible to reschedule orders in. Unexpediting is the most powerful expediting tool.

Some systems include an additional exception message for scheduled receipts that are not needed at all and that are candidates for cancellation. This is a helpful message, although an exception message to reschedule an order out to a later date, in this case the end of the planning horizon, provides the same function.

Today, a question about the generation of rescheduling exception messages is, "Why not let the computer reschedule the orders automatically?" There has been a good deal of discussion on this subject, arguing the pros and cons of allowing the computer to automatically change the dates on scheduled receipts. The biggest problem in this question is the terminology. The term automatic rescheduling gives people the impression that rescheduling happens automatically, that it is done by the computer, and that people are not a part of the process.

Automatic rescheduling is not and cannot be automatic. The computer is incapable of determining whether an order can be rescheduled. A computer does not possess the capabilities to evaluate whether rescheduling an order makes sense, and a computer is unable to determine whether an order can be completed by the date the order is needed. Also, the computer cannot take the responsibility for making sure that an order is completed on time. The question of whether the computer can or cannot reschedule orders is the wrong one—the computer cannot. The real question is, "What is the best way to handle the responsibility requirements for making the decisions on rescheduling orders?"

In most MRP systems today, the computer generates rescheduling exception messages for any orders that are needed earlier or later. The due date of the order is not changed except by the planner, and only after the planner has determined that the reschedule makes sense and that the order can be completed by the new due date. For example, in the case of an order needed at an earlier date, the planner and the shop people are responsible for determining whether the order can be completed by the new due date. In the case of an order needed at a later date, the planner still has a responsibility to determine that the reschedule will not create a problem with a vendor or a capacity problem in the factory. The responsibility is clear in this type of system. The planner and the shop people are responsible for analyzing the rescheduling exception message and deciding what to do.

There are some systems, however, that do work, and where the computer automatically changes the due date of the scheduled receipts. A message is also given which indicates that the due date of an order has been changed by the computer. In such a system, the responsibility of the planner and the shop people is to review all the orders where the due dates have been changed. They must verify that the reschedule makes sense and that the new due date can be met. If not, the change must be reversed. Responsibility still exists in this method, but the responsibility is more difficult to maintain. In this case, the computer has done something, and if it is wrong, people must go back and reverse it. In the other situation, the computer highlights problems, and people take action to solve the problems: here the accountability is clearer. Appendix 4 is a more detailed explanation of what has been called automatic rescheduling.

ADDITIONAL EXCEPTION MESSAGES

Rescheduling exception messages are not the only messages generated by MRP. Other types of exception messages should also be generated. These include:

1. Past Due Scheduled Receipt.

2. Planned Order Due for Release.

3. Planning Parameter Violations.

A past due scheduled receipt exception message indicates an order that is overdue. This is a serious condition. If the order is needed, then a shortage exists because the order was needed and is not in the stockroom. If the order is not needed, then it should be rescheduled to the date it is needed. Either way, a past due scheduled receipt is a situation the planner should review.

A planned order due for release exception message indicates that a computer planned order has come within the normal order release horizon. The release horizon provides a few days to a week of visibility for the planner to review the order and verify that the order makes sense before releasing it. He should make sure that the order is not being generated based on some error in the system like a negative on-hand balance, or gross requirements from an obsolete product. The planner should also check to make sure the order quantity is reasonable. If order and order quantity are reasonable, the planner should release the planned order, creating a scheduled receipt in the system.

Parameter violations are conditions in the system where a reasonableness check has been violated. Examples are: beginning available balance is less than zero, planned order exceeds planned order maximum quantity, no order policy specified, and technical problems with the computer logic such as decimal field overflows. These are situations that the planner should review.

Some systems contain as many as twenty or more types of exception messages. However, the exceptions covered by the messages all fall into the categories listed above. They are either rescheduling exceptions, past due scheduled receipt exceptions, planned orders due for release exceptions, or parameter violations. For example, a system may have three planned order due for release exception messages: one for a planned order that is overdue, one for a planned order where the start date of the order is overdue, but the due date is not, and one for a normal planned order due for release. In this case, it isn't really necessary to have three different planned order due for release exception messages. One exception message would identify the situation for a planner, and the planner could then analyze the situation. In general, people seem to make the most effective use of systems that have the necessary features (like a planned order due for release exception message) but are no more complicated than is necessary to provide the needed functions.

Some systems also produce exception messages in different sections of computer logic. Some exceptions are generated in the MRP replanning logic and others are generated in special sections of logic designed to find and report certain types of exception conditions.

In a regenerative system, all exceptions can be generated as part of the MRP planning logic. All items are processed through the regeneration and this is where all exception checking is done. No special logic beyond the normal material requirements planning logic is needed to produce these exception messages.

In a net change system, the situation is different. Unlike a regeneration, net change processing does not include all items. Only items affected by transactions or changes in related material plans are processed. In such a system the rescheduling exceptions and the parameter violations are generated as part of the net change replanning logic.

Yet other items may have exceptions that result from the passage of time. For example, both past due scheduled receipts and planned orders due for release are exceptions caused by the passage of time. There is no assurance that these items will be included into net change planning since there is no assurance that transactions have occurred on these items. Consequently, net change systems typically have a section of logic designed to scan the files and find these exceptions that result from the passage of time.

The follow-up mechanism for messages is another difference in the exception logic for net change and regenerative systems. A regenerative system tends to be fail-safe in exception reporting. Because the system destroys the old plan and generates a completely new one, any exception messages that were not acted upon will come back to the planner each time the regeneration is run. This is a valuable feature since the planner may forget to take action on an item or lose the exception notice.

In a net change system, there must be a way to remind the planner of any exception messages that have not been acted on after some specified period of time. If the planner forgets to take action on an item or loses the exception notice, there is no assurance that the item will be replanned in the near future.

Most net change systems have a special section of logic, called fail-safe logic, to remind the planner of an exception after some specified period of time. Typically, this logic works by storing the date an exception message was given for an item. If no action is taken on the item after so many days, the logic in this section of the system generates a reminder exception message. The delay of several days is needed to give the planner a chance to clear up any backlog of work.

Chapter 28 is a detailed specification for the netting logic in a regenerative MRP system.

Chapter 7

Order Planning and Explosion

Order planning logic provides the method for satisfying demands not covered by the on-hand balance or scheduled receipts. Planned orders are created to satisfy these demands. Planned orders exist only in the computer files. No shop paperwork or purchase order has been created for these orders. They are an anticipation of what will be manufactured or purchased. This anticipation must be a valid simulation of these manufacturing or purchasing events. The due date, start date, and the order quantity of the planned orders must simulate as accurately as possible the due date, start date, and order quantity of the orders that will eventually be released as manufacturing orders and purchase orders. These planned orders are then used to generate component gross requirements and capacity requirements.

The order planning logic in MRP is done after the netting and exception checking of scheduled receipts. The gross requirements that remain at the end of the netting calculation are those not covered by the on-hand balance and scheduled receipts. Planned orders are created to cover these requirements. Some ordering rules are used to determine the due date, start date, and order quantity of the planned orders.

PLANNED ORDER DUE DATES

The due date of each planned order is the date of the unsatisfied gross requirements. The date of the first unsatisfied gross requirement is the date of the first planned order. Remaining requirements are computed based on the planned order quantity, and the date of the next unsatisfied requirement is calculated. This date becomes the date of the next planned order. In each case, the date of the unsatisfied gross requirements is when the item is needed and it is used as the due date of the planned order.

In some systems, safety time is used to calculate the planned order due date. Safety time asks for the completion of an order a number of days or weeks before the order is really needed. In these cases, the due date of the order is earlier than the date the parts are really needed by the amount of the safety time.

Safety time acts like safety stock: both ask for items when they are not really needed. For this reason, there are many situations where both safety stock and safety time are totally unsuitable. However, there are also some limited situations where either safety stock or safety time are acceptable. These are situations where there is an uncertainty of demand or an uncertainty of supply. Independent demand items, for example, have an uncertainty of demand. The demand for these items varies unpredictably from week to week, and for these items it would make sense to allow some safety time or safety stock. In other situations, the supply of an item is uncertain. This is not because the vendor occasionally fails to deliver on time. An example of this kind of supply uncertainty would be an item that is shipped a great distance, or an item with a history of severe quality problems. These situations are not normal and should be an extremely small percentage of all items.

While safety stock is there to be used, and safety time is there to act as a cushion, a good question to ask is, ''If the on-hand balance falls below the safety stock level or delivery is not made within safety time, are we prepared to treat this much like an assembly shortage?'' Such treatment might justify air freight, special handling, or sending a truck to get quick delivery. If these types of things would not be done when the on-hand balance falls below the safety stock or safety time, then the item might not have a legitimate use for safety stock or safety time.

If safety stock or safety time are used were they are not really needed, the system is no longer a simulation of reality. This is because the logic of MRP treats all potential shortages alike whether they are due to an assembly shortage or because the on-hand balance is projected to go below safety stock. A more detailed explanation of safety stock and safety time is contained in Appendix 5.

PLANNED ORDER QUANTITY

The planned order quantity is calculated using an order policy for an item. An order policy is really just a set of rules that are used to determine the order quantity, and many times the order policy is used with some other information (such as the order quantity or lot size) to calculate the order quantity. Order policies are exclusive of one another: one order policy is specified for each item and an item cannot have several order policies at the same time. Order policies generally fall into the six groupings listed below:

1. Lot-for-lot ordering.

2. Ordering using a fixed lot size.

3. Economic order quantity (EOQ).

4. Dynamic lot sizing.

5. Period order quantity (POQ).

6. Specialized ordering rules for one-time activities like scheduling engineering, design, software development, or construction projects.

Lot-for-lot ordering creates a planned order for each unsatisfied gross requirement. The planned order quantity is the quantity of the unsatisfied requirement (after adjusting for anticipated scrap). This ordering policy is the planner's instruction to order only what is needed: if ten are needed, order ten; if sixty-five are needed, order sixty-five.

In most systems, the lot-for-lot ordering rule accumulates all the unsatisfied requirements for the smallest time period (day or week) before creating a planned order. In other systems, the lot-for-lot ordering rule creates a single planned order for each unsatisfied requirement: if there are five unsatisfied requirements on a single day, the system would create five individual planned orders.

Lot-for-lot ordering is generally used for items that are expensive, bulky, or require little or no setup or ordering cost. Some examples of these items include large highly engineered and custom built items, finished products that are assembled from stocked subassemblies, or a product that has a limited lifetime after the ingredients have been mixed.

Lot-for-lot ordering is also used for handling self-consumed assemblies, and for helping in the implementation of engineering changes. Lot-for-lot ordering might be used in an engineering change where several items are being phased out. It may be necessary to run a short lot of one of the items being phased out as a way of balancing the inventory. This situation requires that the planner be able to have planned orders that are equal to the unsatisfied gross requirements. In other words, a planner must have a lot-for-lot order policy.

The normal fixed order policy logic makes the planned orders equal to the fixed order quantity: if the unsatisfied requirement exceeds the fixed order quantity, then the planned order is a multiple of the fixed order quantity. In some systems, however, the fixed order quantity operates as a type of cut-off. If the unsatisfied requirement exceeds the fixed order quantity, then two planned orders, each for the fixed order quantity, are created.

A fixed order policy is intended for items that are normally manufactured or purchased in lots that cover more than a single gross requirement. These items typically have setup or ordering costs that make it sensible to manufacture or purchase more than just the immediate needs. A fixed order quantity or lot size is determined by the planner and entered into the system. The planner is responsible for evaluating things like the EOQ, a practical quantity that can be handled on the shop floor, any deterioration or limited lifetime on the item, container size, and a number of other intangibles to determine a reasonable lot size.

Chapter 28 includes a detailed technical discussion of the order planning logic that is part of an MRP system.

The economic order quantity is an order policy where the economic order quantity is recalculated during the MRP planning run. This EOQ is then used as a fixed order quantity.

An automatic EOQ order policy has three serious problems. The first problem is that the calculation takes place outside the planner's control and the planner cannot be realistically held accountable for any problems that result from the use of this order quantity. The second problem is that the order quantity is based solely on the balancing of ordering and carrying costs assuming the usage is the same each week. Actually, usage is rarely the same, and more importantly, the carrying cost and ordering cost are only two of many factors that should be considered when deciding on an order quantity. Other factors to consider include a practical quantity to have on the shop floor, pending engineering changes, running time on a critical piece of equipment, etc. The third problem is that the order quantity will continue to change even after vendor deliveries have been firmed up. The rescheduling and ordering to rearrange vendor deliveries so they keep up with a changing order quantity costs far more than any anticipated savings that might come from using the calculated economic order quantity.

Dynamic order policies are those where a type of EOQ calculation is done to optimize the planned order quantity. These calculations are like the EOQ calculation since they attempt to balance the ordering and carrying costs for an order. These calculations are different from the EOQ calculation, however, since they balance the ordering and carrying costs while taking into account lumpy demand. The EOQ calculation assumes that the demand is the same for each week. Another way to look at this is that the dynamic order quantity calculations and EOQ calculation come up with the same order quantity when the demand is the same each week.

There are different types of dynamic order policies. These include part period balancing, part period balancing with look ahead and look back logic, least total cost, least unit cost, etc. The calculation in each of these methods is slightly different, but the fundamentals are all the same. The calculation attempts to calculate the optimum order quantity based on the ordering and carrying costs.

The same three problems exist in using these dynamic ordering policies that exist in using the automatically calculated EOQ order policy. The calculation of the order quantity is still outside the planner's control. As a result, it is not realistic to expect that the planner can be held accountable for any problems that result from the order quantity. Also, the order quantity is based solely on the balancing of ordering and carrying costs without regard to the many other factors that should be used to make up the order quantity. The third problem is that the order quantity continues to change even after the component supply schedules have been firmed up. This can result in a flood of virtually useless exception messages. The planner is being asked to order and reschedule just to satisfy a changing order quantity. The dollar savings that come from using the optimum order quantity do not begin to compensate for the confusion, the wasted time, and the unnecessary effort that result from using these order policies. Appendix 6 is a more complete explanation of the problems that exist in using these dynamic order policies.

In the period order quantity order policy, gross requirements over a specified number of days or weeks are lumped together into a single planned order. The planned order quantity starts out as the quantity of the first unsatisfied gross requirement. Looking ahead, the program finds and includes all gross requirements for a specified number of days or weeks to give the total planned order quantity.

A period order quantity order policy is necessary in some bucketless systems for purely technical reasons based on the way the lot-for-lot ordering rule has been programmed. In bucketless systems where the lot-for-lot ordering rule creates a planned order for each unsatisfied requirement, it is possible to create several planned orders for the same day or many planned orders for the same week.

Each of these planned orders will then be exploded and a number of gross requirements will be created. Each of these may in turn become a planned order and generate multiple gross requirements.

The geometric expansion of planned orders and gross requirements caused by this kind of lot-for-lot ordering rule can cause problems with the computer hardware, the MRP software, and the people that make up the system. For example, the number of planned orders and requirements may exceed the disk space available, or the number of planned orders and gross requirements that have to be maintained by the software may cause long run times or other poor performance that limit the number of times the system can be run. Furthermore, but having multiple planned orders for the same date is usually not a simulation of reality since the planner typically will not release several orders for the same item in the same day, or many orders for the same item in the same week.

The solution to the problem is to change the order policy on these items from lot-for-lot to period order quantity. By specifying a period order quantity of a day, several days, or a week, this geometric expansion of gross requirements will be stopped.

A specialized ordering rule is required to handle one-time events. One-time events (or activities) occur once and only once during a project. One-time events do not reoccur after they have been completed the first time. For example, new product engineering, structuring of bills of material and routings, tool design and toolmaking, methods engineering, design, software development, FDA certification, and excavation of a construction site are all one-time events in various projects. While ongoing improvements often continue to be made even after the initial engineering, design, and documentation effort, one-time events are those like these where the major effort occurs once and only once.

The due date of a one-time event is the earliest date that the item is required to support the master production schedule. This date may change during the life of the project as the event is added to or deleted from bills of material, as the master schedule changes, as parent lead times are increased or decreased, etc. For example, if a one-time event (say the design of an IC chip) supports several new products, the due date of the chip design may change as the schedules for the new product introductions change. One week the design of the IC chip may be needed in week sixteen to support the master schedule for one product. The next week the master schedules may have changed, and the chip design may be needed in week twelve to support a different product.

The one-time ordering rule used for scheduling one-time events creates a single planned order. The due date of the planned order is the date of the earliest unsatisfied requirement. The planned order quantity is for a quantity of one. Any future requirements for this item do not create any planned orders. Because these are one-time events, they only need to be done once. If the same IC chip design is needed in two products, once the design is done for the first, it is done for the second. It isn't necessary to design the item again for the second product. This logic provides a way to schedule these activities and make the schedule an accurate reflection of the nonrecurring events that must take place in the future.

In addition to order policies, many systems also contain order modifiers. These order modifiers take the planned order quantity, which has been calculated based on the order policy, and change it. Order modifiers generally include a minimum order quantity, an order multiple, and a maximum order quantity. These order modifiers are not used on all items but only where the need for an order modifier exists.

The minimum order quantity increases a planned order quantity up to the minimum. If the planned order quantity is already larger than the minimum order quantity, no change is made to the quantity. A minimum is used where a price break, setup, transportation, or design change makes it impractical to order less than a certain quantity.

An order multiple rounds each planned order up to the next multiple. The calculation always rounds the order up and never down. An order multiple would be used where a certain number of items make up a basket, skid, oven rack, or truck load and the planner wants the order to fill up the container.

An order maximum represents the maximum quantity that can normally be ordered. If, for example, the receiving dock can handle only two thousand pounds, the order maximum on material should be two thousand pounds. Normally, if gross requirements exist for more than the maximum, a planned order will be created for the required quantity. At the same time, an exception message will be generated to warn the planner that a planned order has been created which exceeds the order maximum. In this case, the planner can have the material packaged so each bundle is two thousand pounds or less. Another use of the maximum is as a warning on a planned order that is clearly in error. A maximum of one year's usage will flag planned orders that may be in error.

A note of perspective is appropriate here to put the correct emphasis on order policies. The only ordering policies that are absolutely needed to operate MRP are lot-for-lot, fixed order quantity, one-time ordering (if scheduling activities), and, in the case of bucketless system, a period order quantity. And companies aggressively pursuing Just-in-Time methods are demonstrating that lot-for-lot ordering (or a POQ of one day) may be sufficient to operate MRP effectively once problems like high setups and too much paperwork are addressed.

All the dynamic ordering policies and elaborate lot-sizing schemes are holdovers from the conventional wisdom of inventory management. The overwhelming question was, "How much to order?" In an MRP system this question is not as important as two others: "Is the material coming in at the right time to satisfy requirements?" and "Is the quantity large enough to satisfy the requirements until we can get some more?" Once these problems have been solved, it makes sense to worry about a reasonable lot size. The paybacks in MRP do not come from optimizing the lot sizes. They come from planning, and then executing schedules.

To some degree, fixed order quantities and large period order quantities are also holdovers from the conventional wisdom that "big is better when it comes to order quantities." In the conventional view, larger order quantities lower the cost per piece by amortizing the setup over many pieces, provide higher efficiency because equipment runs more (instead of being setup or in changeover), and reduce the paperwork because of fewer manufacturing orders.

EXPLOSION PROCESS

Explosion is the process where planned orders are used to create gross requirements for the component parts. The component parts are, in effect, notified of the needs of the parent item. These needs are gross requirements, and the process of explosion takes the parent planned order, reads the bill of material for the parent item to determine the components required, and extends the planned order quantity by the bill of material quantity per to generate component gross requirements.

To generate the proper gross requirements, the date the component parts are needed must be determined. In nearly all cases, this is the start date of the planned order. The start date of the planned order is the due date offset by the lead time of the item. This lead time should include the time to prepare the paperwork, the time to pick the component parts, move and queue times, setup and running times, and inspection time. The start date of the order is the date component parts will be picked from stock and issued to manufacturing. The start date of the order is the date of the component gross requirements.

The mechanics of planned order explosion are different in net change and regenerative systems. In a regenerative system, all old gross requirements and all old planned orders are destroyed at the beginning of the planning run. These gross requirements and planned orders are erased completely. Planned order explosion in a regenerative system is concerned only with generating gross requirements. As planned orders are exploded, new gross requirements are created and added to the files. The product structure record for each component on the bill of material is accessed. The gross requirements quantity is calculated by extending the planned order quantity by the quantity per assembly in the bill of material. This is the new gross requirement: the quantity is the planned order quantity extended by the bill of material, and the date is the planned order start date. Each component is posted with gross requirements in the same way. All of the planned orders for a parent item are exploded.

In a net change system, there are several options. One option is to destroy all the old planned orders and gross requirements for each item as the item is entered into the planning sequence, with the order planning logic generating new component requirements based on the new planned orders. Another option is to maintain the existing planned orders and update them and their associated gross requirements based on the new need dates.

In the first method, the first step in the replanning process of an item is to read all of its planned orders and associated gross requirements and erase them. At the same time, each component is marked for replanning. The planned order explosion logic in the system is then similar to that in a regenerative system: it is concerned only with generating gross requirements. The product structure is accessed to determine the components in the bill of material. The gross requirement quantity is computed from the planned order quantity and the quantity per in the bill of material; the requirement date is the planned order start date.

The other option is to leave any existing planned orders and associated gross requirements and update them as needed, based on the new material requirements plan. The planned orders would exist with the dates and quantities that were assigned the last time they were changed by the computer. This means that the planned order explosion logic in this type of net change system has to include not only the ability to create new planned orders and gross requirements, but also the logic to update existing gross requirements when planned orders are changed and the logic to delete gross requirements when planned orders are deleted.

Changing gross requirements is done either by using the bill of material to find the component gross requirements, or by directly locating the gross requirements. In some systems, the bill of material is used by the planned order explosion logic to find the gross requirements for updating. If, for example, the start date and due date of a planned order are changed during net change replanning, the bill of material would be used to find the component gross requirements and they would be updated. In other systems, the gross requirements for a planned order are linked directly to the planned order and the bill of material is not needed to find the gross requirements. When a planned order is changed in such a system, the gross requirements are located and updated based on the new date and quantity. Deleting gross requirements in a net change system is similar to changing them. The gross requirements for a planned order are found and deleted either by using the bill of material or by directly locating them.

Some systems include an option to handle situations where the component requirement date is not the start date of the planned order. This may happen in situations where some of the components are added to the assembly significantly later, usually a week or more, from the start date of the order.

This option, called a product structure lead time offset, can be useful in situations like the final assembly or finishing process of the product. However, a product structure lead time offset should not be used to avoid the proper restructuring of the bills of material. Nor should such a feature be used as an excuse for not actively and aggressively trying to reduce lead times to the bare minimum. Appendix 7 is an explanation of this feature.

The explosion logic of MRP should provide a way to handle a scrap factor for each parent-component relationship. The objective of this type of scrap factor is to increase the gross requirements for a component when that component has a scrap or loss rate different from the other components. For example, when a particular component (say a screw) is normally lost or damaged in the process of assembly, the scrap factor is used to increase the gross requirements by the amount of the scrap.

Chapter 8

Entry into the Planning
Sequence for Processing

The logic explained in this chapter acts as a controller or scheduler to the netting and order planning logic. Its purpose is to ensure that all items that should be planned in MRP are planned, and that they are planned at the proper time.

PLANNING PROCESS SELECTION

Because regenerative systems are status driven, most people assume that such a system includes all items in MRP planning. In fact, this is not true. There is no reason to process certain items; an inactive item, for example, does not have to be processed in MRP. This item has no gross requirements, no allocations, no scheduled receipts, no firm planned orders, and no safety stock. There is no reason for MRP to do netting or order planning on this type of item. No exception messages would be generated and no planned orders would be created.

Consequently, most regenerative systems begin by checking each item against some rules, and entering those items requiring replanning into the planning sequence. The general rule is: If the potential for an exception message or a planned order exists, then the item should be planned in MRP. In other words, any items with gross requirements, orders of any type (scheduled receipts or firm planned orders), allocations, or safety stock should be entered into the planning sequence for processing.

Typically, two sections of logic are used to enter items into the planning sequence. In the first section, planned orders and gross requirements from the previous regeneration are destroyed. Each item is checked for requirements, scheduled receipts, firm planned orders, and safety stock, and those that require planning are entered into the planning sequence. Later, a second check occurs during the planned order explosion routine in the system. As planned orders are exploded, gross requirements are posted to items that may not have been entered into the planning sequence already. If so, these items are entered into the planning sequence.

In a net change system, items are entered into the planning sequence based on transactions. If a transaction has caused a change to the plan for an item, then the item should be entered into the planning sequence for net change processing.

Generally, the items are entered into the planning sequence at the time a transaction is processed. Transaction processing routines contain a section of logic that can enter items into the planning sequence. Some transactions execute this logic; others do not. A change in the description of an item, for example, does not cause replanning, while an adjustment to the on-hand balance does.

One of the requirements in designing a net change system is to determine which transactions should enter items into the net change planning sequence. The rule for entering items into the planning sequence is similar to the rule used in a regenerative system: any transactions that have the potential to create an exception message or to cause a change to a planned order should cause the item to be entered into the planning sequence. A few examples of the types of transactions that should cause replanning are: an adjustment to the on-hand balance, a change in order policy or order quantity, a change in lead time, and the release of an unplanned order. In the last example, both the parent item as well as each of the components must be replanned.

Other types of transactions that cause replanning are internal to the system and are not made by the users. For example, posting gross requirements to a component is an internal transaction. If the gross requirements for an item are changed as part of the net change planning run, then the item should be entered into the planning sequence.

PLANNING SEQUENCE

Logic must also exist in the system to properly sequence items for planning. An item must not be planned in MRP until all gross requirements have been posted to the item. If an item is planned before all gross requirements have been posted, the planning will be incorrect because the netting, exception checking, and order planning will be based on incomplete information.

The mechanics of this logic are based on a concept called "low-level coding." The low-level code records the lowest level at which an item appears in any bill of material. For example, an item which is five levels down from the top in one product, and six levels down from the top in another product, has a low level code of six (six levels down).

The MRP logic that uses the low-level codes holds an item out of planning until all items with low-level codes closer to the top of the product structure have been processed. For example, in the case of the item above, the logic in the system would hold that item out of MRP planning until all items with low-level codes of five have been processed. This logic has the effect of making sure, for each item, that all parent items have been planned in MRP and all gross requirements have been posted before the item is planned.

Different software systems handle low-level coding differently. Some software systems number the levels from the top of the product structure down, starting with low-level code zero. Other software systems number the levels from the top of the product structure down, starting with low-level code one. Still other software systems number the levels from the bottom up, starting with either low-level code zero or low-level code one. Regardless of the numbering convention, the principles of operation are the same.

Appendix 8 explains the most common mechanism for scheduling items for replanning. This is a fairly technical discussion and may not be of interest to the typical reader.

Chapter 9

Firm Planned Orders

The firm planned order provides a tool for the planner to override the normal logic of the system. The normal order planning logic works well in an overwhelming number of cases. In most situations, the calculated planned order due date is the date the items are really needed. The start date of the order should be the due date offset to an earlier date by the lead time of the item, and the planned order quantity should be based on the order policy for the item.

Yet there are situations where these normal rules do not apply. There are cases when the due date of an order is not the date the items are needed in the stockroom, when the start date of an order is not the due date offset by the normal lead time, or when the order quantity is not based on the order policy. It may be necessary to manufacture some items earlier than required because of a capacity problem. Sometimes a component part is late, but the lost time can be made up by pushing a parent item through in less than the normal lead time. A lot that is larger or smaller than the normal lot size may have to be run because of a partial delivery of one component, or as a way to balance stock. In these and many other situations, the normal ordering rules do not give an accurate simulation of reality.

The firm planned order gives the planner the ability to override the normal ordering rules and lead times. He can freeze a planned order using the date and quantity he chooses. If the normal ordering rules do not apply to a specific situation, the firm planned order can be used to accurately represent the events of the future. When larger or smaller lots are run or the start date is changed, a firm planned order is used to communicate the new information to the lower level items. The system is then a simulation of reality and represents what will really happen. (Appendix 9 gives a more detailed explanation of the uses of the firm planned order.)

A firm planned order combines the characteristics of a scheduled receipt and a planned order. Like a scheduled receipt, a firm planned order is not rescheduled automatically to earlier or later dates; instead, exception messages are produced so that a planner can review the situation. Unlike a scheduled receipt, however, a firm planned order does not generate component allocations: firm planned orders are exploded into component gross requirements. The generation of component requirements is like that done for planned orders.

ABILITY FOR FIRM PLANNED ORDER

A planner must be able to specify a firm planned order for any start or due date, quantity, or lead time. In some cases, the planner may wish to specify a due date and use the existing lead time and order quantity, or the planner may wish to specify both the due date and the start date (or the due date and a lead time override) and use the normal order quantity. In other cases, the planner may specify the planned due date but a larger or smaller than normal lot size, or specify the due date and order quantity and an override code indicating that the order will be purchased even though the item is normally manufactured (or vice versa).

Firm planned orders are treated like scheduled receipts in the netting and exception logic of MRP. After the scheduled receipts have been processed through the netting logic, firm planned orders are brought into the calculation and used to satisfy requirements. Like the section of netting that handles scheduled receipts, the logic that processes firm planned orders makes the rescheduling assumption.

Rescheduling exception messages are generated for firm planned orders based on the netting calculation. MRP produces exception messages for firm planned orders that need to be rescheduled to an earlier date, firm planned orders that need to be rescheduled to a later date, and firm planned orders that are candidates for cancellation.

A minor problem in some software systems is the sequence of processing for firm planned orders. To generate the proper exception messages, scheduled receipts should be used to satisfy the earliest requirements. Then firm planned orders should be used to satisfy any remaining requirements. This is really just a simulation of reality. Scheduled receipts can be completed at earlier dates than firm planned orders because scheduled receipts are already in process.

In some systems, the scheduled receipts and firm planned orders are processed in due date sequence. If a firm planned order exists for an item and a scheduled receipt also exists but at a later date, these systems will generate an exception message to move the firm planned order to satisfy the earliest requirement. This message can be somewhat confusing. In this specific situation, it makes more sense to reschedule the scheduled receipt to satisfy the earliest requirement since the scheduled receipt is already in process.

Technically, netting scheduled receipts and firm planned orders in due date sequence is incorrect. However, the problem is probably not serious for most companies. In most cases, firm planned orders do not exist at dates earlier than scheduled receipts. And, a planner typically looks at the entire situation for an item before taking any action. In such a case, the planner will see the existing scheduled receipt and reschedule it. Consequently, in most cases, companies will probably choose not to correct such a problem in a software system because it is a large modification with little practical benefit.

Additional exception messages for firm planned orders due for release are also produced in the logic of MRP. Firm planned order start dates are checked against a release horizon (a few days or a week) and firm planned orders due to start during that time are reported along with other planned orders due for release.

In a net change system, the mechanism for handling problems caused by the passage of time must provide a way to identify firm planned orders due for release. These exception messages should be listed along with the other exception messages for planned orders due for release and past due scheduled receipts.

The logic for generating and maintaining the gross requirements coming from firm planned orders can be done in several different ways. One method is to treat firm planned orders like planned orders in the explosion logic: the order remains unreleased (like a planned order) and is exploded to create gross requirements like planned orders. Another method is to generate gross requirements and attach them to the firm planned order just as time phased allocations are attached to scheduled receipts. In this method, the order is bypassed in the order planning and explosion logic and a transaction system exists to add, change, and delete component requirements.

Chapter 17 explains the transaction system required to create and maintain firm planned orders, and the additional capabilities needed when gross requirements are not generated from the MRP explosion logic.

Chapter 10

Pegging

Explosion is the process where planned orders generate gross requirements. Pegging is the reverse: taking gross requirements and determining where they came from.

Finding where requirements are coming from is an essential part of a closed loop system. In a closed loop system, priorities are planned in both directions: from the top down and from the bottom up. In top down planning, a master production schedule is exploded. Gross requirements are generated, netting and exception checking is done for each item, planned orders are created and exploded to the components. Planning moves from the top of the bill of material to the bottom.

Planning is also done from the bottom up. When an unanticipated problem occurs and a vendor cannot deliver, or a quality problem or production delay prevents the plan from being executed, planning moves from the bottom up. This planning is done by a person. His or her primary responsibility is to make the supply meet the demands. Failing that, the demands must be made to meet the available supply. This is done by finding the parent items causing the gross requirements and changing some of their schedules to match the availability of components.

PEGGING

In order to do bottom up planning, a planner needs a way to find out the source of the demands. This information is single-level pegging. The minimum amount of pegging information needed by the planner includes the date, quantity, and parent item number.

Typically, pegging is arranged so the planner can look up an item number and a date to determine quickly which parent items are causing the gross requirements and what quantity each parent requires. There are two ways to produce this detailed listing of gross requirements:

1. Create a history of gross requirements as the planned order are exploded.

2. Recreate the pegging using where-used logic in the bill of material system.

The first method is to create a history record of the gross requirements as planned orders are exploded. This record is normally stored in a separate computer file used exclusively for pegging. In a bucketless system, the pegging record is usually the same as the individual gross requirements record being used in MRP; in a bucketed system, the pegging record is usually stored in a work file that is separate from the gross requirements buckets used in the netting calculations of MRP. In each case, however, the pegging information identifies each gross requirement by item number, date, quantity, and parent item number.

The second method for providing pegging does not store the pegging information as planned orders are exploded. Instead, pegging is recreated using the where-used logic in the bill of material system. For an item and a date or a range of dates, this logic searches through the parent item numbers to find the ones that are causing specific gross requirements. These parent item numbers are then displayed.

Some systems provide both single-level pegging and full pegging. Full pegging is a way to see not only the parent item number causing the gross requirements, but to have the computer trace it all the way back up the product structure to the master production schedule.

Full pegging can be helpful for government contractors and other companies with stringent accounting requirements like in the Federal Acquisition Regulations (FAR). Defense Acquisition Regulations (DAR), and Cost Schedule Control System Criteria (CSCSC). For many companies, however, there are some reasons for avoiding full pegging.

The primary difficulty with full pegging is that it does not represent the way a planner should solve a problem. The planner should work his way up the product structure one level at a time looking for ways to solve the problem at each level. Full pegging makes it easy to go directly to the master production schedule and change it. In practice, most problems can be solved as the planner works through the product structure and the master production schedule may not have to be changed at all.

For this reason full pegging is not considered to be essential or even beneficial unless a company has FAR, DAR, or CSCSC requirements. Appendix 10 is a more complete explanation of full pegging and shows the reasons it is not considered helpful.

ALLOCATIONS

Pegging also provides the details of allocations, requirements coming from firm planned orders, customer orders, and forecasts. Just as there are situations where the planner needs to know the source of gross requirements, the planner will also need to know the source of the other requirements. This is especially true when the firm planned order has been used and requirements are attached to the order directly.

The requirement for allocation pegging and pegging for customer orders and forecasts is much the same as gross requirements pegging. Allocation details should be presented for the planner so that he or she can look up an item number and a date (or a range of dates, or no date at all) and be able to quickly find the parent item numbers causing the allocations. The pegging information must include the parent item number, date, and quantity: the parent order number is also helpful and is required in the case of pegging for customer orders.

Unlike gross requirements pegging, allocation pegging cannot be recreated through a where-used search to find the parent items. A where-used chase is unable to determine which scheduled receipts have had some or all of the components issued from stock. To provide allocation pegging, allocation details must be stored in a file. These details can then be displayed when the pegging is required.

The requirements for pegging for gross requirements and allocations have been described separately in this section. However, the pegging information for both gross requirements and allocations should be presented together. This is the simplest way for people to use the system. The planners should not be required to go to one report or display for the gross requirements pegging and another report or display for the allocation pegging. A more complete explanation of how the pegging information should be displayed is part of the next chapter, Human Engineering.

Chapter 11

Human Engineering

The prior five chapters were concerned with how the right dates, quantities, orders, and comparisons are computed. This chapter looks at how that information should be presented to people working with the system and explains the human engineering that needs to be a part of an MRP II system.

Unfortunately, it is all too common to have a system that is impressive as it streams off a high-speed printer, but which is an exercise in tongue biting frustration as someone tries to squeeze all the reports, books, and binders onto a single desk to do the job.

Yet it is possible to design a system that not only displays the proper information, but also presents it in a well-organized and readable set of reports or on-line displays. Good human engineering in a system can make the difference between a system that's difficult to use and one that's uncomplicated, easy to understand, and simple to operate effectively.

INFORMATION DISPLAY

The information that needs to be displayed for MRP planning can be broken into three logical categories. These are:

1. The time-phased display.

2. Exception messages.

3. Supporting details to any summary information.

The time-phased display is a way to show the picture on an item. It displays the future showing the gross requirements, scheduled receipts, firm planned orders, planned orders, and projected on-hand balance, either by date or by time period.

There are two formats for the time-phased report. One format shows the future horizontally across the display using one or more sets of horizontal blocks. In this presentation, time is shown as a series of buckets, usually weekly, that cover the horizon being displayed to the planner. If there is no activity in a bucket, it is left blank; if there is more than one gross requirement, scheduled receipt, etc. in a bucket, the total is shown. This type of display is a logical outgrowth of a bucketed system, although some bucketless systems also use this type of display.

The other format displays the time-phased information vertically. This method shows the future down the display rather than horizontally across the page or display screen. Only the dates that have any activity (gross requirements, scheduled receipts, etc.) are shown. Dates with more than one event are shown several times, once for each order or demand. This display is a logical outgrowth of a bucketless system. In addition, this type of display is the more popular method of displaying the time-phased information on a CRT screen.

Both the vertical and horizontal displays have their supporters. Each group tends to feel that their display presents the information most logically. Actually, both vertical and horizontal formats show the future in a way that is both acceptable and workable. Appendix 11 explains the advantages and disadvantages of each, and contains examples of the different reports.

The objective of the time-phased display is to allow the planner to see into the system. All the gross requirements, scheduled receipts, planned and firm planned orders are shown by date and each is labeled clearly so the planner can easily distinguish one from the other. In addition, totals for gross requirements, scheduled receipts, etc. are helpful and can be listed at the end of the planning horizon.

A time-phased projected on-hand balance is part of the time-phased report. This projection is based on the beginning on-hand balance and the time-phased information (gross requirements, allocations, scheduled receipts, planned and firm planned orders).

The projected on-hand balance shows the balance on hand at the end of every time period. This calculation is based on the current due dates of scheduled receipts and firm planned orders and the need dates for gross requirements and allocations.

The projected on-hand balance is a necessary tool for the planner. The projected on-hand balance provides visibility to a planner: the planner can get a clear understanding of why certain exception messages were produced, and what the specific problems are. This way, the planner can use his intelligence to develop a solution to the problem. This solution may be to reschedule the orders according to the exception messages, or it may be to split a lot instead of rescheduling the entire quantity, or it may be to use a firm planned order to change the lead time or lot size for the parent order.

The projected on-hand balance also provides visibility into the dates to which scheduled receipts or firm planned orders should be rescheduled. It also shows the projected inventory for an item, which in turn indicates whether enough inventory will exist to satisfy the master production schedule.

Some systems include a calculation of the projected on-hand balance assuming that all the rescheduling recommended by MRP can and will be done. Unfortunately, there are any number of situations where the planner cannot make the reschedules recommended by MRP. For example, an order may be needed earlier than its current due date. However, it may not be possible to get an earlier delivery.

A projected on-hand balance that assumes that this reschedule has been made does not display the problem clearly so that a planner can immediately begin to develop other solutions. Instead, the planner is forced to reconstruct the problem before working on a solution. Since reconstructing the problem is not only time consuming and may lead to errors, a projected on-hand balance calculation that assumes that all rescheduling will occur as recommended is not a good feature in any system.

Normally, the reporting horizon for the time-phased information is the same as the planning horizon. However, sometimes companies may wish to display a shorter horizon on the time-phased MRP reports and make the remainder of the information available through inquiries. In situations where the reporting horizon is less than the planning horizon, the displays show all the time-phased information for an item at least through its lead time. In a horizontal display, the time buckets through the lead time are weekly or smaller.

The time-phased display also gives some descriptive information for an item. Information like the description, unit of measure, order policy, lead time, on-hand balance, etc. is listed for each item. The descriptive information includes anything the planner might need to interpret the time-phased information. This is necessary to make the system transparent or visible to the people using it. The planner must be able to pick up the report and see clearly what is happening and where the numbers and exception messages came from. He must be able to see why planned orders are in a given week, or why an exception message is given. This visibility is one of the basic and fundamental principles of systems design.

Exception messages are the next category of information that must be presented to the planner. The objective is to make effective use of the planner's time by concentrating on the exception conditions without forcing the planner to analyze the whole mass of current information.

The exception messages must be problem oriented. It is more effective for the computer to analyze and list each problem in the form of an exception message than to merely point the planner to an item with exceptions and leave it to him to reconstruct the problems. This means that there should be one exception for each problem, and not several exceptions for the same problem, or one exception that covers many problems. Three exception messages should indicate that there are three problems. Then the planner can locate the problems and begin to solve them, rather than having to go through the intermediate step of determining which exceptions go with which problems.

A common example of exceptions that are not problem oriented occurs when two exception messages are generated for the same problem. This happens, for example, when a rescheduling exception message is given for an order that should be rescheduled to an earlier date and another exception message is given for the unsatisfied gross requirements. These two exception messages are redundant. There is only one problem, an order that should be rescheduled to an earlier date. Therefore, there should be only one exception message.

Exception messages should point out problems by describing the situation in words. Exceptions should be in words even though the planners who work with the system every day soon learn the meanings of any numbers or codes that identify the exception messages. A message in English will be obvious to anyone whether they work with the system regularly or not. People in marketing, engineering, and other departments will all have occasion to review problems with the planner from time to time. Uninterpreted exception codes only serve to make the system seem mysterious and complicated. The objective must be the opposite, to make the system as simple and easy-to-use as possible.

An exception message must direct attention to the problem, giving the date and quantity so it can be found easily in the time-phased display. The message is most helpful if any additional information, such as the date the order needs to be rescheduled to, is listed along with the message.

The best arrangement for listing exception messages is to display all exceptions for the same item together and to group the items by planner. A good rule for the planner to follow is to look at and recognize all exceptions for an item before making any decisions on how to solve the problems. Unless all the exceptions for an item are listed together, a planner may overlook an exception and make decisions on how to solve the problems for an item based on an incomplete evaluation of the situation.

The third category of information is the details to any summary information. Whenever any summary information is displayed, like the gross requirements presented in buckets for example, the details should be available to back up this summary.

Pegging is one type of supporting detail. The display of pegging information should include the date, quantity, and parent item number for gross requirements and allocations. The parent item number is a helpful addition to the pegging display for allocations, and the pegging display for any customer orders should include the date, quantity, and customer order number.

Detailed information is also needed for scheduled receipts and firm planned orders. The due date, quantity remaining on order, and order number should all be available to the planner. This information is needed to be able to reschedule an order.

PRESENTATION OF INFORMATION

Unfortunately, the physical presentation of information is something that is commonly ignored in the design of MRP II software. In some software packages, all the information that a planner needs is in the system, but the number of printed reports or displays is excessive. And in many on-line systems, planners are continually forced to reenter part numbers, transaction codes, order numbers, dates, etc. in order to move from display to display.

The human engineering that is part of an MRP II system is as important to the success of the system as any other part of the software. In general, the human engineering aspects of an MRP II system fall into three categories:

1. Whether the information is presented in a convenient number of reports or displays.

2. Whether the information is displayed in a logical manner.

3. Whether the planners have easy and timely access to the information, that is, the ability to move easily from display screen to display screen without having numerous intermediate steps or rekeying of data.

Some elements of the human engineering of MRP software depend upon whether information is displayed on cathode ray tube displays or in printed reports; other elements are the same regardless of whether the displays are printed reports or CRT displays. Consequently, the physical display of information is described in three parts: one for the common elements of human engineering, one for systems where the MRP planning information is displayed on line, and another for systems where the information is displayed in reports.

COMMON ELEMENTS

The human engineering that is common to all MRP systems falls into two categories:

1. A way to work by exception.

2. Presentation of the information in a logical format.

A planner needs to work by exception. Without this ability, a planner would spend most of his time scanning time-phased displays trying to determine whether there is a problem, what the problem is, etc. In some companies, it may be possible for a planner to do this; he can look at the printed MRP report for every item or key in each of his item numbers and scan the on-line displays. In most companies, however, this is a poor use of a planner's time; there are too many items, and the number of items with activity is low compared to the total number of items in the system.

Consequently, a planner needs a display of the items with exceptions. Such an exception report or on-line display prints or displays a list of items with exceptions, or it displays one item at a time, showing all the exceptions for the item. In either case, the exception display allows a planner to go directly to the items that require evaluation.

The exception report or display serves as an index for the planner. The planner can look at each item with exception messages. From the exception display the planner can go to the time-phased report or on-line display for the time-phased information, pegging, order details, etc. Once the planner understands the problem and its solution, he can reschedule an order, check component availability, release an order, etc.

The organization of reports and displays is also important. Even when the system provides all the information and a way to work by exception, a planner may have difficulty if the information is presented in a poorly organized or cluttered format. For example, some systems try to fit too much information into too small a space, resulting in two, three, four, or more different formats jammed together on a report or CRT screen.

Reading such a display is an exercise in frustration as the planner's eye is forced to switch back and forth between the different formats and information. Consequently, it is generally better to provide displays that are organized in logical, uncluttered blocks of information and presented in a standard format, rather than trying to jam all the information together in one place or mixing different pieces of unrelated information together. A good organization for the time-phased MRP report is to display separate blocks for descriptive information, time-phased data, pegging, scheduled receipts details, exception messages, etc.

ON-LINE ELEMENTS

When cathode ray tubes (as opposed to printed reports) are used for displaying the MRP planning information, there is less room for information. It is typically not possible to display all the descriptive and time-phased information, exception messages, pegging information, supporting details for scheduled receipts and firm planned orders, etc. on a single screen. Instead, this information is typically displayed in two, three, or four screens of information for an item.

When information is split among different displays, three features are part of a well-engineered on-line system:

1. The ability to use menus to move from one display to another.

2. The ability to move from display to display based on the way a planner would logically work.

3. The ability to retrieve information without constantly reentering part numbers, order numbers, etc.

A well-engineered system includes some method for assisting new users in understanding the functions that are part of the system and in moving from function to function. Generally this takes the form of a menu or menus that list the different capabilities. A user can review the menu, select the function needed, go to the appropriate on-line screen to perform the desired transaction or get an inquiry, and then return back to the menu. Menus perform an important function in making the capabilities of the system visible to its users and leading new users through the various steps of performing their jobs.

Eventually, new users become experienced users. At that point, the system should be designed so that a planner does not have to constantly go back and forth between menus and on-line display screens, or constantly reenter transaction codes in order to move from display to display. Instead the system would provide a way to get information based on the way a planner would logically work.

A planner should be able to go directly from the time-phased MRP display to the pegging screen, the rescheduling display, the firm planned order maintenance display, and the order release screens. These are the typical displays that a planner uses in reviewing and solving exception conditions, so direct paths should be provided to them. Other displays, like a bill of material or routing display, might be used occasionally in the process of solving these kinds of problems. However, these other displays are not typical of those needed to solve material planning problems, so that direct paths to them from the MRP display are not as critical.

In a well-designed system, a planner has a method for retrieving the information and transactions that he needs without going through an individual procedure for each display and without reentering part numbers and order numbers. A planner can go directly from the exception display to the MRP time-phased display for the same item by pressing one key. From the time-phased display, he may choose to jump to an order release or order rescheduling screen by pressing another key. Or, he can jump from the time-phased display on one item to the time-phased display on a parent by pressing still another key. In those cases where a planner goes directly from one display on an item to another display for the same item, he is not forced to reenter the item number. The system carries along item numbers, order numbers, dates, etc. and retrieve and display information for the planner immediately. There is no need to require a planner to look at a blank format, enter this information, and then wait for the display.

In general, a well-designed on-line system seems to make the paths that a planner would take in finding and evaluating information easily available without the constant rekeying of transaction codes, without going back and forth to the menus, and without having to reenter item numbers, order numbers, dates, etc.

While this provides an easy method for the planner to access and display information, the limitation in cathode ray tube displays currently is that only one display can be presented at a time. It is not possible, in most systems, to have two or more displays on the CRT screen in front of a planner at the same time. Yet, regardless of the paths that have been programmed into the software for retrieving and displaying information, there are still times and situations where a planner will want to be able to refer back and forth between two displays, or will want a printed copy of the information on which to make notes or do trial calculations.

One good solution to the problem of referring back and forth between displays is the capability to split the CRT screen and show several different displays simultaneously. A special set of commands and a key on the CRT keyboard allows a planner to specify that the screen is to be split into two or more sections, each displaying some portion of a normal display.

Once the screen is split, a planner can control each section independently; scrolling up and down to look at additional information or requesting additional inquiry displays like pegging, exception messages, time-phased information, etc. This way, for example, a planner could display both the time-phased display for a component in the top section of the display screen, and the time-phased display for one of its parents at the bottom. This makes solving problems much easier as the amount of jumping back and forth between display screens is reduced dramatically.

Another solution is the capability to produce a printed copy of the cathode ray tube screens. A key on the cathode ray tube keyboard typically allows a planner to print a page containing the information shown on a display. These pages are printed immediately, either on the main printer for the system or on a small work station printer near the cathode ray tubes.

PRINTED REPORT ELEMENTS

Experience has shown that two or, at the very most, three reports are all that can be used at the same time on one desk. Since the planner may also want some work area for making notes or calculations, or room for last week's time-phased display, the three categories of information explained above should not be presented on any more than two reports. Generally, if two reports are used, they are the time-phased report and the exception report. The supporting details can be included into either of the two reports. Another way to present the information would be to include all three categories of information in the same report. As long as the information is presented in one or two reports, it really doesn't matter which categories of information are presented in which reports.

It is best to sequence the reports by responsibility. Each planner should receive a report that includes only the items for which that planner is responsible, or at least a report that separates that planner's items from the others in the report. Confusion over who is responsible for what is eliminated this way and no time is lost by a planner who must page through someone else's items.

Even when the reports are organized so the information is presented in a minimum number of reports, it is still possible to overwhelm the planner with the volume of information that is generated each week (or each day in a net change system). In some companies, the planners are responsible for relatively few items and they can easily manage a printed report for each item. In other companies, a planner may be responsible for several thousand item numbers. Printing volumes of information like this is not only expensive, but also awkward as the planner struggles to work with a report that is as high as it is wide. The information in these types of reports is basically reference material, like a dictionary or an encyclopedia. The level of activity is low and the planner will not look at all the items that are printed.

The most common solution to this problem is to print only the items with exception messages and to make the remaining items available through an on-line inquiry using cathode ray tubes. This way the planner does not have to handle printed reports for the items that he is not likely to look at, and the volume of printed material for each planner is reduced to a reasonable level.

Another way to provide quick access to items that were not printed is microfiche. This is an alternative for companies without cathode ray tubes. The entire report containing all items can be listed to microfiche. The items with exceptions should be printed, however. When the planner needs information on an item that was not printed, it is available by using a microfiche reader. Also, the entire report for several weeks can be stored very conveniently on microfiche. This allows the planner to go back and review a report from last week or the week before.

In either a net change or a regenerative system with printed reports, the volume of pegging information can also be a problem. The amount of pegging information for some items can be quite large, consuming large amounts of time as it is generated and maintained in the system, and large quantities of paper as it is printed. Common hardware is an example of an item that generates lots of pegging information, but usually without much practical value.

An option to prevent or limit pegging for certain items like common hardware is generally a helpful feature. Preventing or limiting the pegging in this way, in addition to using cathode ray tubes or microfiche, will reduce the volume of pegging to manageable levels.

The human engineering aspects of the system are not limited to the material requirements planning reports and displays. The same basic principles of transaction driven rather than menu driven, not having to reenter the same data over and over, and having a convenient number of well-organized reports or displays, apply not only to MRP, but also to the other planning systems, master production scheduling and capacity requirements planning, and also, possibly to a lesser degree, to the supporting systems like inventory transactions, scheduled receipts, etc.

The reports explained in this topic are the main MRP planning reports. There are a number of other reports that will be specified as functional requirements in the explanations of other topics. Appendix 12 is a summary of all the reports which are listed as functional requirements in the Standard System.

PART IV

Subsystems to Material Requirements Planning

Chapter 12

Bill of Material Subsystem

The bill of material subsystem, like the inventory transaction subsystem, the scheduled receipts subsystem, and the firm planned order subsystem, provides MRP the information needed to calculate and determine priorities. These are considered supporting systems to MRP because they provide information to MRP, but are not a part of the MRP calculations.

PARENT-COMPONENT RELATIONSHIP

A bill of material system defines how one or more component parts are brought together to make up a parent item. These component parts can be manufactured or purchased items, or raw materials. The list of components that make up an item is a single-level bill of material.

A bill of material system provides the capabilities to add, change, and delete single-level bills of material. The system allows an unlimited number of components in any single-level bill of material and allows an item to appear more than a single time in the bill of material. In addition, the system normally provides a way to define a bill of material for a purchased part as a way to handle situations where either the item is purchased but some material is supplied, or the item is currently purchased but has been manufactured in the past.

To maintain the single-level bill of material relationships, the bill of material system must include transactions to add a component to a bill of material, to delete components from a bill of material, and to change the bill of material information for a parent-component relationship.

Each parent-component relationship must include a quantity per assembly. The quantity per assembly is the quantity of the component that is required to make one parent item. The quantity per assembly must have enough digits to both the left and the right of the decimal point to accurately define the quantity of the component required. For example, a quantity per defines as xxxx.xxxxx handles many if not most products, but a quantity per field of xx.xx will not handle many at all.

Generally, the quantity per assembly has no unit of measure itself, but uses the units of measure of the parent and component items. For example, a unit of measure of each on the parent, a unit of measure of pounds on the component, and a quantity of 3.2 means that 3.2 pounds of the component are needed to make each parent item.

In many bill of material systems, there is also some other information stored for a parent-component relationship. This typically includes a scrap factor, operation number, and reference designators or balloon numbers. In addition, effectivity dates are normally stored in the bill of material as one of several methods of handling engineering changes. Effectivity dates are explained in detail later in this chapter.

Most systems include a scrap quantity for a component. This scrap quantity is meant to represent any losses for that component during the process of parts issue and assembly. For example, a fastener is used to make a subassembly and 5% of the fasteners are lost due to the automatic machine that does one of the assembly operations. In this situation, a scrap factor of 5% would be used for that component. If a bill of material system does not include a scrap factor it is possible to handle this situation by increasing the quantity per assembly for the fastener from 1.00 to 1.05, although this would not be the preferred method.

Some bills of material also carry reference designators or balloon numbers. A reference designator or balloon number provides a cross-reference to the drawing. By providing such a cross-reference, it is possible to eliminate bill of material information from the drawing.

Single-level bills of material define the parent-to-component relationship: a where-used relationship defines a component-to-parent relationship. It lists all the parent items that a component goes into. Some bill of material systems keep the where-used information up-to-date at all times. When a change is made by adding or deleting components, the where-used relationships are updated at that time. Other systems do not maintain this information and must recreate the where-used relationships periodically. In many companies, bills of material are changed frequently as the accuracy is checked and the bills of material restructured for MRP. Bill of material systems that keep the where-used information up-to-date have a distinct advantage during this period.

Some bill of material systems contain specialized transactions for reducing the clerical time required to maintain the bills of material. Multiple-delete, same-as-except, and multiple-replace are transactions of this type. While these transactions are not essential in a system, when they are used correctly they do make it possible to avoid some clerical work and can be helpful in certain situations. However, if the transactions are used incorrectly, it may take hours to reconstruct what was changed automatically in a matter of seconds.

The multiple-delete transaction deletes all relationships for that parent item, rather than a single parent-component relationship. This transaction removes a complete bill of material. The transaction is used most often when an item is obsolete.

A multiple-replace transaction searches the where-used list and replaces one component with another in all its uses. This transaction is used where one component is replacing another in every bill of material where the original item is used.

The same-as-except transaction copies a bill of material and attaches it to another parent item. This is normally followed by some transactions to change a few of the items in the copied bill of material. An extensive use of this transaction means that many bills of material are being constructed with similar characteristics. This generally means that the bills of material should be restructured into modular bills of material.

Modular bills of material offer a number of advantages over simply using a same-as-except transaction to generate large numbers of similar bills of material. Appendix 13 is a more complete explanation of the reasons for using modular bills of material instead of the same-as-except transaction.

REPORTING

The bill of material system must also provide some reporting capabilities. Normal functions include:

1. Single-level bills of material.

2. Single-level where-used listings.

3. Multi-level bills of material.

4. Multi-level where-used listings.

The single-level bills of material and where-used listings are simply lists of the components and the parents for an item. A single-level bill of material lists the components for the item. A single-level where-used listing lists the parent items where this component is used. Multi-level reporting takes the bill of material information which is stored in the computer as single-level bills of material and combines it.

A multi-level bill of material starts with the single-level bill of material for an item. Each component in this bill of material is checked to see if it has a bill of material. If so, the component is exploded. If the components on this second level bill have a bill of material, that bill of material is exploded in the same fashion. The explosion of bills of material continues until the lowest levels are reached. The process is one where the total product structure is shown from the top level down.

The multi-level where-used listing goes through the same process in the other direction. It starts with a component, showing all the places it is used, and then in turn, shows all the places each parent item is used, and so on.

Only three of these reporting functions are essential. They are the single-level bill of material, single-level where-used, and multi-level bill of material. The multi-level where-used is interesting but not vital. Some systems have summarized bills of material and where-used listings. There are some limited uses for these, but they are not needed to run the system. Appendix 12 includes examples of single-level bill of material, single-level where-used, and multi-level bill of material.

LOW-LEVEL CODE LOGIC

The bill of material subsystem usually contains the low-level code logic. Low-level codes are the position that an item occupies in the total product structure, and the purpose of low-level codes was explained in the topic on entry into the planning sequence.

Like the where-used relationships, the low-level codes can be maintained as changes to the product structure occur or they can be recreated periodically. If they are created, this should be done before a regeneration or a net change run. If this is not done, items may be planned incorrectly because their location in the total product structure may be incorrect.

Many software systems contain the logic to increase the low-level codes when changes are made to the product structure, but not to decrease the low-level codes. This does not cause a problem in using the system and makes the low-level code logic much simpler.

NET CHANGE GROSS REQUIREMENT UPDATE

In a net change system, a mechanism is required to maintain gross requirements whenever the bills of material change. This mechanism can be provided in a number of different ways.

One way to maintain the gross requirements is to update them at the time the bills of material are changed. This method is frequently used because the bills of material are an easy way to find and update the gross requirements. Once the bill of material has changed, finding and updating the gross requirements is more difficult unless the proper architecture exists in the system.

So, in many net change systems the component gross requirements are updated whenever a parent-component relationship is added, changed, or deleted. If a parent-component relationship is added, new component gross requirements are added for each parent planned order. If a parent-component relationship is changed (for example the quantity per assembly is changed), the gross requirements are found and updated. If a component is deleted, the gross requirements are found and deleted.

A second way to provide this function is to include logic that completely destroys all gross requirements and planned orders when a change is made to the bill of material. At the time the bill of material is changed, the parent item is marked indicating that a bill of material change has been made for the item. Then the planned orders for the parent item are destroyed and all gross requirements are erased as well. During net change planning, new planned orders are created for the parent item and exploded using the new version of the bill of material. This has the same effect as finding and correcting the gross requirements when the bill of material is changed.

The third method for providing the function is to flag items with bill of material changes, and then, during net change planning, match the current bill of material against the old gross requirements. As differences between the bill of material and the gross requirements are found, this logic adds, changes, and deletes gross requirements. This method also has the effect of finding and correcting the gross requirements when the bill of material is changed. The only disadvantage to the method is that developing the matching logic is generally more complicated than developing the logic needed for the other two approaches. Consequently, this method tends to be the least popular way to provide the function of correcting the gross requirements when the bills of material change.

ENGINEERING CHANGE OUTPUT

Bill of material systems originally defined a static product structure. They represented the way the product was made, and it was assumed that the bill of material would continue to represent the product for an indefinite period of time into the future. As MRP systems began to use the bills of material for planning a year or so into the future, some problems developed. The bills of material are not static. They change and the bill of material that represents the product today may not be the same one that will represent it a year from now. In some situations there is no way to know this, but in others the new bill of material may already be known. The engineering change may have been made, however, and the implementation of the change may not actually change the way the product is being manufactured for some time. Examples are situations where the existing stock of old components should be used up before the change is made or where tooling or a new piece of machinery are needed to implement the change.

As it became obvious that bills of material are constantly changing, the first solution was to tie the changes in the bills of material to a date. This feature is a part of most systems and is generally called bill of material effectivity dates. The dates are stored as part of the descriptive information for a parent-component relationship. The dates are used to determine when a component is active as a part of the bill of material. Generally, effectivity dates are set up as a start date and an end date. The component is active as part of the bill of material between the two dates. The planned order explosion logic in MRP checks the planned order start date against the effectivity dates in the bill of material. If the component is active on the start date of the planned order, gross requirements are generated and posted. If the component is not active on the date of the planned order, the component is bypassed and no gross requirements are generated.

Effectivity dates provide a date driven bill of material change system. In practice, some bill of material changes are driven by a date, but most are not. An example of a date driven bill of material change would be a change that must be made on March 1 regardless of the component inventories. However, a more common situation is where the bill of material change is determined more by an event than a date. An example of this type of change would be where existing component inventories should be used up or the completion of some tooling determines when the bill of material will change. These bill of material changes are determined by the event, the date is just an estimation of when the event will occur. As a result, any inventory adjustments, changes to the master production schedule, scrap, or other engineering changes can cause the date to change. These types of things are a way of life in a manufacturing environment and so the date a change is to be implemented always seems to be changing. The date of implementation is a moving target and the effectivity date is trying to keep up with it.

This makes it difficult for the planners to work with the system. The events are always changing and so the effectivity dates must be changed as well. This is even more of a problem because inventory adjustments, changes to the master production schedule, etc. can cause gross requirements to be generated incorrectly. If a planned order moves from one side of the effectivity date to the other, the gross requirements will be incorrect until the planner changes the effectivity date. This arrangement can be made to work, but is difficult to work with at best and in most cases quite confusing.

There is also another problem in using effectivity dates. Effectivity dates do not allow for temporary material substitutions. In some companies, these types of substitutions are not common, but in other companies they are a way of life. Effectivity date logic assumes that there is a start date and an end date for a component. No provision is made for an item that may be used for one order, then not used for some time, and then used again. What is needed in this situation is a way to allow a nearly unlimited number of substitutions on a bill of material.

Fortunately, there is another way to handle engineering changes and material substitutions. The technique is to allow a deviation to the normal bill of material, and to have this deviation tied to the order. A deviation to a bill of material is a change to one or more components. It could be the addition, deletion, or change in quantity for a component. The deviations are tied to an order which means they are for this order and do not apply to all orders. Because the deviations are tied to the order and not determined by date, if the order is rescheduled, the bill of material deviation moves as well. This eliminates the need for the planners to continually update effectivity dates as scrap, inventory adjustments, and changes to the master schedule change the date. This method also eliminates the incorrect gross requirements that occur when planned orders cross the effectivity dates.

Bill of material deviations that are tied to an order are normally provided in any of several ways:

1. Allowing the planner to maintain gross requirements attached to a firm planned order.

2. Serial number effectivity logic.

3. Lot number effectivity.

4. Other methods based on revision numbers or letters, etc.

Typically bill of material deviations tied to an order are provided by allowing the planner to maintain the component gross requirements for firm planned orders (and in some cases planned orders), and to maintain the allocations for scheduled receipts. The planner is able to add component gross requirements to an order, delete gross requirements from an order, or change the gross requirements for an order. (Allowing this type of maintenance for planned orders would only make sense in a net change system since both the gross requirements and planned orders are destroyed in a regenerative system.)

Using this method to implement an engineering change, a planner could make all orders after a certain order use the new bill of material. Another way to accomplish the same thing would be to change the bill of material to the new version, and to have all the orders earlier than the first new order show the old version of the bill of material. If the planner is going to make a material substitution, he could delete the gross requirement for the normal material and add a gross requirement for the substitution.

Another method for providing a bill of material deviation on a specific order is to tie the bill of material deviation to a specific serial number or serial number range. This is similar to the date effectivity logic in the system. A serial number is stored as part of the descriptive information for a parent-component relationship and for a firm planned order. The serial numbers are then used to determine when a component is active as a part of the bill of material for an order. Generally, serial numbers are set up as a start serial number and an end serial number. The component is active as part of the bill of material between the two serial numbers. The planned order explosion logic in MRP checks the firm planned or planned order serial number against the serial number effectivity information in the bill of material. If the component is active, gross requirements are generated and posted. If the component is not active, the component is bypassed and no gross requirements are generated.

Using this method to implement an engineering change, a planner could specify a serial number on a firm planned order as a way to use the new bill of material. Another way to accomplish the same thing would be to change the bill of material to the new version, and to have some orders with serial numbers that call out the old version of the bill of material.

The other methods (lot number effectivity, revision level effectivity, etc.) are similar to serial number effectivity. A range of lot numbers or a revision number or letter is stored for each order. In addition, each parent-component relationship includes a start and end lot number or start and end revision letter. The planned order explosion logic checks each order against the lot number or revision level range to determine whether the component is active. Components that are active have gross requirements generated. Components that are inactive are bypassed.

DISASSEMBLY, SORTING, AND BY-PRODUCTS

The fundamental assumption behind most bill of material systems is that one or more components come together to create a parent item. However, this is not always the case. In some companies, producing one item creates several other items. In other companies, an item may be pulled out of stock and torn down to yield several other items.

In a company that rebuilds or refurbishes copying machines, for example, a core (in this case, a used copying machine) is torn down to yield a number of component parts and subassemblies. These components may be reworked, put back into stock, and used later to build refurbished machines. The disassembly of cores also requires labor and equipment, some of which is also used in reassembling machines and producing components.

Consequently, in this kind of company, the schedule for buying or producing additional component parts needs to take into account the scheduled receipt of components that come from disassembling the items. In addition, the capacity requirements for labor and equipment need to be calculated based on both the disassembly schedule for used machines and the master production schedule for refurbished copying machines.

A similar situation exists in companies who have extensive sorting or grading operations. For example, in a company that produces semiconductor chips, the chips are sorted based on electronic characteristics. Based on the sorting operation, an item may be classified as one of several different item numbers. These different semiconductor chips can then be put into stock and sold or used in higher level assemblies.

Producing bulk chemicals is also a similar situation. Here, a bulk product is created through a series of chemical processes. These processes may result in the desired bulk chemical, and also yield a number of other chemicals, each of which may be put into stock and then sold or used in other chemical processes.

In both of these situations, the system needs to provide a method for showing the by-products in MRP, and for predicting the capacity required for sorting operations and chemical processing. Consequently, in a company where sorting or disassembly operations or chemical processes are a significant part of the business, the bill of material subsystem requires some additional capabilities to show by-products or scheduled receipts from disassembly. In a company where sorting, disassembly, and chemical processes aren't a significant part of the business, these capabilities would be optional. Having them would be helpful, but not essential to making the system work.

To handle disassembly, sorting, and chemical processes, the system needs a capability to define both a normal bill of material, and a disassembly, sorting, or by-product bill of material. The normal bill of material lists the component items that come together to make the parent item. The disassembly bill of material lists the item numbers that result from disassembling the item.

The system should also provide a method for showing, in MRP, the receipt of any components coming from disassembly or any by-products. In addition, the system should show the capacity requirements from the disassembly or sorting operation or chemical process. This way, MRP would take the scheduled receipts for by-products into account before planning additional orders to purchase or manufacture these items. In addition, the capacity requirements planning system should show the proper requirements for labor and equipment, taking into account both normal production and the disassembly or sorting.

An explanation of the logic needed to support a disassembly schedule is provided in Appendix 15. This is a high-level discussion of the typical changes in MRP and capacity requirements planning.

Chapter 13

Inventory Transaction Subsystem

ISSUE AND RECEIPT TRANSACTIONS

Stockroom transactions can be broken into two basic categories: planned and unplanned. Planned transactions are those where some type of allocation, scheduled receipt, or inspection information must be found and updated. Examples of planned transactions include:

1. Issue of component parts on a manufacturing order.

2. Receipt into stock of an item on a manufacturing order.

3. Receipt of an item on a purchase order.

A planned issue reduces the on-hand balance of the component and reduces (or close out) the allocation.

A planned receipt on a manufacturing order increases the on-hand balance and reduces or closes out the order.

A planned receipt transaction for purchase orders can work in several different ways depending upon whether inspection is required for the item. Many systems assume that purchase order receipts go directly into the stockroom. In some situations this is so, but in general, this is not the case. In many companies material goes through an inspection process and it is common for inspection to hold the material long enough to require some record of the material's location. The material in inspection is not on order any longer, and it is not in the stockroom either.

The transaction system must support moving material directly to stock and bypassing inspection or receiving material into the inspection area and subsequently moving material from the inspection area to stock. Receipts for material not being inspected increase the on-hand balance and reduce the quantity outstanding on order. Receipts into inspection reduce the outstanding quantity on order and increase the amount in inspection. Moves from inspection to stock increase the on-hand balance and reduce the quantity in inspection.

The way material in inspection is recorded is usually done in one of two ways. One way is to maintain an inspection inventory: material received against a purchase order would reduce the purchase order quantity on order and increase the inspection inventory. The other way is to leave the purchase order open, but to show the quantity of material in the inspection area as part of the descriptive information for the purchase order. Either of these two methods is workable.

The transaction system for maintaining an inspection inventory must include additional transactions for rejection, return, scrap, and rework. A reject and return transaction reduces the quantity in inspection and reopens the purchase order. A reject and scrap transaction reduces the inspection quantity and scraps the material—the purchase order is not reopened. Reject and rework transactions reduce the inspection quantity and create a manufacturing order to cover the rework.

Planned transactions normally support those situations where the transaction is made for a quantity different from the planned quantity. There are any number of reasons why a transaction would be made for more or less than the planned quantity. Planned issues are made for less than the planned quantity when a partial issue is made. This would be done, for example, when the assembly area does not have enough room to accept the planned issue quantity. Planned issues can also be made for more than the planned quantity. This happens most often when certain types of items, like corrugated boxes for example, are packaged or wrapped in bundles, and issued in whole bundles. Planned issue transactions should provide a partial issue, issuing a component complete at less than the planned quantity, and issuing more than the planned quantity.

A planned receipt on a manufacturing or purchase order may be a partial receipt, or the receipt could be for more than the quantity of the order if the vendor overshipped or if some allowance was made for scrap and no scrap occurred. Planned receipt transactions should provide for partial receipts on manufacturing or purchase orders, receiving an order complete at less than the planned quantity, and receiving an order for more than the planned quantity.

Unplanned transactions update only the on-hand balance. Examples of unplanned transactions include:

1. Unplanned receipts.

2. Unplanned issues.

3. Scrap.

4. Inventory adjustments.

An unplanned issue transaction reduces the on-hand balance. Unplanned issues are used to replace lost or scrapped parts, for spare parts issue, and for issues to engineering or inspection.

An unplanned receipt transaction increases the on-hand balance. Unplanned receipts are used for returns from engineering, marketing, etc.

A scrap transaction works differently depending upon what is being scrapped. If material is scrapped from stock, the scrap transaction reduces the balance on hand. If a component is being scrapped from a shop order, then the allocation is increased to show that additional material is needed. If an item is being scrapped from a shop order to manufacture it, then the scheduled receipt quantity is reduced.

An inventory adjustment transaction may increase or decrease the on-hand balance. Generally this transaction is used for adjustments identified during cycle counting, although it could also be used to report scrap or loss that occurred in the stockroom.

In some systems, a single general purpose transaction exists to report all unplanned activity. In this method, a reason code is provided as part of the transaction so that people can indicate why inventory is being adjusted. A reason code would exist for unplanned issues, unplanned receipts, scrap, adjustments from cycle counting, etc.

The inventory transaction system should also provide some method of handling fractional or decimal units. For example, someone may need 1.5 pounds of steel, leaving 17.5 pounds in stock. It should be possible to issue exactly 1.5 pounds, not 1 or 2, and store 17.5 pounds as the on-hand balance.

MULTIPLE INVENTORY LOCATIONS

An inventory transaction subsystem normally includes transactions to support multiple inventory locations. An unlimited number of locations are typically available for each item, and the system normally allows more than one item to be stored in each location.

Any transactions that update the on-hand balance also update the quantity stored in the inventory location. For example, a planned issue transaction of ten pieces reduces both the on-hand balance and the location quantity by ten. A planned receipt for twenty-five increases both the balance on hand and the location quantity by twenty-five.

An additional transaction is required to handle transfers from location to location. A transfer transaction reduces the balance in the sending location and increases the balance in the receiving location.

One helpful feature in a system is a way to identify a primary or preferred location. Identifying such a location aids in showing where material should be put away, even when the balance on hand for the item is currently zero. This primary location is a way ot help in organizing and running the stockroom more efficiently.

The system normally should assist in identifying and purging temporary locations when the balance on hand is zero. In many systems, an inventory location for an item is deleted whenever a cycle count for the item in the location verifies that the quantity in the location is zero. However, the primary location or other locations identified as permanent is not deleted even when the on hand is zero.

Each location record includes a way to identify the status of the material being stored there. For example, there is typically some way to identify an item in a location as rejected and awaiting final disposition (and therefore excluded from the beginning available balance in MRP). And there is a way to identify material that is waiting for inspection or in quarantine so that it is part of the beginning available balance in MRP, but excluded from the on hand used in component availability check that is part of order release.

CYCLE COUNTING

Cycle counting is a way to sample inventory records and measure inventory record accuracy. A number of items are counted each day, and the count is compared to the inventory balance stored in the computer. Inventory records that differ from the actual counts by more than some small tolerance (tolerances are explained in Chapter 25, Performance Measurements) are incorrect. Inventory records that are within the tolerance are correct. If 100 items are counted, and ninety-five are within the counting tolerance, then the inventory record accuracy is 95%.

The main goals of cycle counting are:

1. To assist in identifying the causes of inventory record errors, so the causes of errors can be corrected.

2. To improve the accuracy of the inventory records by purging any existing errors.

3. To measure inventory record accuracy.

A number of different methods for cycle counting have been developed over the years. Random sample cycle counting, ABC cycle counting, process control cycle counting, and control group cycle counting are all different methods for sampling the inventory records. Because each of these methods achieves somewhat different goals, most companies use a combination of sampling methods. The most popular combinations seem to be:

1. Control group and ABC cycle counting.

2. Control group, process control, and random sample cycle counting.

CONTROL GROUP CYCLE COUNTING

Control group cycle counting helps in researching inventory errors. The system should include a special group of items, called the control group, which is counted frequently (like once every ten days for example).

The control group is a small sample of about 100 item numbers which is used to find and correct the causes of inventory errors. By counting these items frequently, it is possible to determine the cause of the error in almost all cases. Only ten days worth of transactions have to be researched, and normally this means that it is possible to find the specific cause of the error. The improvement (or lack of improvement) in the level of inventory record accuracy can be monitored easily using this approach because new information is available every ten days on whether the inventory accuracy is getting better or worse.

If a control group is part of the cycle counting system, the system should provide a notification listing the items in the control group that are to be counted each day. This notification could be a separate listing, or it could be part of a combined listing which specifies the other items that are to be cycle counted.

Control group cycle counting is an excellent way to assist in identifying the causes of inventory inaccuracies, but is not a measure of overall inventory accuracy. The accuracy of a control group is typically higher than the accuracy of the other items in inventory because the control group is counted more frequently. The other limitation in control group cycle counting is that it is not an effective method for purging the inventory records of existing errors. Because the sample is so small, many items have inventory record errors that are not caught in the 100 item sample. Consequently, other sampling methods would be used for purging the inventory records of existing errors.

RANDOM SAMPLE AND ABC CYCLE COUNTING

In a random sample cycle counting system, items are selected for counting at random. Each day a certain number of items are selected. All items are candidates for counting. Some items may never have been counted; others may have been counted the prior day or during the prior week.

In a random sample cycle counting system, there is no guarantee that all items will be counted each year. While this is workable, many people prefer that all inventory records be verified at least yearly. These people generally prefer to use a slightly different method of sampling. This sampling method is called ABC cycle counting.

In an ABC cycle counting system, all items are counted periodically and generally with varying frequencies for different types of items. For example, a common cycle counting program is to count the A items four times a year, B items twice a year, and C items once a year. Cycle counting can also be triggered based on other conditions like a negative on-hand balance, a low point in inventory, etc., although the main selection criteria is the date of the last cycle count and the counting frequency for each class of item.

In both the random and ABC approaches, the cycle counting system should provide some type of notification listing the items which are due to be cycle counted. In most systems based on ABC classifications, this is done by specifying how often each of the different classes of items is to be counted over the course of a year. The system then assigns a cycle count date to each item and produces a listing each day of the items due to be cycle counted.

While random sample and ABC cycle counting systems provide fairly accurate measures of overall inventory accuracy and a way to purge the existing errors in the records, there is one limitation. In a company with 95% inventory accuracy, it's necessary to count 100 items to find the five items that are in error. There isn't any way to direct the cycle counter to those items that are most likely in error. Instead, a cycle counter spends most of his time counting items that are correct, rather than concentrating on the items in error.

PROCESS CONTROL CYCLE COUNTING

Process control cycle counting is a cycle counting approach designed to direct the cycle counter to the items most likely to be in error and are easiest to count.

Instead of sampling items based on random selection or fixed intervals, process control cycle counting samples items based on the likelihood of error in the inventory record. This way, the cycle counter's attention is concentrated on the items that may be in error. Being able to concentrate on the items likely to be in error makes the cycle counter tremendously effective in finding errors in the inventory records and purging them.

In process control cycle counting, two types of items are cycle counted:

1. Items that are easy to count (low balances, sealed cartons or boxes, etc.)

2. Items that are obviously in error.

In a process control cycle counting system, the cycle count report lists all the items stored in an location or area. While all these items are candidates for counting, only those which have obvious errors or which are easy to count are actually counted. An example of an item with an obvious error would be one where the computer inventory balance is ten and where the actual quantity on hand is obviously over 100.

Items that are easy to count typically have low inventory balances, or are packaged in sealed cartons, boxes, or tubs. Since most of the items that will be counted will be items with low inventory balances, the result of these sampling rules is to concentrate on the items with the highest probability of inventory errors. Items with low on-hand balances will have had the highest number of transactions, and therefore the greatest exposure to error.

The procedure for cycle counting using a process control technique is simple and consists mainly of checking the balance on hand against the cycle count report by item. Each item within the location is checked. Items that are easy to count are counted, and, if in error, corrected. Items that are not easy to count are checked against the cycle count listing for an obvious error. If there isn't an obvious error, the item is skipped. If there is an obvious error, then the item is counted and the balance on hand corrected.

Besides directing the cycle counter to the records most likely in error, process control cycle counting has an additional advantage. Because the items that are easiest to count represent a high percentage of the items counted in this method, more items can be counted in a day than in other methods. This in turn means that any errors that exist in the inventory records can be purged faster in this cycle counting approach.

To implement process control cycle counting there are two assumptions. One assumption is that inventory records are kept by stockroom location. Keeping records by location and cycle counting by location prevents the cycle counter from having to walk back and forth across the stockroom to count an item. All the cycle counter's time is spent cycle counting, making it possible to count a higher number of items per day. The other assumption is that the cycle counter has easy access to the on-hand balance for each item and location. Access to the on-hand balance allows the cycle counter to identify obvious errors easily. These errors can be corrected, and the cycle counter can move on to the next item.

Some companies may be concerned about giving the cycle counter access to the on-hand balance prior to the cycle count. A blind count assures the integrity of the cycle counting activity. However, most companies do not experience a problem, and in general, this is a worthwhile trade-off when considering the benefits of process control cycle counting.

The one limitation in a cycle counting system based on process control sampling is that it does not measure inventory record accuracy. The only items that are actually counted are those most likely to be or obviously in error. Consequently, the accuracy measurement is skewed, and appears to be lower than it really is. To determine the true inventory record accuracy, most companies periodically take a random sample of the records.

CYCLE COUNTING AS A TWO-STEP PROCESS

Regardless of what system is used for sampling, cycle counting is a two-step process. When items are cycle counted, the inventory should not be immediately updated with the cycle counted quantity. One reason is that the effects of an inventory adjustment are serious enough to warrant a double check whenever a sizeable discrepancy appears. Another reason is that there may be a few transactions in the paperwork pipeline between the stockroom shelves and the computer inventory record. This can happen, for example, when someone forgets to turn in a transaction or when a transaction is rejected. With some effort, the number of transactions in this state of suspension can be drastically reduced, but in many cases, the pipeline will not be cleared entirely.

The second step in the cycle counting process is to make a double check on any cycle counts where the cycle count and the on-hand balance for the item are out of agreement by a sizeable amount. In some cases the discrepancy is due to a transaction which is in this paperwork pipeline and has not been processed yet. If this is not the reason for the discrepancy, then the item should be cycle counted again, perhaps by someone else. If this second count verifies the first count, the on-hand balance should be updated. This is normally done using an inventory adjustment transaction. The inventory adjustment transaction can be one which replaces the on-hand balance or one which adjusts the on-hand balance up or down.

In some cycle counting systems, inventory transactions are done on-line, so the transaction cut-off problems in a batch processing system do not exist. Cycle counting can go on throughout the day. As items are counted, the on-hand balance can be checked using a stock status inquiry before the adjustment is made. If the adjustment is a large one, the physical count can be double checked before the inventory is updated.

In other cycle counting systems, the cycle count listing shows the items to be counted and the on-hand balance for each. In a process control cycle counting system, this is typical. It may also be true in other cycle counting systems. The cycle count listing is used when the cycle counts are made. The count is compared to the on-hand balance listed on the report. Records that are significantly in error are double checked. In order to use this method, the on-hand balance must be up-to-date at the time the cycle count listing is printed, and the on-hand balance must be updated fairly close to the time the cycle counting is done.

AUDIT TRAIL

Once the on-hand balance has been adjusted, the job is not done. In practice, the job of investigating and finding the causes of inventory errors is more difficult and time consuming than the job of counting. This investigation typically starts with a search of all inventory transactions for an item back to the time of the last cycle count.

Normally, control group items are the only items researched for the cause of inventory errors. Control group items are counted frequently, say once every ten days, as a way to minimize the number of transactions that have to be researched to find an error. Most of the time, the transactions for ten days or so have to be searched. However, there are times when items that are not part of the control group have to be researched, and in these situations more transactions have to be searched through.

Consequently, a transaction history by item showing all the transactions that affected the on hand balance is needed for investigating inventory errors. This transaction history should list all the inventory transactions for some specified time frame (day, week, month) in one report and show the type of transaction, transaction quantity, and on-hand balance before and after the transaction.

Some systems also include a transaction history by item and location. This type of transaction history shows only those transactions that affected the balance on hand in the specified inventory location. The transaction history report or display would show the same type of information as the main transaction history inquiry.

One additional type of transaction history display may be helpful in a system. This type of display shows all the transactions that updated the balances, quantities, and fields affecting the master scheduling, material requirements planning, and capacity planning calculations. Such a display can help in situations where there is a major change in the material requirements plan for an item (for example) and a planner wants to see whether the change may have been caused by changing order quantities, safety stock levels. etc.

Chapter 14

Scheduled Receipts Subsystem

The scheduled receipts system maintains the manufacturing and purchase orders. A shop dispatching system may expand on this system or replace it; a purchasing system may do the same. A separate scheduled receipts system is explained here for several reasons. First, a number of software packages do not have a shop dispatching system, or else they have a dispatching but it is separate from the scheduled receipts system. Second, most companies implement MRP II in stages starting with the supporting systems to MRP (including the scheduled receipts subsystem), master production scheduling, and the MRP logic. Later they implement shop dispatching, capacity planning, input/output control, and purchasing.

SCHEDULED RECEIPT TRANSACTIONS

The scheduled receipts system is used to add, delete, and change scheduled receipts. Depending upon whether the item is planned by MRP or controlled through the master scheduling system, these scheduled receipts will then be presented to the MRP netting and exception checking logic or to the master production scheduling netting and exception logic.

Three pieces of information are needed for each scheduled receipt. These are the item number, due date, and quantity. The item number is used to present the scheduled receipts information to MRP and master scheduling. The due date and quantity are used in the netting and exception logic.

In addition, in most systems, a fourth piece of information is required. This piece of information is a unique identifier used to distinguish one order from another. The unique identifier is often called an order number or authorization number. In the case of purchase orders, the unique identifier may be a purchase order number and line number, so that each purchase order can have several scheduled receipts. In many companies the unique identifier is assigned automatically when the order is released.

Scheduled receipts for items planned in MRP may be added by releasing an existing planned or firm planned order, or they may be unplanned and simply entered into the system. Scheduled receipts for master schedule items that are finished products are normally added by releasing an existing master schedule order, although it is possible that the scheduled receipt could be unplanned and entered directly into the system. In cases where an existing planned or firm planned order is being released, it should be possible to change the date or quantity. Some of the normal methods for creating scheduled receipts and the mechanics of handling existing planned and firm planned orders are explained in the following paragraphs.

When a scheduled receipt is created by releasing a planned order from MRP, many systems find the planned order and delete it. Although this is logical, it is not always necessary. It is possible to leave the planned order in the system and use the logic of MRP to delete it during the next planning run. The mechanics of how and when planned orders should be deleted are explained in Appendix 16.

When firm planned orders for items in MRP or master schedule orders for finished items are released to create scheduled receipts, the firm planned order must be found and deleted. Firm planned orders are not changed in any way by the computer, and, unless firm planned orders are deleted at the time an order is released, the firm planned order will continue to create gross requirements. So while it may be possible to avoid finding and deleting planned orders under some circumstances, it is not possible to do the same with firm planned orders.

When scheduled receipts for purchased items are released, the scheduled receipts system must be able to create multiple scheduled receipts on a single purchase order. These multiple scheduled receipts may be for different items or for the same item on different delivery dates.

Besides having the capability to create scheduled receipts, the scheduled receipts system must be able to change and delete existing orders. Once a scheduled receipt has been created, the information must be available for change. It must be possible to change the due date and the order quantity, and changes to the date or quantity should be reflected in the component allocations. If the order is rescheduled earlier or later, the component allocations should be dated earlier or later. If the order quantity increases or decreases, then the component allocation quantities should increase or decrease. When a scheduled receipt is deleted, the system should close the scheduled receipt and remove the component allocations, regardless of the order status.

A split transaction is normally part of a scheduled receipt subsystem. This type of transaction splits an existing scheduled receipt into two or more scheduled receipts, each with its own delivery date and quantity. The split transaction usually reschedules the existing order to the earliest date and creates a new scheduled receipt or receipts for the other later dates. In addition, the split transaction includes logic to apply any prior issues and shop movement transactions to the new set of orders.

A rework order release transaction is also normally part of a scheduled receipt subsystem. A rework order release handles the situation where an item is being pulled from stock and reworked to make it usable. In this situation new sets of components are not required. The components are already built into the item being issued and reworked. Consequently, a rework order release transaction bypasses the normal component allocation logic and creates a scheduled receipt without component allocations. If additional components are required, then a planner can add individual allocations using transactions.

Paperwork to assist the stockroom people may be helpful and can be produced when the scheduled receipt is created. This computer generated paperwork typically includes a picking list. Some systems also produce a picking list that summarizes certain types of orders.

This is a helpful feature for efficient picking of components, particularly when there is a high degree of commonality across different orders and when those orders are going through the same assembly or subassembly areas. For example, it might make a lot of sense to summarize all the scheduled receipts for different types of fork lift trucks and pick them all at once, rather than picking each one individually. On the other hand, it doesn't make sense to summarize all the fabrication, subassembly, and assembly orders since all the components are going to different areas in the shop.

Some scheduled receipts systems include simple logic to assist in picking components efficiently or in running a stockroom more effectively. This logic attempts to predict the locations from which components should be picked. Some sample rules include:

1. List inventory locations with small on-hand balances. By eliminating locations with small on-hand balances, material can be consolidated into fewer locations.

2. List inventory locations with on-hand balances sufficient to cover the required quantity. By picking these locations, picking can be done more efficiently.

3. List all locations for each item. Let a human choose the best picking method.

4. List all locations with a non-zero on-hand balance. Let a human choose the best picking method.

Frequently, turn-around documents like planned issue transactions for the components and a planned receipt for receiving the order back into stock are also generated by the computer. These documents can be helpful in reducing the amount of information that must be written on a transaction form or document.

Logic for producing hardcopy purchase orders may be helpful. Purchase orders are typically printed immediately following the creation of all the scheduled receipts.

ALLOCATIONS AND COMPONENT AVAILABILITY

When a manufacturing scheduled receipt is created, component allocations are also generated. Allocations are requirements for component parts and as such are similar to gross requirements. Allocations are requirements for component parts coming from scheduled receipts. Gross requirements are requirements for component parts coming from planned or firm planned orders. Allocations are uncashed requisitions on the stockroom and they exist only from the time a scheduled receipt is created until the components have been issued on the order.

There are some limited situations where it is possible to operate a system without allocations. However, there are a number of limitations in operating this way and it is not recommended.

There are several reasons for needing allocations in an MRP II system:

1. To properly reflect the requirements for component parts during the time that an order is waiting to be picked.

2. To assist in running the stockroom in a more organized way.

Primarily, allocations are needed to allow MRP to properly reflect the requirements for component parts. In a regenerative system, all gross requirements are deleted each time MRP is run. As planned orders are created, they are exploded and posted to the component parts. Yet there are requirements coming from scheduled receipts that have not been pulled from stock and must be represented in the system. Allocations are a way to show these requirements.

In a net change system, the mechanics of how gross requirements are handled is somewhat different. Gross requirements are not deleted as part of the MRP planning run. In a net change system, it would be possible to leave gross requirements attached to the scheduled receipts until the components are issued to manufacturing. These individual allocations could be used in the MRP calculations for each of the components.

Even in a net change system, however, there are good reasons for keeping an allocation total for each item. This is because one important use of allocations is to help run the stockroom in an organized way. Using allocations, there is no reason to stage orders in the stockroom to determine shortages. Instead, orders can be picked and sent to the manufacturing floor. Eliminating staging is a major improvement in the way a stockroom is run. Staged material is a nightmare to control. It is generally cannibalized, mixed-up, or lost. The way to avoid this situation is to make sure that all the components are on hand and available before the order is sent to the stockroom for picking.

Allocations are normally stored as both a total quantity allocated and as individual requirements that can be traced back to the scheduled receipts that created them. The individual allocations are the pegging, and the total allocation is the total quantity of the item that has been reserved for orders that have been released but not picked. It is not mandatory to maintain a total quantity allocated: some systems compute the total quantity allocated by summarizing the individual allocations. Either method is workable, but the method where both an allocation total and the allocation details are stored makes the component availability logic, explained below, much simpler.

A transaction system to add, change, and delete individual allocations must be part of the scheduled receipt subsystem. The transaction that adds an allocation creates an individual allocation and updates the total quantity allocated. The transaction that changes an allocation can change the date or quantity in the individual allocation, and in the case of a quantity change, updates the total allocated quantity. The delete transaction removes the individual allocation and reduces the total allocated.

These transactions are used primarily to handle temporary material substitutions, although they can also be used to help in the implementation of engineering changes. For example, a higher grade, more expensive steel might be used as a temporary substitute for a less expensive material due to material availability problems. In this situation, the allocation for the less expensive material would be deleted, and an allocation added for the higher grade steel.

Components can be checked to make sure that they are on hand and available using a component availability check. A component check should be run on each order before it is released and sent to the stockroom for picking. The component check works by checking each of the components, making sure that the quantity required by the order is available in the stockroom. The available quantity for each component is the on-hand balance less any allocations for other orders that have not yet been picked.

In most systems today, the component availability check is an on-line display. A planner requests a component check for an item or for a specific order for an item. The system explodes the bill of material for the item (or for the specific order) and checks availability. Components that are short are flagged for the planner's review.

A component availability check does not require that the planner create a firm planned order or scheduled receipt first. The component check logic accepts either an item number and quantity as input, or an order identifier. By specifying an item number and quantity, a planner can check component availability for a planned order or for an unplanned order release. By specifying an order identifier, a planner can check component availability for a firm planned order.

The component availability check includes logic for handling nonstocked or pseudo modules, for phantoms, transients, and self-consumed assemblies. The component check on these types of items compares the quantity required for the order to the quantity available. If the phantom item is not available, then the bill of material for the phantom is exploded and the component availability check performed on its components.

The order release process in the scheduled receipts systems is usually done in two steps. The first step is the component availability check. Each component is checked comparing the available quantity to the quantity required. If the order passes the component check, or if the planner decides to release the order in spite of the component availability, the second step takes place. This is the actual order release and allocation of the components. Allocations are created for each component.

The system should not prevent a planner from creating an order for an item when the components are not available. If a planner specifies that an order should be released, then the system should create the order and allocate the components.

This kind of manual override or forced release should be used only in exceptional situations and not routinely. Use of the override makes sense when a component is coming into the stockroom today or tomorrow, and the planner wants to have the assembly order ready so that it can be issued as soon as the component arrives in the stockroom. The override also makes sense when a component is short and the decision is to begin building the assembly anyway. This might be done, for example, when the seats for a tractor are still missing on the date the order is due to start. The decision is to go ahead and build the tractors without the seats and to install them later. This will keep the assembly department going and will probably not delay any shipments since the seats are due to be in by the time the tractors are built.

A note of perspective is appropriate here on the purpose of the component availability check. The component check is a way to help operate the stockroom in an organized manner by sending orders out to be picked only when the parts are available. The component availability check is not meant to be used as a type of priority planning tool, or as a type of automated shortage list for expediting parts. Such a shortage list cannot be used as a priority planning tool any more than manually produced shortage list can. The failure of a shortage list is not that it needs to be automated, but that it cannot look out into the future, it cannot show relative priorities, and it is not recalculated frequently. The component availability check is a way to help run the stockroom and not a way to determine what is needed and when. The determination of what is needed and when is done in MRP.

FINAL ASSEMBLY SCHEDULING

The scheduled receipt subsystem requires some additional capabilities to handle scheduled receipts for products made-to-order from a number of options. This type of product is like the automobile described in the master production scheduling topic. For automobiles, modules exist for V-8 and V-6 engines, AM/FM radios, accessory trim packages, etc. These modules may be actual subassemblies that are stocked and then put into the automobile (for example, the V-6 and V-8 engine options), or they may be logical groupings of parts that cannot physically be assembled (like accessory trim packages). The parts associated with this type of module are put together with the parts of other modules to create a number of different subassemblies, like the front and rear door subassemblies.

In this type of product, the master production schedule and the final assembly schedule are different. The master production schedule is stated in terms of the logical groupings of parts. When the time actually comes to build a product for a specific customer order, a schedule must be produced to pull the proper parts (produce a picking list), show the proper operations (produce a shop routing), and provide for receipt into stock or shipment to the customer. This manufacturing schedule for the finished product is called a final assembly schedule. This final assembly schedule, stated in terms of the final product configuration (say a silver Buick Skylark automobile with V-6 engine, AM/FM cassette stereo, special trim, etc.), calls for all the parts to build the car and also shows the assembly operations required. In effect, the final assembly schedule provides a way to build the product to a customer's specification.

In addition, the final assembly schedule must keep the numbers in the master production schedule in balance. This means one of two things. If the customer orders are left in the master scheduling system, then a scheduled receipt must be shown in the master scheduling system. This balances the customer order (a demand) with the scheduled receipt (a production order). The other method removes both the customer order and the master schedule orders from the master scheduling system.

The following explanation of final assembly scheduling covers the most common method. In this method, customer orders are left in the master scheduling system until the order is shipped. This method makes it easier for the master scheduler and sales people to see the status of each customer's order and the final assembly schedule that will produce it. Companies interested in other methods for handling final assembly scheduling can refer to Appendix 17.

This method for final assembly scheduling uses the customer order both as a unique identifier (item number) and as a listing of options (bill of material). The customer order number is unique and can therefore be used instead of an item number. The listing of options the customer has selected shows what is needed to produce the product and can therefore become the bill of material. There is no need to create a new item number and bill of material for this customer's specific configuration.

When the time comes to create the final assembly schedule, the customer order can also be converted to a type of scheduled receipt. This final assembly scheduled receipt is like a normal scheduled receipt except that the part number is the customer order number and the bill of material would be the line items on the customer order. In addition, a routing for the type of product can be used to show the operations needed to produce the item. This routing is attached to the final assembly order and backscheduled to compute operation schedule dates. The shop paperwork for the final assembly order includes a picking list, shop routing, and, in some cases, move and operation transactions. In this method, there would be one final assembly schedule order for each customer order.

Like any other scheduled receipts, final assembly orders have a release process that includes component availability checking, authorization, and allocation of the components. In the automobile example, the customer order for the Buick Skylark with V-6 engine, special trim, etc. is released to become the final assembly order. The customer order is used as the bill of material for checking component availability, and, assuming that all components were available, the order is released. The V-6 engine option, which is a physical subassembly, is allocated and listed on the picking list. The special trim option, which is just a logical grouping of parts (phantom item), is exploded to its components (say side-trim strips, pinstriping, etc.) and these individual components are allocated. The individual trim strips, pinstriping, etc. are listed on the picking list for the final assembly schedule order.

Whenever an option is a pseudo or phantom, some additional bookkeeping logic is required in the system. A dummy type of scheduled receipt is required on the pseudo or phantom item to replace the master schedule orders. These dummy scheduled receipts are necessary because the customer orders for these options are still in the master scheduling system and consequently they are still creating demand. The dummy scheduled receipts offset this customer order demand. These scheduled receipts are different from normal scheduled receipts because there are no allocations attached to them. The components have already been allocated as part of the final assembly order.

When the final assembly order is released, the dummy scheduled receipts that are created for each option replace the existing master schedule orders. If this were not the case, double requirements would be created for the components; one set of requirements from the final assembly order and one set from the master schedule order.

When a customer order is shipped, all the remaining items must be removed from the master scheduling system. This includes the customer order demands, scheduled receipts, and allocations (if not already gone). The allocations are typically gone by this time since they are reduced as the component parts are issued from the stockroom.

STATUS REPORTING

A scheduled receipts system must have a status reporting function that includes a simple status report listing the information for each order and arranged in item number sequence for easy reference. By sorting this status report by due date, a simple dispatch list can be produced. This simple dispatch list is many times used for shop dispatching during the span of time when MRP is operating, but before detailed shop scheduling and dispatching is on the air. Once shop scheduling and dispatching is available, the daily dispatch list provides this function.

Chapter 15

Firm Planned Order Subsystem

FIRM PLANNED ORDER TRANSACTIONS

The firm planned order system is used to add, delete, and change firm planned orders. If the item is planned by MRP, these firm planned orders will be presented to the netting and exception checking logic of material requirements planning. If the item is controlled through the master scheduling system, these firm planned orders will be passed to the master production scheduling netting and exception logic.

In many systems, the transactions to add, change, and delete scheduled receipts are modified to create firm planned order maintenance transactions. In fact, in some cases, the same transactions are used, and firm planned orders are coded as a special type of scheduled receipt.

When the scheduled receipts system transactions are used to create and maintain firm planned orders, the system must include time phased allocations and the ability to separate firm planned orders from normal scheduled receipts. Time phased allocations are needed as a way to show the proper requirements for sets of component parts. The ability to distinguish firm planned orders from scheduled receipts is needed so that the system produces the proper paperwork and exception messages and excludes requirements generated from firm planned orders from the component availability check.

Scheduled receipts are ready to be worked on, so that the system produces shop paperwork, allocates the component parts so that they are unavailable for any other orders, and shows the scheduled receipts in the shop dispatching system. Firm planned orders must be handled somewhat differently, however. Shop paperwork should not be produced for firm planned orders. Components should not be allocated to firm planned orders. And the shop dispatching system should not include firm planned orders. Additionally, an exception message, a firm planned order due for release message, should be produced when the order is ready for release.

Several pieces of information are needed for each firm planned order. The minimum information includes the item number, due date, and quantity. The firm planned order start date is also helpful for situations where the normal lead time is being compressed or expanded.

The item number is used to present the firm planned order information to MRP and master scheduling. The start and due dates and quantity are used in the netting and exception logic and the explosion calculations. By setting the start date, the planner is able to specify the date of the component gross requirements. Setting the due date allows the planner to specify the date that the firm planned order will be included into the netting calculation. By setting the order quantity, the planner is able to override the normal calculated lot size.

A few systems also include some other information for firm planned orders. This can include:

1. The lead time for the firm planned order (this is an alternative to specifying the start date).

2. A unique identifier (order number, authorization number).

3. A code identifying whether or not the firm planned order deviates from the normal bill of material or normal routing. This code may also indicate that the order is a purchase order where the item is normally manufactured, or vice versa.

Firm planned orders for items planned in MRP may be added by firming an existing planned order, or they may be simply entered into the system without an existing planned order. Firm planned orders for master schedule items that are finished products are normally entered directly into the system, although it is possible for a firm planned order to be created by firming up a suggested master schedule order. In cases where an existing planned order is being firmed, it should be possible to change the date or quantity.

When a firm planned order is created by firming a planned order from MRP, many systems find the planned order and delete it. Yet while this is logical, it is not always necessary. It is possible to leave the planned order in the system and use the logic of MRP to delete it during the next planning run.

FIRM PLANNED ORDER COMPONENT UPDATE

The system must provide a mechanism to update component gross requirements when firm planned orders are added, changed, or deleted. When a firm planned order is added, component requirements that reflect the firm planned order dates and order quantity must be created. Subsequent changes to the start or due date, or the order quantity, must also be reflected in the component gross requirements. If the order is due earlier or later, the component requirements must be dated earlier or later. If the order quantity increases or decreases, then the component requirement quantities must increase or decrease. When a firm planned order is deleted, the system must close the order and remove the component requirements.

Several methods are available for creating and maintaining the timing and quantity of component gross requirements coming from firm planned orders:

1. By exploding the firm planned orders in the explosion logic of MRP (if no bill of material deviations are indicated).

2. By updating the component requirements as part of the firm planned order maintenance transaction logic.

In some systems, including most regenerative systems, both planned and firm planned orders are exploded in the planned order explosion logic. Consequently, no special logic is needed to create and maintain component gross requirements coming from firm planned orders: each time MRP is run, the system re-explodes the existing firm planned orders to create component requirements.

In other systems, including many net change systems, the component gross requirements are attached to the order and consequently must be maintained in the transaction system that adds, changes, and deletes the order. Generally, the firm planned order add transaction creates the component gross requirements by exploding the bill of material and attaching the requirements to the order. The firm planned order change transaction reschedules component requirements by reading the requirements attached to the order and changing them to earlier or later dates or larger or smaller quantities. The firm planned order delete transaction removes the component requirements.

PART V

Executing the Material Plan

Chapter 16

Routing Subsystem

The routing subsystem provides the information needed to calculate capacity requirements in the future. It also provides the basic data needed to translate the priorities from MRP, such as due dates, into more detailed milestones for shop scheduling and dispatching.

ROUTING TRANSACTIONS

The routing subsystem maintains the relationships between items and the resources required to manufacture or acquire them. In other words, the routing system defines the process needed to make or buy every item.

A routing system must provide the capabilities to maintain both the resources (work centers) and the routing operation records that relate the resource to an item.

Transactions must exist to add, change, and delete work centers; in addition, transactions must exist to add, change, or delete an operation in the routing for an item. The routing system allows an unlimited number of operations in any routing. And the system normally provides a way to define a routing for a purchased part as a way to handle situations where either the item is purchased but some material is supplied, or the item is currently purchased but has been manufactured in the past.

The information that is stored for an item-work center relationship must include the run time and a time basis code. The time basis code allows a flexibile method for defining the run time. For example, one time basis code might indicate that the operation run time is per item; another time basis code indicates that the operation run time is per ten thousand pieces.

Some routing subsystems contain specialized transactions for reducing the clerical time required to maintain the routing. Multiple-delete, same-as-except, and multiple-replace are such transactions. While these transactions are not essential in a system, when they are used correctly they do make it possible to avoid some clerical work.

The multiple-delete transaction deletes all the operations in a routing, in effect removing the entire routing. The transaction is used most often when an item is obsolete. The same-as-except transaction copies a routing and attaches it to another parent item. This is normally followed by some transactions to change a few of the operations in the copied routing. A multiple-replace transaction replaces one work center with another work center in every operation that it appears.

The routing defines the item-work center relationships. A work center where-used relationship is just the opposite. The work center where-used lists all the items where a work center is used.

Some routing systems keep the work center where-used relationships up-to-date at all times. When a change is made by adding or deleting operations, the where-used information is updated immediately. However, in other systems, the where-used information is not maintained at the time the routing changes. Instead, the where-used information is recreated periodically.

REPORTING

The routing system should also provide some reporting capabilities. Normal functions include:

1. Routing inquiry.

2. Work center where-used listing.

The routing inquiry simply lists all of the operations and work centers for an item. The work center where-used listing displays all of the operations and items that use a specified work center.

UPDATE IN NET CHANGE SYSTEM

In a net change capacity planning system, a mechanism is required to maintain the capacity requirements whenever the routings change. This mechanism can be provided in a number of different ways.

One way to maintain the capacity requirements is to update them at the time the operation in the routing changes. This method is frequently used because the routings are an easy way to find and update the capacity requirements. Once the routing has changed, finding and updating the capacity requirements is more difficult.

So, in some net change capacity planning systems the capacity requirements are updated whenever an operation is added, changed, or deleted. If an operation is added, new capacity requirements are added for each planned order for the item. If an operation is changed, like a different run time or setup time, the capacity requirements are found and updated. If an operation is deleted, the capacity requirements are found and deleted.

A second way to provide this function is to include logic, which completely destroys all the capacity requirements when a change is made to the routing. At the time the routing is changed, the item is marked indicating that a routing has been made for the item, and all the capacity requirements coming from the item are erased. During net change capacity planning, the planned orders are exploded using the new version of the routing. This has the same effect as finding and correcting the capacity requirements when the routing is changed.

The third method for providing the function is to flag items with routing changes, and then, during net change capacity planning, match the current routing against the old capacity requirements. As differences between the routing and the capacity requirements are found, this logic adds, changes, and deletes capacity requirements. This method also has the effect of finding and correcting the capacity requirements when the routing is changed. The only disadvantage to the method is that developing the matching logic is generally more complicated than developing the logic needed for the other two approaches. Consequently, this method tends to be the least popular way to provide the function of correcting the capacity requirements when the routings change.

Chapter 17

Shop Scheduling and Dispatching

A shop scheduling and dispatching system provides a way to communicate priorities between the planner and the shop floor. Using shop dispatching, the shop schedule can be shown by department or by work center and operation, instead of showing only the manufacturing orders and their due dates.

The ability to see where the orders are and where they should be is a tremendous benefit to the people on the shop floor. They are being held accountable for meeting the scheduled due dates, and the more closely they can monitor progress against the schedule, the better they will be at meeting the dates.

Another way to look at this is that shop scheduling and dispatching provides the people on the floor with more detailed milestones to use in measuring progress against the plan. Like any large project, meeting the shop schedule requires that people have an accurate way to gauge their progress against the plan.

In some cases, however, having a very detailed shop schedule and operation-by-operation dispatching would not be particularly helpful. This would be the case in paced or dedicated assembly areas, for packaging and process lines, for other areas where orders flow from work station to work station without delays from queues or move time between operations, or for products where only one operation is performed. For example, in a pharmaceutical company, orders flow down packaging lines consisting of fillers, cappers, labelers, and boxers. When the filling operation starts, the other operations (capping, labeling, boxing) start simultaneously. Having individual shop schedules for the filler, capper, labeler, and boxer isn't of much value in this situation. Instead, having a shop schedule showing the start date and due date of the order or showing the start date and due date of the order in the packaging department would probably be adequate and make more sense.

Consequently, companies with high volume assembly operations or processes may not need the complete capabilities for scheduling by operation and dispatching by work center and operation. These companies may only need a simplified type of shop scheduling system. This simplified scheduling system would show, by department, the jobs that need to be completed in a given week or day.

Companies in these situations might be wise to review this explanation of shop floor control for any points that are not necessary in their operation. During the review of the explanation of shop floor control, these companies may also find it helpful to substitute the word "department" for the word "operation." Sometimes the detailed schedules and dispatch lists by operation don't make sense, but schedules by department do.

Presenting schedules by operation or by department only makes sense if the basic scheduling information is correct. All scheduling in a shop scheduling and dispatching system is based on the due dates of the scheduled receipts. If these due dates do not represent the real need dates, extending the dates to a finer level of detail is of no value. MRP is the way to plan and maintain valid due dates. Consequently, a shop scheduling and dispatching system without an MRP system is of little value.

In some systems, shop scheduling and dispatching may replace the scheduled receipts system as a way to maintain the scheduled receipts for manufactured items. In other systems, the shop scheduling and dispatching system is added to the already existing functions of the scheduled receipts system. It makes no difference how the system handles this as long as the required functions are provided. This explanation of the Standard System has already covered the functions of the scheduled receipts subsystem, and so only the additional functions needed for shop scheduling and dispatching will be explained here.

SHOP SCHEDULING TRANSACTIONS

The manufacturing operations for scheduled receipts are stored and maintained by the shop scheduling and dispatching system. When a scheduled receipt is created for a manufactured item, a copy of the routing for that item is made and attached to the scheduled receipt. Generally, the routing is copied and attached as part of the order release transaction, or is done later in a batch run for all the orders released that day.

The information normally stored in the routing file includes:

1. Operation number.

2. Description of the operation.

3. Work center.

4. Setup hours.

5. Labor hours.

6. Scheduling time (this will be explained later).

When the routing is copied and attached to the scheduled receipt, it is normally stored in an open shop order file or segment. This is just a routing file of the operations for active manufacturing scheduled receipts. The logic to maintain this open shop order file must include the logic explained above to copy the routing and attach it to the scheduled receipt, as well as logic to handle phantom, transient, or self-consumed assemblies that are components. In this situation, the routing for the phantom component will be copied and merged into the routing for the assembly. This provides a way to properly handle intermediate assemblies produced on an assembly line and which are immediately used in another assembly.

The maintenance logic also includes transactions to add, delete, and change the operations attached to an order. An operation will be changed, for example, where the operation will actually be run at a different work center. An example of an operation that must be added is where a rework operation is needed for a particular order.

Shop paperwork may be produced when the scheduled receipt is created and the routing is copied and attached to the order. The shop paperwork is optional, and many companies with active Just-in-Time programs choose to eliminate all the shop paperwork that they had been producing in the past. As they move to daily or more frequent deliveries and scheduled receipts that cover shorter and shorter periods of time, the shop paperwork becomes less and less useful.

In companies who choose to generate shop paperwork, the computer-generated paperwork may include a routing, as well as the picking list described in the topic on the scheduled receipts subsystem. In some systems, stockroom and shop turnaround documents are also produced. These could include planned issue transactions for issuing the component parts, a planned receipt transaction for receiving the order back into the stockroom, shop move transactions to indicate movement of the job from one operation to the next, and operation complete transactions to indicate that an operation has been finished.

OPERATION SCHEDULE DATES

Operation schedule dates should be calculated for each operation. The operation schedule dates are the shop schedule. They are what will be used by the people in the shop to determine whether they are ahead of schedule, behind schedule, or on time.

Operation schedule dates normally include both an operation start date and an operation due date. These dates are back scheduled from the order due date using some simple scheduling rules. Back scheduling means that the scheduling calculation starts with the order due date and backs through the operations. The order due date less the move time to receive the order into the stockroom gives the operation due date for the last operation. The operation due date for this operation less the setup and run time give the operation start date. The operation start date less the move and queue time give the operation due date for the previous operation, and so on.

The back scheduling rules should not be complicated. Complicated rules only make the system difficult to use, and the people using the system have trouble understanding how the schedule was calculated. Some examples of the types of typical scheduling rules (that may not fit every company) are the following:

1. CATEGORY: Number of shifts and hours per shift used for scheduling.

   RULE: Schedule one shift at eight hours per shift each week.

2. CATEGORY: Number of men or machines in the work center and the number used in this operation.

   RULE: Schedule with the assumption that all the machines in the work center will be used for processing, unless overridden by the information in the routing.

3. CATEGORY: Paperwork preparation and parts issue time.

   RULE: Allow three days for preparation of paperwork and parts issue.

4. CATEGORY: Move and queue times between operations.

   RULE 1: Allow two days for move and queue between departments.

   RULE 2: Allow one day for move and queue for operations in the same department.

   RULE 3: Allow no move and queue time for successive operations in the same work center.

5. CATEGORY: Outside processing.

   RULE: Allow two weeks for any outside processing operations.

6. CATEGORY: Scheduling deviations and overlapping operations.

   RULE: Schedule overlapping based on overrides specified by operation.

There may be situations where these sample scheduling rules do not apply. For example, a fully manned two or three shift operation should not be scheduled forty hours a week. In other situations, some types of outside vendor operations will need more than two weeks. However, the categories of scheduling rules listed above are ones where rules must be agreed upon—the sample rules are ones that are used commonly and seem to work well. The important thing in these scheduling rules is that they are simple and easy for everyone to understand.

The shop scheduling and dispatching system must make some provision for special circumstances where the planner or shop people want to override the normal scheduling rules. For example, an item where two or more of the operations are normally overlapped, or a product manufactured on an assembly line don't fit the normal scheduling rules. Instead of waiting for the first operation to be completed, the second operation and possibly third or fourth operations are started as soon as enough material is available. In another situation, a machined casting may have to be water tested, and many times the casting fails the water test and has to be reworked before going on to the next operation. Both of these are situations of a recurring nature and the shop people want to be able to show reasonably correct operation schedule dates on these orders. This can be done by allowing deviations to the normal scheduling rules to be stored in the routing.

A deviation is typically stored by operation as a scheduling time override. In the case of the overlapping operations above, a negative scheduling time, less two days, for example, can be used on the overlapping operations (second, third, and fourth). This schedules the second, third, and fourth operations two days before they would normally have been scheduled to start. In the case of the machined casting that normally needs rework, a positive scheduling time could be used. A scheduling time of four days, for example, schedules the operation for an extra four days in addition to the setup and running time. This extra time can be used to rework the castings if they fail the water test.

When scheduling time overrides are used in the routing, they apply to all orders. As each new scheduled receipt is created, the routing is copied and the scheduling time is used in the calculation of operation schedule dates.

The back scheduling logic in the system must also include the ability to update the operation schedule dates when the order is rescheduled. This logic generally operates by calculating the difference between the old due date and the new due date. This difference is then applied to the operation start and operation due dates.

The back scheduling logic must also provide a way to recompute the operation schedule dates in two other situations:

1. When operations are added, changed, or deleted from the order.

2. When the rules or factors change. For example, if the queue time being used for a work center changes, the orders in that work center should have their operation schedule dates recomputed.

A helpful capability in a system is a way to compare the computed lead time from back scheduling to the lead time being used for material planning. In situations where there is a significant difference, the item should be flagged for a planner's review. In some cases the planner may need to change the lead time for material planning. In other cases the rules or factors being used in back scheduling may be incorrect and need to be updated.

DAILY DISPATCH LIST

Two operation transactions are normally part of the shop scheduling and dispatching system. One transaction records the movement of material from one operation to another (often called the move transaction), and the other transaction updates the system to show that the work at an operation is complete (usually called the operation complete transaction).

These transactions are needed for the system to operate as a tool for scheduling. Move transactions signal the arrival, and operation complete transactions signal the end of an order through each operation. The move transaction says that the material has been moved to the work center for an operation, and it is now available to be started. The operation complete transaction says that the work is done at this operation, and it should be taken off the schedule of work to be completed.

Some companies find it helpful to include some additional transactions in the shop scheduling and dispatching system. For example, one transaction that is helpful but much less critical is the one to report labor on an operation. This transaction shows that an operation is partially completed. Another transaction that is sometimes helpful is one that combines the functions of the operation complete or labor transaction with those of the move transaction. This transaction shows that an operation is complete or partially complete and has immediately moved to the next work center.

The shop transactions generally work by updating a status for each operation. The operation status has values like:

1. NOT AVAILABLE. The job has not been moved to this work center and it is not available to be worked on.

2. AVAILABLE. The job has been moved to this operation and is now available to be worked on.

3. WORKING. Labor has been reported on the operation. This means the job is either setup or running.

4. COMPLETE. The operation has been reported as complete.

5. HOLD. The job is on hold. This could be due to a rejection, broken tool, etc.

The most important report in the shop scheduling and dispatching system is the shop schedule. The daily dispatch list is the most useful form of the shop schedule and Figure 22 is an example of this report.

The daily dispatch list shows the jobs that are in each work center or department ready to be worked on. It also looks ahead a few days and, in a separate section of the report, shows the jobs that will be coming to the work center or the department.

The dispatch list, like any other shop schedule, is a list of the jobs to be done showing the operation start and due dates as well as the order due date. The operation start dates are used to determine what job to work on next. The opera-

Figure 22
Daily Dispatch List

WORK CENTER: 3001 PUNCH PRESS
TODAY'S DATE: 1/16/88
PRIORITY: OPERATION DUE DATE

Item #	Order #	Operation #	Operation Description	Operation Dates Start	Operation Dates Due	Order Due Date	Hours Set Up	Hours Run	Qty. REM	Prev Op #	Prev Op W/C	Next Op #	Next Op W/C
JOBS AT THIS WORK CENTER													
L930	1326	10	Punch	1/11/88	1/13/88	1/30/88	.0	4.0	1500	—	—	20	4510
K421	2937	10	Punch	1/12/88	1/13/88	1/27/88	2.0	6.0	2000	—	—	20	4775
D430	2561	10	Punch	1/17/88	1/18/88	1/23/88	1.0	1.0	500	10	3000	20	4510
N862	3817	20	Punch	1/19/88	1/20/88	1/24/88	.5	3.5	1000	—	—	20	4000
G315	4123	10	Punch	1/26/88	1/27/88	2/15/88	.5	3.5	1200	—	—	15	4100
JOBS COMING TO THIS WORK CENTER IN THE NEXT 3 DAYS													
K319	2497	15	Punch	1/17/88	1/18/88	1/27/88	1.0	3.0	800		Stock	20	4510
B412	3515	20	Punch	1/17/88	1/20/88	2/08/88	2.0	20.0	10,000	10	3000	30	9500

tion due dates and order due dates are the vital pieces of information. They are the shop schedule. These due dates are the dates the shop people are responsible for meeting. In some companies, schedule dates are shown by department instead of by operation. In such a case, the daily dispatch list shows the department start date and department due date for each order as well as the order due date. This presentation makes sense where a number of operations are done in each department and where the operations are very short running. An example of this would be in a pharmaceutical company where mixing, blending, and granulating all take place in the same department and on the same day. Another example would be in a wood working plant where planing, sanding, and gluing all take place within several hours.

The order due date is included in the dispatch list to help the shop people determine when to feed back information to the planners. If an order is behind schedule by five days, but the order due date is not for another twenty days, there is still time to make up the five days. As the order moves through each operation, the fact that it is behind schedule will cause it to appear near the top of the dispatch list and, if possible, will be worked on quickly. This helps to make up the time that the order is behind schedule. However, if an order is five days behind schedule and is due into the stockroom tomorrow, the shop people need to notify the planners if the order will not be completed on time. The due date of an order is the date the order is needed back in the stockroom. If an order is going to be late by more than a day or so, the planners need to begin to make alternate plans.

Many shop scheduling and dispatching systems include a priority tool that is a numerical ratio, like critical ratio or slack time per operation. This explanation of the Standard System does not include such a tool.

The best way to show priorities in a shop scheduling and dispatching system is in the form of dates. Scheduling ratios like critical ratio and slack time per operation will give the same kind of priority information: both show which job to do first, second, and so on. However, shop dates are a better way to present the shop schedule for two reasons. One is that shop dates are easy to relate to. The shop schedule is clear and easy to understand if it says an order should be through this operation by Wednesday, or that an order is four days behind schedule. These are things that everyone in a shop is used to relating to and working with.

A numerical ratio is an abstraction without meaning from everyday experience. A ratio of .78 or 1.05 doesn't really say much. It may indicate that a job is ahead of schedule or behind schedule, but that is about all. It doesn't really give a person in the shop an idea of how far behind schedule the job is in terms of things that he can relate to. To say that a job is .22 behind schedule is just about meaningless. To say that the job is three days behind schedule or sixteen hours behind schedule makes much more sense.

The second advantage in using operation schedule dates instead of a ratio is that working on the jobs in the right relative priorities is not enough to meet the assembly schedule. A work center can be working on the jobs in the correct sequence (the most urgent job first, the next most urgent job after that, etc.), but that does not mean that the assembly schedule will be met. One work center could be two weeks behind schedule and still be working on the jobs in the right sequence. If the work center is two weeks behind schedule, the parts will be two weeks late. So, in addition to working on jobs in the right sequence, the shop must also work to meet the due dates; the dates the parts are needed. The shop people should accept and be held accountable for meeting the due dates of the orders. Think of someone running to catch a plane. The fact that he is hurrying, and that he is doing things in the right sequence (getting into the car, driving to the airport, parking the car, etc.) doesn't count for much if he gets there an hour late.

STATUS REPORT

An order status report should be a part of the shop scheduling and dispatching system. This status report is a listing of all the open manufacturing scheduled receipts. The report should show the summary information for each order as well as the details of each operation. The summary information would be things such as:

1. Item number.

2. Order quantity.

3. Due date.

4. Order number.

The detailed information for each operation should include:

1. Operation number.

2. Operation description.

3. Setup and run hours.

4. Operation start date.

5. Operation due date.

6. Operation status (not available, available, working, etc.).

This report is used by the planners and shop people to evaluate shop orders. In some cases they will be trying to determine whether an order can be rescheduled to an earlier date. In other cases they will be trying to find a way to complete an order that is behind schedule by the due date of the order. Typically, this report is sequenced by item number.

Chapter 18

Vendor Scheduling and Related Purchasing Activities

A well-managed MRP II system allows a dramatic improvement in the productivity of purchasing people. In the past, most of the purchasing people's time was spent ordering parts in less than quoted lead times, expediting overdue items, rescheduling items to earlier dates, etc. With an effective MRP II system, that time can be spent more productively because:

1. Expediting is reduced from the routine to the exception. This makes more time available for purchasing people to do effective purchasing.

2. Valid schedules exist for purchased items and raw material. This allows improved delivery performance since both the customer and the vendor know what the schedules are well enough in advance to meet the due dates.

3. Accurate projections of future purchases can be displayed for the buyer to use in effective negotiation, value analysis, and cost reduction.

VENDOR SCHEDULING TRANSACTIONS

Vendor scheduling is similar to shop scheduling: both are part of the execution systems for MRP II. The shop schedule or dispatch list is part of the shop floor control system and communicates the schedule dates on manufacturing orders to the shop. The vendor schedule is part of the purchasing system and communicates the due dates for purchased items to the vendors.

A sample vendor scheduling report is shown in Figure 23. This vendor scheduling report shows the scheduled receipts that have been authorized for the vendor, and it looks ahead, beyond the vendor's quoted lead time, to display any planned purchase orders in the future. This forward visibility provides a way for a vendor to see the customer's real needs far in advance. By showing a vendor the schedule in the future, it is possible for him to do a better job of planning and of hitting the dates for which he is responsible.

Regardless of whether vendor scheduling is done, a vendor has to do some type of planning beyond the backlog of customer orders. Without vendor scheduling, this planning out beyond the backlog of customer orders would have to be based

Figure 23
Vendor Schedule

VENDOR: 1540 ACME AND CO.
VENDOR SCHEDULER: A. GRAY
BUYER: A. FARRAGHER

SCHEDULING HORIZON INFORMATION:
FIRM ZONE — FIRST 4 WEEKS
MATERIAL COMMITMENT ZONE - NEXT 6 WEEKS

Item#/ Description	Order Detail	Past Due 1/16/88	Week of 1/23/88	Week of 1/30/88	Week of 2/06/88	Week of 2/13/88	Week of 2/20/88	Month of 2/27/88	Month of 3/26/88	Qtr of 4/23/88
F11249	Quantity: Order#:		100 Q1178				100	100	300	200
H87877	Quantity: Order#:	20 P1178	20 P1178	20 P1435	20 P1510	20	20	80	80	80
M42215	Quantity: Order#:		300 P1435		500 P1510			1100		3500
R97232	Quantity: Order#:			40 P1619			200			

on forecasts of requirements that may or may not be close to the real purchasing schedules. With vendor scheduling it is possible to show the vendor planned purchase orders before they would normally be placed. This allows the vendor to plan both material and capacity out beyond the backlog of customer orders, which in turn makes the vendor more effective in executing the schedule once an order is finally authorized.

There could be as many as three time zones in the vendor schedule, and the degree of commitment to the vendor may vary depending upon which zone a particular order is in:

1. Close to the current date, the commitment is like an authorized purchase order.

2. Out near the end of the planning horizon, planned orders in the vendor schedule are for the vendor's planning information only. The customer makes no commitment to these planned orders.

3. Between the two there may be a zone of semicommitment. The commitment is typically for the material only, not for the labor needed to produce the items. When these planned orders are authorized or come into the current zone, then the commitment is for both the material and labor. This middle zone may not exist, although some companies find it helpful.

The timing of where these time zones start and end may vary from company to company, from vendor to vendor, and from item to item. These are decisions each company must make when setting up its vendor scheduling function.

Without a vendor schedule and a working relationship based on it, a company may have problems when lead times change. For example, if the lead time on an item changes from ten weeks to fifteen weeks, five weeks of orders are now overdue to be placed. Consequently, the vendor may not be able to deliver these orders on time. On the other hand, if the vendor and customer are working using the vendor schedule, the vendor already knows about the five weeks of orders and has the responsibility to respond to the customer if these orders cannot be met.

For certain products that are ordered from several different vendors, a company may want to show that no one vendor will get all the business. This can be done in several ways. One approach would be to use a percentage to split each of the planned orders among several vendors. Another approach would be to show every other or every third planned order to a vendor. A third approach would be to show each vendor the total quantity the customer will be buying from all suppliers and also show each vendor the percentage that that vendor will supply. Companies who take this approach generally feel that showing the total quantity is good incentive for the vendor to improve service, price, or quality to get a bigger percentage.

The vendor scheduling report can be mailed to each vendor periodically or communicated electronically from computer to computer. This is a desirable method that reduces paperwork and, consequently, reduces cost.

One of the responsibilities in working with vendors is to properly follow-up with the vendor to assure on-time delivery. Depending on the relationship with the vendor, how well the vendor works with the vendor schedule, etc., this responsibility may require extensive follow-up or no follow-up at all. If follow-up is needed, it would be done using a follow-up date in the purchasing system. This date is typically stored for each line item on a purchase order. When the date is due, a message appears to remind the buyer or vendor scheduler that follow-up is required. The buyer or vendor scheduler can then reset the follow-up date if another follow-up is required, or leave the date blank if no other follow-up is needed. The follow-up date would typically appear on the vendor schedule, although it could also appear on a separate listing or exception report.

In some cases, it can also be helpful to do some capacity planning for vendors. Such capacity planning can be done in units, hours, molds, etc. This would be especially helpful in the case of a vendor who is not operating an MRP II system. However, there could be some limitations in this approach. For example, if some customers (but not all customers) provide capacity planning information, it may be hard for the vendor to make effective use of the information.

NEGOTIATION

One of the areas of greatest productivity improvement in purchasing is in negotiation, value analysis, and cost reduction. The problem in companies without MRP II is that the right information on what will be purchased and when is not easily available, and cannot be updated easily. In MRP II, such information is available and current. Planned purchases are in the system because they are the planned orders. In addition, these planned orders are updated each time MRP is run. This information can be extracted from the system and displayed for negotiation, value analysis, etc. Normally, this display would take the form of a vendor negotiation report showing the planned purchases over the next quarter, next six months, next year, and so forth. A buyer can use this report to concentrate on the big dollar purchases, on large variance items, etc.

Figure 24 is an example of a vendor negotiation report. In this report, the planned purchase orders due for release in the next quarter are listed. In addition, in the sample report, planned purchases are sorted by greatest dollar amount per year. Items listed in the sample report are:

1. Item number.

2. Planned order quantity.

3. Yearly planned order total.

4. Planned order release date (the date the negotiations must be completed and the order placed).

5. Cost.

6. Variance.

7. Projected yearly purchase dollars (based on the cost and the planned order total for the year).

8. Projected yearly variance (based on the variance and the planned order total).

PURCHASE ORDER CONTROLS

The delivery date on a purchase order and the date items are due to arrive in the stockroom may be two different dates, and the system should recognize this. The time required to receive and inspect a purchase order accounts for any difference in the two dates. Generally, vendors work in terms of the delivery date for an order, and MRP is concerned with the date the items will be available in the stockroom.

The way to recognize these two dates is to provide two dates for each purchase order line item: a purchase order delivery date and a date the items are expected to be available in the stockroom. The purchase order delivery date is the date that

Figure 24
Vendor Negotiation Report—Purchase Orders Due for Release in the Next 12 Weeks

4/2/88
NEGOTIATOR LANE

Part Number	Planned Order Quantity	Yearly Planned Order Total	Planned Order Release Date	Cost/100	Variance	Projected Yearly Purchases	Projected Yearly Variance
G391	3,000	30,000	4/29/88	$60.00	$9.00	$1,800,000	$270,000
K392	1,500	12,000	5/3/88	70.00	3.00	840,000	36,000
L138	10,000	100,000	4/7/88	8.00	.50	800,000	50,000

is used in all dealings with the vendor (delivery date, all rescheduling, etc.). The stockroom date is the date that is used in the MRP netting and exception logic.

A receiving/inspection lead time is the difference between the two dates. A buyer or vendor scheduler can specify both dates (the delivery date and the stockroom date) for each order (based on the normal receiving/inspection time), or the buyer or vendor scheduler can specify one of the dates and have the system calculate the other date using the receiving/inspection lead time. Either method is workable.

It is essential to provide a type of dispatch list for those items in the inspection area. Inspection needs to be able to determine what is needed and when just like any production area. A dispatch list can be provided by sorting and listing the items in the inspection area by stockroom date. Another approach would be to allow a routing on purchased items, and then use the shop floor control system to provide a dispatch list for items in inspection. This second approach would make sense where there are several inspection steps on a purchased item or raw material. An example of an inspection dispatch list is shown in Figure 25.

Many times manufacturing orders are routed to vendors for some type of outside processing. For example, an item may be routed through the machine shop, outside for plating, and then back to the machine shop for additional machining. In this situation, the shop floor control system includes a shop order and routing that covers all the inside and outside operations. The purchasing system should provide a way to store and maintain an additional purchase order to record the purchase of the outside operation.

The purchase orders that cover outside operations must be handled somewhat differently from normal purchase orders. This is because a scheduled receipt already exists in MRP for these items. The scheduled receipt is the manufacturing order showing all the different operations, some done in the inside shop and some done at an outside shop. Therefore, purchase orders for outside operations should

Figure 25
Inspection Dispatch List

WORK CENTER: 9890 INCOMING INSPECTION
TODAY'S DATE: 1/16/88
PRIORITY: OPERATION DUE DATE

Item #	Order #	Operation #	Operation Description	Operation Dates Start	Due	Order Due Date	Hours Set Up	Run	Qty. REM	Prev Op #	W/C	Next Op #	W/C
JOBS AT THIS WORK CENTER													
Q20591	15408	10	Inspect	1/15/88	1/16/88	1/16/88		4.0	1000	—	—		Stock
E00011	15408	10	Inspect	1/18/88	1/19/88	1/20/88		8.0	2000	—	—		Whse
M42215	17101	10	Inspect	1/17/88	1/20/88	1/23/88		17.0	5000	—	—		Whse
JOBS COMING TO THIS WORK CENTER IN THE NEXT 3 DAYS													
R97232	17101	10	Inspect	1/17/88	1/20/88	1/20/88		17.0	5000	—	—		Stock
H87877	19652	10	Inspect	1/18/88	1/23/88	1/23/88		18.0	6000	—	—		Stock

not appear in MRP. They have to exist in the purchase order files for vendor scheduling, accounting, and receiving purposes. However, if these purchase orders are included in MRP, the same scheduled receipt will be shown twice: once on the manufacturing order and once on the purchase order for the outside operation.

Consequently, the normal way to handle purchase orders for outside operations is to ignore them in the netting and exception logic of MRP. However, in most other respects these purchase orders would be treated normally in the system. They would be treated as scheduled receipts for vendor scheduling purposes, as purchase commitments for accounting and financial planning, etc.

One difference between these purchase orders and normal purchase orders is that purchase orders for outside operations are tied directly to manufacturing orders in the shop floor control system. As a manufacturing order is rescheduled, the operation due dates are recalculated for all operations, including outside vendor operations. These operation schedule dates are compared to the due dates of the corresponding purchase orders for outside operations and exception messages generated for any where the dates are different.

The transaction to receive material against a purchase order for an outside operation is also somewhat different from the normal receipt transaction. The receipt against a purchase order for an outside operation normally works more like the operation complete transaction in shop scheduling and dispatching than like a receipt into stock. The receipt against an outside processing purchase order marks the operation complete but does not update the on-hand balance. Material will be moved to the next operation on the routing and may not go back to stock immediately.

PART VI

Capacity Planning and Control

Chapter 19

Capacity Requirements Planning

Capacity Requirements Planning is a tool to show the capacity picture for a work center in the same way that the material requirements planning reports show the picture for material. This type of planning is needed if shop schedules are to be met. Shop floor control is a way to develop shop schedules that people will be accountable for meeting. Yet it is a lot to ask of someone to have them agree to meet a due date and not provide them with a picture of the total capacity requirements in the future. By producing a capacity picture, one section of the planning loop is closed. Instead of reacting to capacity problems, people are able to anticipate these problems and solve them while there is still time.

Capacity Requirements Planning is a tool that shows the capacity requirements and does not attempt to solve the capacity problems. That is a job for people, typically the capacity planner working with people in the factory. These people are provided with information showing any capacity problems, however, the computer does not automatically attempt to solve these problems.

An example of a system that attempts to solve capacity problems is a finite loading system. The term "finite loading" means that the work centers are loaded to their stated capacities, at which point the computer begins to take action to solve projected overload conditions. The Standard System does not include an explanation of these types of systems because they have not been demonstrated to work.

Do finite scheduling systems produce results? Yes and no. Yes, in that there are companies where things are better after the implementation of a finite scheduling system, and no, in that the finite scheduling logic did not cause the improvements. Years ago, Oliver Wight articulated the thought that when a company changes five things at once and things get better the tendency is to attribute the improvement to the most complex thing that was changed. In fact, the results are typically due to the simplest thing that was changed. The improvements in companies with finite scheduling systems come from better material planning and capacity planning rather than finite loading.

The primary problem with finite loading seems to be the lack of accountability in such a system. A planner or shop foreman looking at a schedule developed in a finite loading calculation is unable to verify that the plan makes sense. Because of the volume of calculations and the different interacting options that are taken in the computer program, the people using the system are unable to duplicate the calculation and verify that it is correct. If they are going to use the system, it will have to be on faith: faith that the computer used the right numbers, and faith that the computer took the right options to develop the schedule. Few people are willing to be held accountable under these circumstances, and those who are willing are just buying time until something goes wrong. Since the calculations cannot be duplicated by the planners using the system, quite a few things could go wrong without becoming obvious. Yet, when the results of such an error manifest themselves in missed shipping schedules or out of control inventories, people are still going to be held accountable for the results.

These accountability problems are the same as those that would exist if the automatic pilots on an airliner required that all other instruments be turned off. If this type of autopilot actually existed, the pilots would be unable to see the altitude, speed, on or off course indications from the navigation system, or any of the engine instruments. While someone could argue that the pilots who refused to use this autopilot lacked faith and confidence in the system, few people are likely to be persuaded. When an autopilot is used, the instruments are still on. This is for a very simple reason: regardless of whether the autopilot is on or off, the pilot is still responsible for flying the airplane, and he will be accountable if something goes wrong.

Another problem with the type of capacity planning systems that attempt to solve capacity problems is that the solutions to these types of problems do not lend themselves well to the computer. The solutions are basically human, and the judgment and evaluation of a planner or shop person is the best way to handle them. In fact, many of the ways to solve capacity problems will probably never be programmed into a computer. Subcontracting, running a job on a different piece of equipment, changing order quantities, overtime, extra shifts, reducing the lead time for the parent item, running jobs early, and many others are common ways to solve capacity problems. For the most part, these are human decisions.

However, there may be a potential use for finite loading logic as a simulator. In this manner, the finite loader could help determine the master production schedule or the sequence of orders through a key work center. Then a person could evaluate the output and, if appropriate, enter it into the normal MRP logic where there is transparency and clearly defined accountabilities.

Capacity problems all have one thing in common: someone needs to know about the problem before it appears on the shop floor. The function of the Capacity Requirements Planning system is to identify these problems and present them to the planner. The responsibility of the planner is to find solutions to these problems.

CAPACITY PLANNING TRANSACTIONS

Capacity requirements are calculated using both the planned and released orders. The capacity requirements for released orders are extracted from the shop scheduling and dispatching system. The open shop order file contains all the manufacturing operations by date. The operations that are not complete are the capacity requirements for scheduled receipts.

The planned and firm planned orders are back scheduled through the routing to give the capacity requirements for these orders. This back scheduling calculation takes into account the order quantity, run time, setup time, tear down time, etc. to compute the capacity requirements.

The back scheduling calculations for planned and firm planned orders must be the same as that used when a scheduled receipt is created in the shop scheduling system. The system must do the same calculations consistently, regardless of whether the order is planned or released, otherwise there may be transparency or accountability problems in using the system—such as, why did the system generate these numbers this time and not the last?

The routing is used to create operation records for each planned and firm planned order. These operation records are written to a capacity requirements work file. Then the capacity requirements from the shop scheduling and dispatching system are combined with the capacity requirements from the planned and firm planned orders to give the total capacity requirements.

In some systems, capacity requirements for firm planned orders can be extracted from the shop scheduling system. If the routing is attached to a firm planned order when it is created, then the open order detail file contains the operations which should be used for capacity requirements generation.

Capacity requirements are normally calculated in standard hours. The order quantity multiplied by the standard hours required for the operation gives the standard hours. No efficiency calculation or percentage is typically used. The reason for this is that the output of the work center will be stated in standard hours of output. These hours of output are the number of standard hours that a work center is producing, which can differ significantly from the number of hours the work center is manned.

The advantage in working with standard hours of output and not using efficiency calculations is that standard hours gives the simplest and most fundamental measurement of capacity. Most companies use demonstrated capacity as the measure of output. Demonstrated capacity is the actual standard hours of output produced, regardless of the actual clock time required to do the work. For example, if a work center is operating for thirty hours, producing twenty parts with a value of one standard hour per part, the demonstrated capacity is twenty standard hours.

Using the actual standard hours of output for a work center takes into account all the factors that can affect the output of a work center. It includes time the machine is down for repairs, lost production due to a broken tool, bad standards, time that the machine is available and an operator is not, etc.

The capacity planning calculations need to handle the situation where several men (a crew) or machines are being used in an operation. In this situation, the capacity requirement should be increased by the number of men in the crew or the number of machines being used.

Sometimes it is necessary to calculate capacity requirements for more than one resource needed in an operation. For example, in some companies, a single operator may run several different NC machines simultaneously. In this situation, it's essential to be able to see both the capacity requirements for labor (Do we have enough operators?) and the capacity requirements for NC machines (Do we have enough equipment?). Another example of this problem is in a pharmaceutical company with high-volume packaging lines. These lines, which may consist of a filler, capper, labeler, and boxer are assembled from four distinct work centers or resources. These same work centers can be moved into a different configuration with other equipment to form new types of packaging lines. For scheduling purposes, there is a single operation: packaging. For capacity planning purposes, however, it is necessary to know the capacity requirements for fillers, cappers, labelers, and boxers.

Many software packages are limited to planning one work center or resource per operation. For companies where there are only a few operations that affect more than one resource, this would probably not be a problem. These companies should be able to use the normal Capacity Requirements Planning system without modifying it. On the other hand, if a company has a significant number of operations that affect two or more resources, then this capability should be provided in the system. Otherwise, the capacity planners will not have all the tools needed to plan and get the required labor and equipment.

Some method must be provided for slotting the capacity requirements based on the operation schedule dates. In some systems, capacity requirements are shown spread over the entire run time of the operation. In other words, the capacity requirement is prorated over the number of days between the operation start and operation due dates. In other systems, a single capacity requirement is shown at the start date of the operation. In still other systems, the capacity requirement is shown at the due date of the operation.

REPORTS

Three reports display the capacity planning information. The capacity requirements should be totalled and displayed for each work center, and also listed individually to back up the totals. For grouping orders with common set-ups, a third report should display all the orders in a manufacturing family.

A capacity planning summary report displays the totals of the capacity requirements by work center and time period. The totals are calculated by sorting and summarizing the detailed capacity requirements by work center and date. Figure 10 is an example of a capacity planning summary report. The planner can find capacity problems using this report by comparing the normal capacity in standard hours to the capacity requirements.

Some companies can argue that displaying capacity requirements in weekly time buckets is an illusion of accuracy that doesn't exist. For example, in a machine shop where an order goes through cut off, milling, drilling, and grinding operations, the order may sit in a queue in front of each machine before being processed. In this case, capacity requirements are calculated by estimating the date that an order will arrive at a work center. Normal scheduling rules are used to develop these dates, and deviations from the dates will occur causing some of the jobs to arrive sooner than anticipated and others later than expected. For this reason, the planner is generally not expected to react to spikes in the capacity

Figure 26
Capacity Requirements Plan

WORK CENTER: 3001 PUNCH PRESS
NORMAL CAPACITY: 37 STANDARD HOURS/WEEK

Week	Past Due	1/16/88	1/23/88	1/30/88	2/06/88
Capacity Requirements	12	32	26	30	16
Four Week Average		29			

Week	2/13/88	2/20/88	2/27/88	3/05/88	3/12/88
Capacity Requirements	9	50	25	16	60
Four Week Average	25				43

Week	3/19/88	3/26/88	4/02/88	4/09/88	4/16/88
Capacity Requirements	52	45	15	37	32
Four Week Average				32	

Week	4/23/88	4/30/88	5/7/88	5/14/88	5/21/88
Capacity Requirements	28	31	20	36	30
Four Week Average			29		

Week	5/28/88
Capacity Requirements	20
Four Week Average	

picture, such as the one shown in Figure 26 on 2/20/88. Chances are quite good that this work will arrive over more than one week and not present a problem.

The exception to this would be in the case of a gateway work center which is the starting work center for many of the items that cross it. In this case, the planner is fairly certain of the flow of work to the center and may want to smooth the load. The capacity planner should be looking more for problem situations over an extended period of time such as the one pictured in Figure 26 between 3/12/88 and 3/26/88.

In other companies, however, the capacity picture is very accurate. For example, in a company making a highly repetitive product in high volumes, the capacity picture is quite reliable. Since there are no queues between work centers, the material flows from operation to operation to operation. In this case, the scheduling rules can predict accurately when the order will reach each work center. In these companies, the capacity planners would be expected to react to spikes in the capacity requirements, and would have to smooth the work load.

Consequently, it is helpful to be able to vary the time periods used for capacity planning. Some companies may choose to show daily or weekly time periods; other companies may elect to use two week or larger periods. In addition, a display of the average capacity requirement over some number of periods is a useful tool to help identify real problem situations (a trend or a long-term overload for example) rather than a spike that a capacity planner will not react to. Generally, the average capacity requirement is computed using a rule similar to that in a moving four-period average calculation.

Another helpful tool in the summary capacity planning report is the ability to vary capacity in the future. If a plan exists to add another shift or purchase additional equipment or hire additional people, then it is helpful in capacity planning to show such information.

For a planner to be able to solve capacity problems, a list of the detailed capacity requirements that make up each weekly total is required. For example, a planner working to reduce an overload on a work center needs a list of the items causing the capacity requirements for that work center in the weeks that are overloaded. Once he knows which orders are causing the capacity requirements, he can begin to solve the problem. The detailed listing of the capacity requirements is much like pegging. The detailed listing shows where the capacity requirements are coming from. This display of detailed capacity requirements (Figure 27) should include:

1. Work center.

2. Date.

3. Item number causing the capacity requirements.

4. Hours.

The hours are needed to allow the planner to work efficiently with the report. By listing the hours, the planner can concentrate on those few orders causing most of the load. Some systems also distinguish the different types of orders causing the requirements (scheduled receipt, planned order, etc.) or list the operation number and operation description. These are helpful features, but are not necessary to be able to use the system.

The volume of detail capacity requirements, such as the volume of pegging in MRP, can be overwhelming in some cases. If the number of detail capacity requirements is too large to print, the simplest solution would be to make them available as a CRT inquiry. Another solution would be to print the detailed capacity requirements for the time periods that exceed the normal work center capacity, and to make the other detail requirements available on a type of inquiry.

Figure 27
Capacity Requirements Planning Details

WORK CENTER: 3001 PUNCH PRESS
DEPARTMENT: 633

Week	Hours	Operation	Quantity	Item #
1/09/88	4	10	200	L930
1/09/88	8	10	400	K421
	12			
1/16/88	2	10	190	D43ſ
1/16/88	4	20	300	N862
1/16/88	4	15	250	K319
1/16/88	22	20	1800	B412
	32			
1/23/88	14	10	900	C692
1/23/88	2	10	400	K361
1/23/88	4	10	500	G315
1/23/88	6	20	630	F410
	26			

A third solution would be to list the details of the capacity requirements to microfiche.

In some companies, a significant portion of the capacity requirements in a work center may come from setup time. When many of the items crossing a work center have common or similar setups, it is possible to eliminate some of the setup time by scheduling similar items together. In this situation, a listing of the items with common setups, and which have planned orders during the next few months, can be helpful for a capacity planner. Once a planner knows which orders have similar setups, he can adjust the schedule, and run items in a manufacturing family one after another. This way, the capacity planner can avoid some setups that would have been required otherwise.

A display of orders by manufacturing family like the one shown in Figure 28 is a way to solve the problem of identifying the planned orders that can be run together. The listing of the planned orders and scheduled receipts by manufacturing family shows each item in the family, and the quantity scheduled for each time period. This report is typically a grid showing item numbers vertically, and time periods horizontally.

It is possible to develop the groups or families of items with common or similar setups in a number of ways. One simple way would be to have the capacity planners assign a family code for any items that are candidates for grouping. Group technology is a system designed to categorize, classify, and code items by manufacturing characteristics. These codes can be used to sort the items together in MRP II reports so that they can be run together. By interfacing MRP II and group technology in this way, it would be possible to identify the items that are really needed (MRP II), see which ones could be grouped for efficient processing

Figure 28
Orders by Manufacturing Family

FAMILY: 015 LEG & POSTS—EARLY FRANCIS

		Weeks								
Item Number		1/16	1/23	1/30	2/06	2/13	2/20	2/27	3/05	3/12
2416	Cherry post		1000							
5639	Walnut post								1200	
3931	Pine post					2100				
8420	Oak post									
6420	Cherry leg								900	
2175	Walnut leg		1600							
9806	Pine leg		800							
1248	Oak leg								1000	

(group technology and the orders by manufacturing family), and make sure the material and capacity are available to run them when planned (MRP II).

ROUTING FLEXIBILITY

The Capacity Requirements Planning system should allow deviations from the normal routing for an order in the same way the bill of material system allows deviations from the normal bills of material. Deviations from the normal routing are situations where an operation is added, deleted, or changed for an order. The order could be a scheduled receipt, firm planned order or planned order. (Allowing deviations to be attached to a planned order only makes sense in a net change system, in a regenerative system all planned orders and gross requirements are destroyed at the beginning of the planning run.) The deviations from the normal routing are attached to the order. If the order is rescheduled, the changed operations move with the order. An operation might be added to an orders as a way to include some rework operations on several orders. This might be because of a problem with the raw material, and a number of orders may require rework to correct the problem.

An operation might be changed as a way to change the work center for an operation as a way to offload work from one work center to another. An example of deleting an operation would be where an engineering change will remove an operation from the routing.

Deviations to the normal routing are normally provided by allowing the routing to be copied for firm planned orders (and sometimes planned orders) and added to the open shop order file. The routing for these orders does not have to be stored in the open shop order file. It is also possible to have a separate file to store the operations for these firm planned orders or planned orders. The capacity planners can maintain these operations by adding, deleting, or changing operations. The operations are then used in Capacity Requirements Planning. The capacity requirements for firm planned (or planned) orders with these deviations from the normal routing are taken from the file of operations. The orders are not extended by the routing to generate capacity requirements.

Another method is to provide a type of serial number or lot number effectivity logic for routings. Each operation record can store a serial number or lot number effectivity range and each firm planned order can store a serial number or lot number. The back scheduling logic can select the proper routing based on these serial numbers or lot numbers and the capacity requirements can be generated in the normal way. By defining the alternate routing using serial or lot numbers, a planner can provide for a routing deviation for a specific order without affecting the other orders for the item.

Chapter 20

Input/Output Control

Input/output control is the way to control the execution of the capacity plan. Capacity requirements planning plans capacities. Input/ output control controls capacity. The relationship is similar to MRP and shop scheduling and dispatching. MRP plans priorities, and shop scheduling and dispatching helps to control the execution of those priorities.

Controlling capacity requires that someone be responsible for executing the capacity plan. It also requires that there be a way to measure whether or not the capacity plan is actually happening. Input/output control does this. A plan is established for the input to a work center, and the output from a work center. This plan is then used to measure what actually happens.

The advantage in input/output control is that the capacity plan can be measured so potential problems can be highlighted before they become crises. By measuring the capacity plan, it is possible to determine where the plan is not being met and why. Using input/output control to show a problem at a work center before it would be obvious otherwise makes it possible to identify and solve a problem before it becomes a crisis that seriously affects schedules.

COMPARING PLAN TO ACTUAL

Input/output control requires several basic categories of historical and future information. These are:

1. Planned input.

2. Actual input.

3. Planned output.

4. Actual output.

5. Planned queue.

6. Actual queue.

7. Tolerances for input, output, and queue comparisons.

Planned input is the average of the capacity requirements over several weeks. This is the work that is projected to come into the work center. The planned input is averaged to remove the peaks and valleys, since the average is easier to work with and makes more sense as a rate of work coming to the work center.

Planned input is generally maintained using transactions. A planner reviews the capacity requirements plan, calculates the average capacity requirement and inputs this for the future periods. However, it is possible to compute the average capacity requirement for future periods (for example, a four week moving average) and automatically update the current and future planned input buckets used for input/output control.

The actual input is the work that is actually moved into the work center during the week. This information is extracted from the shop scheduling and dispatching system. When a job is moved to a work center, the move transaction adds the standard hours for the job to the actual input for that week.

The planned output is the agreed upon rate of output for the work center. This is in standard hours of output as opposed to the number of hours that the work center is manned. This is the number that the shop people agree to produce from the work center. They will be held accountable for meeting this rate of output. Planned output is maintained using transactions.

The actual output is the work that is actually completed at the work center during that week. This information is extracted from the shop scheduling and dispatching system. As jobs are completed at a work center, the operation complete transaction adds the standard hours for the job to the actual output for that week. If labor reporting transactions are used to show the partial completion of an operation in the shop scheduling and dispatching system, these can be used to accumulate the actual output for a work center. In such a system, the number of pieces reported at the work center are multiplied by the standard to give the standard hours of actual output. These hours are added to the actual output for that week.

The planned queue in future periods can be computed from the current queue and the planned input and output. Planned queue in prior periods can be maintained using transactions.

The actual queue for prior periods can be maintained using transactions, or recomputed each time the input/output control system is run. The actual queues can be computed starting from the current queue and the actual input and actual output, working backward from the current date.

Most companies find it most effective to display at least eight periods of input/output control information. These eight periods are usually broken into four past periods for historical comparisons, one current period, and three future periods. Some companies prefer to store and display more history and more future periods, but eight periods seems to be the minimum necessary for effective input/output control.

The work center performance can be evaluated by comparing the planned input to the actual input, comparing the planned output to the actual output, and comparing planned queue to actual queue. Figure 29 is an example of an input/output control report that makes this kind of comparison. The report displays:

INPUT

1. Planned input.

2. Actual input.

3. Cumulative deviation.

OUTPUT

1. Planned output.

2. Actual output.

3. Cumulative deviation.

QUEUE

1. Planned queue.

2. Actual queue.

3. Cumulative deviation.

Figure 29
Input/Output Control Report

WORK CENTER   3001 PUNCH PRESS   PLANNED QUEUE 8 HOURS
TOLERANCE   10 HOURS   ACTUAL QUEUE   8 HOURS

			Past	Current Week	Future	
Week	12/20/87	12/27/87	1/02/88	1/09/88	1/16/88	1/23/88
Planned Input	39	20	16	32	26	30
Actual Input	32	29	14			
Cumulative Deviation	−7	+2	0			

Planned Input	37	37	37	37	37	37
Actual Input	35	40	32			
Cumulative Deviation	−2	+1	−4			

The measure of a problem in input or output is the cumulative deviation. A cumulative deviation is used instead of a simple week by week comparison because of the peaks and variations in input and output from week to week. A cumulative deviation shows whether a work center is running consistently ahead or behind the plan. A planner using input/output control generally looks first at the output. By comparing the planned output with the actual output, the capacity planner is checking to see that the work center is executing the capacity plan. If the actual output is less than what was planned, the planner looks at the input. If the actual input has been coming to the work center as planned, then this work center is the problem. Work has been arriving, but the work center has not been able to meet the capacity plan. In the other situation, if the actual input is less than what was planned, then the problem is at one of the feeding work centers. Some other work center is not meeting the output plan and the work is not being made available to this work center.

It is important to establish some tolerances when using input/output control. These tolerances are cumulative deviations by work center that trigger some type of corrective action. For example, the output tolerance on the horizontal boring mills may be 100 hours. If the actual output is less than the planned output by more than than 100 hours, overtime and extra shifts are immediately authorized. Similar tolerances can also be set up for input and queue. The advantage in establishing these types of tolerances is that it allows problems to be caught early, and allows solutions to be started right away. If tolerances are not established, it generally takes some late orders and missed schedules to identify a problem and begin working to solve it. Some more time is then spent calling a meeting and determining what to do. At this stage the problem is larger than it would be if some corrective action had been taken sooner, and valuable time that could have been spent solving the problem has been wasted.

An input/output control system must also provide some mechanism for shifting the input/output control information to different buckets as time passes. At the end of each week the system should drop the earliest past period of planned and actual input, output, and queue. Then the information in the next period should be moved to the earlier bucket. The current period information is shifted to the past. The first future period is shifted to the current bucket, etc.

PART VII

Distribution and Multiplant Planning

Chapter 21

Distribution Resource Planning

Distribution Resource Planning is MRP II in a distribution environment. A distribution network needs the same kinds of scheduling information that is needed in scheduling a factory. Knowing what is needed and when is just as important in a distribution network as it is in a factory. This same kind of information is also needed for a multiplant operation; each of the plants need to know what is needed and when. Consequently, this explanation of Distribution Resource Planning covers both MRP II in a distribution environment and MRP II in a multiplant operation.

Distribution Resource Planning allows visibility into the entire distribution network. It allows the central facility to see the actual demands for products that will be needed at the distribution centers. The picture of demand at the central facility is like that of any other dependent demand item. The demand is lumpy. In some weeks the requirements far exceed the average, and in others there are few or even no requirements at all. The demands from the distribution centers on the central facility are visible as far into the future as the planning horizon extends.

Distribution Resource Planning also provides an accurate picture of the transportation loading and scheduling needed to support the distribution schedule. Using the projection of transportation requirements by volume, weight, and number of pallets, and the tools of MRP, a transportation planner can do a more effective job of truck and freight car loading.

The same type of advantages exist in a multiplant operation. The supplying plants are able to truly see into the receiving plants. The requirements for material and transportation are clear, and the interplant communication allows planners and master scheduler at the supplying plant to see the requirements as far into the future as the planning horizon extends.

DRP TRANSACTIONS

The basis for Distribution Resource Planning is a material requirements planning calculation done for each item at each distribution center or receiving plant. For each stock keeping unit (SKU) at a distribution center, MRP is run using the forecast and any customer orders that are promised for future delivery as gross requirements. For the receiving plants, the master production schedule would be the source of requirements for component items.

In any case, the normal MRP logic nets these requirements against the on-hand balance, safety stock, and any scheduled receipts (in-transit orders on the way to this branch warehouse or receiving plant) for the stock keeping unit. Planned orders are created to cover the remaining gross requirements using the lot sizing rule for the SKU. These planned orders will be supplied by the central facility, and so they are offset by the lead time for the SKU, exploded, and appear in the master schedule report for the central facility or supplying plant as a type of demand.

There are several different ways to translate the planned orders at the distribution centers and receiving plants into demands on the master production schedule for the supplying facility. They are:

1. Using a single data base and bills of material to represent the distribution network. Each stock keeping unit at each logication has a separate item number, typically the product item number and a location identifier.

2. Using a single data base and a source code on each item/location to identify the manufacturing source for that stock keeping unit. A computer program translates planned orders for one location into demands on the master schedule at the source location.

3. Using separate data bases and a computer program or programs to translate planned orders at the DCs to demand on the master production schedule.

The bill of material method requires that each stock keeping unit in each warehouse has a unique item number. This unique item number is typically the item number at the supplying facility plus the warehouse or receiving plant number. Then a bill of material is created showing the item number at the receiving location being made from the item number at the central supply location. By including a bill of material, the planned orders at the receiving locations will be exploded and gross requirements will be posted to the master schedule at the supply location.

The second method is similar. Each stock keeping unit has a unique item number, typically the item number from the supplying facility and a location identifier. In addition, a code is stored for each SKU to identify the source location. The MRP logic is run for each SKU at a location. Then each planned order is sent to the supplying location as gross requirements. When this method is used, additional explosion logic must be added to the system to properly handle the transfer of the gross requirements.

Another way to show the branch warehouse and multiplant demands is to have separate data bases for the different warehouses or receiving plants and the central supply facility. MRP is run for each of the warehouses or receiving plants. The planned orders are then sent as gross requirements from the branch warehouse or receiving plant MRP systems to the master production schedule at the supplying location. These gross requirements are treated as demands in the master scheduling system for the central facility. When this method is used, logic is included in the system to handle the transfer of the gross requirements.

IN-TRANSIT INFORMATION

In a distribution or multiplant environment it is also necessary to show the material that is in transit to the MRP system. This material is a scheduled receipt for the receiving location. The system that maintains these scheduled receipts functions like the system that maintains manufacturing scheduled receipts. When a movement is created to ship material from the central facility to a distribution center or receiving plant, the items in the central facility are allocated to the shipment and a scheduled receipt is created at the receiving location. When the items are shipped from the central facility, the on-hand balance and the allocation are reduced. When the items are received at the branch warehouse or receiving plant, the scheduled receipt is reduced and the on-hand balance is increased. This same process can also be used when items are shipped from one warehouse to another.

While the system for items that are in transit is similar to the manufacturing scheduled receipts system, there are also some differences. Items that are in transit require that shipment information be stored for the movement. In addition to the movement number, item number, quantity, and date, this information includes things like the shipper, means of shipment, freight cost, value of the shipment, insurance, and an indication of what is in transit and what has not been shipped. For this reason, many times a separate system is used to maintain the information on items that are in transit. Other times, the scheduled receipts system for manufacturing items is modified to allow this type of information to be stored.

TRANSPORTATION PLANNING

Transportation planning is an integral part of DRP. Accurate transportation scheduling and loading, such as accurate capacity requirements planning in a manufacturing environment, is a necessity if a distribution network is to be managed effectively.

Transportation planning is a way to plan the weight, volume, and number of pallets to be shipped based on the distribution resource plan. Transportation planning simulates these transportation requirements for the purpose of taking advantage of freight rates. By simulating the transportation requirements, a company can see which periods have less than full truckloads or railcars. By adjusting the shipping schedule to ship full truckloads or railcars, at the greatest possible weight, a transportation planner can take advantage of the best rates, and, as a result minimize freight costs. A real benefit is that the products that must be shipped early (in order to have full truckloads) can be determined well in advance, rather than left to chance or to what's available at the time the trucks are being loaded.

The logic of transportation planning is similar to that Capacity Requirements Planning. In Capacity Requirements Planning, the planned order quantities are extracted from MRP and extended by the standard hours for each operation in the routing. The capacity requirements are then summarized and displayed for each work center and time period.

In transportation planning, the unshipped distribution orders and firm planned and planned orders for the distribution centers or receiving plants are extracted from DRP and extended by the product weight (for example, pounds) and package volume (cubic feet), and divided by the quantity of the product that will fit on a pallet or container. These transportation requirements are scheduled for the start date of each planned order. After the transportation requirements have been generated, they are summarized and displayed by time period.

A transportation planning report displays the weight, volume, and number of pallets required to ship to each distribution center in each week. Using this report, a distribution planner can see into the DRP system, anticipate problems in freight car loading, and solve them while there is still time enough to ship the right products.

A transportation planning system must include a transportation planning summary report and a report showing the details of the transportation requirements. A transportation planning summary report or display shows the totals of the transportation requirements by destination and shipping method, including:

1. Destination and shipping method descriptive information.

2. Transportation planning periods (days, weeks, etc.).

3. Required weight, volume, and number of pallets.

4. Available transportation capacity in weight, volume, and number of pallets.

5. Amount over/under available capacity.

A display of the transportation requirements details is needed to solve transportation planning problems. This display shows the individual shipments that make up the total transportation requirements.

Many companies plan transportation requirements in weekly time periods, although in some cases it may be essential to plan daily transportation requirements. An example of needing to plan daily transportation requirements is a high volume manufacturer of cigarettes or soft drinks. No finished goods storage space exists, and product must be shipped daily or more frequently to the distribution sites. In this case, planning daily transportation requirements is essential.

One helpful feature in a transportation planning system is a way to vary the transportation capacity in each period. For example, in week twenty a company may be adding an additional truck to its company-owned fleet. In this situation, a transportation planner will want to increase the capacity available in week twenty and each subsequent period.

FIXED SHIPPING SCHEDULES

Many distribution companies work to fixed shipping schedules. A fixed shipping schedule establishes the specific days and weeks on which material is shipped to each distribution center. For example, one shipping schedule might be to ship to the Seattle distribution center every third Thursday, to the Boston distribution center every other Tuesday, and to the Houston distribution center every Wednesday.

Working to a fixed shipping schedule solves several problems in distribution. For example, a fixed shipping schedule is one way to handle limitations in shipping doors and docks and in manpower and equipment at either the sending or receiving facility. A fixed shipping schedule is a simple way of leveling transportation load.

In a company with a fixed shipping schedule, the Distribution Resource Planning system must include a way to define a fixed shipping schedule and logic to adjust the planned shipments to the distribution centers to agree with the fixed shipping schedule. DRP may plan an order to be shipped to the Seattle distribution center on Wednesday of week four. If the shipping schedule for Seattle is Thursday of weeks two, five, and eight, DRP will not be a true simulation of what will actually happen.

In this situation, the planned order should be adjusted to ship on Thursday of week two and an action message indicating that the order is scheduled for shipment earlier than needed should be produced for the planner. This way, DRP will be an accurate simulation for the resupply, and the master scheduler will be able to see that the material is really needed in week two. The action message provides a way for the planner to see into the system and to verify that what the system has done makes sense.

There are two methods for adjusting the planned order dates to the shipping schedule. One method is to calculate the planned orders based on the date the items are needed in the distribution centers. An additional calculation in the order planning logic would then adjust the dates to the shipping schedule. The planned orders would be moved to the next earlier shipping date.

The other method would be to use a separate program that adjusts the planned orders after DRP has created and stored them. This computer program would read the planned orders, adjust them to the next earlier shipping date, and, if necessary, update the distribution demands on the master production schedule. This method of having a separate program is often used when it is difficult, or impractical, to modify the logic of MRP in a software package.

PART VIII

Integration with Other Functions

Chapter 22

Tool Planning and Control

In many companies, scheduling the right tooling at the right time is as important as scheduling material and capacity to support the master production schedule. Having the proper tools, in good condition, when needed and for the number of hours required, is just as critical as material and capacity in meeting the master production schedule (and sometimes just as difficult).

The capabilities listed above are quite similar to MRP, Capacity Requirements Planning, and the related subsystems (inventory transactions, scheduled receipts, etc.). MRP develops a schedule for raw materials, components, and assemblies. Capacity Requirements Planning identifies the equipment needs by time period. The supporting subsystems like inventory transactions, scheduled receipts, etc. supply the supporting information to MRP, Capacity Requirements Planning, and the other systems.

The tooling subsystem does the same for tools. MRP for tooling provides a schedule for replacing, refurbishing, or resharpening tools based on the remaining life of the tools on hand and those on order. Capacity Requirements Planning for tooling shows the number of hours that a tool will be used by time period. This way the system can point out any schedule conflicts in the use of a tool. In order to develop these schedules and capacity plans, like the subsystems for MRP, the tooling subsystem must maintain the basic information on tooling including on-hand balance, scheduled receipts, tooling life, etc.

A tooling subsystem does not have to be a separate set of programs and files from those used for MRP, Capacity Requirements Planning, and the supporting subsystems. For example, it is possible to use the normal MRP and Capacity Requirements Planning systems to handle most of the planning and scheduling needs of tooling. Tooling information can be stored in the normal inventory, bill of material, and routing files. The inventory files store the descriptive information on a tool and the on-hand balance. This on-hand balance can be in terms of numbers of tools (thirty drills), it can be number of tools left where some of these have been partially consumed (two grinding wheels, one half gone, one new), or several tools where refurbishment is needed after some amount of use (one die that will require refurbishment after ten thousand strokes, and one die that has been recently refurbished for the final time and will require replacement after another twenty thousand strokes. So in some cases, the on-hand balance will be in terms of numbers of tools, and in others, in terms of numbers of tools and units of life remaining for each tool. The bill of material links the tool to each item using it, and the quantity per assembly represents the amount of tool life (say the number of drills, or number of strokes) used in producing the item. Similarly, the routing file links a tool to the operation and work center in which it's used for purposes of Capacity Requirements Planning. Normal Material Requirements Planning and Capacity Requirements Planning logic can be used to schedule tool replacement or refurbishment and tool priorities.

Another approach is to have a separate tooling subsystem that is tied to MRP. This subsystem consists of separate programs and files that would be similar to the programs and files used in MRP, Capacity Requirements Planning, and the related subsystems. In this approach, an interface passes the planned orders and scheduled receipts in MRP (by operation) to the tooling subsystem. The advantage in having a separate subsystem is that the programs and files for both MRP (including Capacity Requirements Planning and the supporting subsystems) and the tooling subsystem will be simpler than if all the logic were in one set of software. Sometimes, in designing computer programs to do all things for many different uses, the internal logic of the software becomes overly complex. For example, if the tooling information is stored in the item master file, fields have to be provided for tool life, on-hand balances in strokes, life-to-refurbishment, life-to-replacement, etc. In addition, the MRP logic must be modified to use these fields rather than the normal item information when a tool is being planned. In such situations, it is often better to use copies of the basic programs (MRP, Capacity Requirements Planning, etc.) and make minor adaptations for the different applications. In such a situation, the basic logic stays the same, but the data fields, files, etc. differ.

In this explanation of the tooling subsystem, tooling is handled in a separate system with separate files and separate programs. This is because there are enough minor differences between tooling and items like raw materials, assemblies, etc. to make the internal logic of the software overly complex if all logic were contained in one set of software.

This approach (a separate scheduling subsystem) can also handle other types of activities that need to be planned and scheduled. For example, it is possible to handle the scheduling of engineering design, drafting, software development, etc. using separate subsystems. These subsystems can be tied to MRP using an interface to pass planned orders, scheduled receipts, and descriptive information as needed.

TOOLING TRANSACTIONS

The tooling subsystem stores some descriptive information about each tool. This information normally includes the tool number, tool description, typical lifetime of a new tool (may be in some unit of measure, such as strokes), lead times for replacement or refurbishment of the tool, an indication of whether the tool is expendable or nonexpendable, and the number of hours the tool is available in a normal week. This is similar to the way item and work center information is maintained.

The tooling subsystem stores and maintains the tools required for each part number by operation number and the usage required per item. This usage may be one-tenth of a drill, or one stroke per item, or whatever other unit makes sense. This is similar to the way routings are maintained.

The tooling subsystem contains transactions to maintain the on-hand balance for each tool. This on-hand balance may be in terms of tools (thirty drills), or tools and life remaining (one die that is new and one die that will require refurbishment after ten thousand strokes). This is similar to the inventory transaction subsystem.

The tooling subsystem contains transactions to maintain the scheduled receipts for each tool. Typically, it is not necessary to store the scheduled receipts in terms of remaining life on the tool (as was the case in the inventory transaction subsystem) since the system stores the typical lifetime for a new tool. The logic for maintaining tooling scheduled receipts is similar to the scheduled receipts subsystem.

The shop paperwork for a shop order lists the tooling that needs to be issued by operation. This would be done by accessing the tooling file mentioned above. Listing the tooling as part of the shop paperwork gives the tool room a picking list for tooling, and gives the people on the shop floor a listing of what tools are required for each operation.

MRP FOR TOOLING

The MRP logic for scheduling tooling is the same as the MRP logic for any other item. The on-hand balance is netted against the gross requirements, scheduled receipts are included, planned orders are created if necessary, and exception messages are produced as required. These programs are nearly the same as the normal MRP programs. The difference is the fields and files used, and for some tools, the MRP calculations are done using usage instead of units. For example, the gross requirements, on-hand balance, and scheduled receipts are all stated in terms of strokes instead of numbers of tools. Consequently, the netting calculation, planned orders, and exception messages are also in terms of strokes rather than numbers of tools.

The interface to MRP for tooling is from the Capacity Requirements Planning system. This interface passes the item number, operation number, order quantity, operation schedule dates (start and due dates), and the number of setup and run hours for the operation. The item number and operation number are used to access the tool file. The order quantity is extended by the usage to generate the gross requirements. The operation schedule dates are used to put dates on these gross requirements.

CRP FOR TOOLING

The Capacity Requirements Planning logic for tooling is the same as the Capacity Requirements Planning logic for any work center. The capacity requirements for the tool are compared to the number of hours the tool is available in each time period.

The same interface is used for Capacity Requirements Planning for tooling as was used for MRP for tooling. In this case, the item number and operation number are used to access the tool file. The setup and run hours are used to generate the capacity requirements. The operation schedule dates are used to put dates on the capacity requirements.

In many situations, there are many more tools than work centers. In fact, some companies have more tools than they have item numbers. For this reason, a tooling subsystem will typically need some exception logic as part of the Capacity Requirements Planning for tooling. This logic identifies situations where the capacity requirements for a tool exceed the hours the tool will be available in that time period, and generates an exception message for the capacity planner to review.

Chapter 23

Financial Planning Interfaces

This explanation of the financial planning interface describes how MRP II can develop some of the information used in financial planning. The financial information from MRP II consists of projections of inventory levels, cash disbursements for labor and direct labor, cash receipts, etc. These projections can be combined with other financial information to develop a complete financial plan.

The type of information that MRP II provides is not financial planning, nor is it an attempt to develop profit and loss statements or balance sheets. Instead, the interface from MRP II provides a simple way to extract certain kinds of financial data, organize it, and present it to people who can use it in their financial planning. People develop financial plans, MRP II gives them the information to do it well. MRP II provides detailed and accurate financial information on:

1. Projected inventory value.

2. Cash disbursements for material, direct labor, and variable overhead.

3. Cash receipts.

4. Fixed overhead allocation.

In a company without MRP II, this kind of information is typically difficult to develop accurately or in a reasonable period of time. As a result, financial projections are often based on historical relationships and fudge factors (like "the cost of sales is 50% of sales dollars," or "about 65% of all the purchase orders due in the current week (including past dues) will actually be received this week.") Unfortunately, anyone who's introduced a new product, seen a shift in product mix, experienced the effects of a recession, etc., knows that historical factors aren't very effective methods in projecting future financial requirements. These factors seem to break down just at the time they are needed most—when the business is changing.

With MRP II, information for financial planning is calculated directly from the numbers in the operating system. The financial planning interface to MRP II takes the company game plan expressed in manufacturing terms like units, pounds, and hours, and converts it into dollars and other units meaningful to top management, financial people, and even non-manufacturing executives outside the company. In MRP II, the financial projections are developed by taking the details on each individual item, order, manufacturing event, etc., and extending them by the cost information for the item, order, etc. The details of the company game plan are costed and summarized to show the overall financial effects of the plan.

The software in the financial planning interface can prepare accurate projections of the material, direct labor, and variable overhead costs based on the company game plan. As the company game plan changes, the financial plans from MRP II change also. And since the financial plans were developed directly from the manufacturing numbers, it is possible to look into the system and track a financial number back to the individual manufacturing events that caused it. A top manager or financial planner can take a number like the projected value of finished goods inventory in week ten, trace it back to the projected value of finished goods inventory in week ten for each end item, and trace this back to the master production schedule that caused it. If there is a problem with the financial plan, it is possible to see it in advance and attempt to correct it before it happens.

To develop a total financial plan, the financial data from MRP II are combined with other financial information like principal and interest payments, depreciation, taxes, research and development expense, general administrative expense, etc. However, in other cases, the financial data could be fed into computer programs or spreadsheets to assist in developing the financial projections. In either case, when the data from MRP II is combined with the other financial information on the business, it is possible to develop a very accurate overall financial plan for the company.

The financial projections made possible by MRP II are typically used by a number of people within a company. Financial planners use it to plan cash flow, project profits, develop prices, evaluate make/buy decisions, etc. Top management uses it to evaluate different business strategies, obtain lines of credit, justify new equipment and facilities, etc. The explanation of the software in the financial interface does not assume any specific type of costing system. It is possible to develop the tools for financial planning using any of a number of cost systems, including standard cost, job cost, direct cost, etc.

This explanation of the software in the financial planning interface assumes that a cost system exists, and that unit cost information is available for each item.

CURRENT AND PROJECTED INVENTORY VALUE CALCULATIONS

The financial planning interface should provide a way to develop both the present value of inventory and the projected value of inventory in the future. The present inventory value represents the value of the inventory in the stockroom, in inspection, in transit, in field service, on the shop floor, etc. All balances included in MRP II are included in the present inventory value. The projected value of inventory is a projection of the inventory that will be on hand plus the orders that will be in process in the future. This projected value of inventory includes both stockroom and finished goods inventories, as well as the work-in-process inventory projected for the future. The inventory value in future time periods is the sum of the projected stockroom inventory (based on the projected on-hand balances from MRP), the projected finished goods inventory (from the projected on-hand balances in the master scheduling system), and the projected work-in-process inventory (based on planned and released orders from MRP).

The present value of inventory is calculated by adding the value of the inventory on hand to the value of work-in-process. The value of the inventory on hand is found by taking the balance in the stockroom plus any additional inventory (inspection, in transit, etc.) for each item and extending it by the unit cost. This cost it totalled for all items in stock to develop the value of the on-hand inventory. The value of work-in-process is developed by taking the material costs for each order and adding in any labor that has been reported on the order. In addition, an overhead cost based on the work centers and departments through which the order has been processed is added. All orders are summed to give the total value of work on the shop floor.

The projected inventory value is calculated from the projected on-hand balances and from the orders in the MRP II system. The projected on-hand balances in MRP are extended by the unit costs to give the inventory value of raw material and completed components in the stockroom. The projected on-hand balances in the master scheduling system is extended by the unit costs to give the finished goods inventory. The projected value of work-in-process is developed by taking all scheduled receipts, firm planned orders and planned orders, and extending them by the proper material, labor, and overhead costs. Each order is extended by the material cost, and by the prorated labor and overhead cost based on the start and due date of the order.

There are several ways to prorate labor and overhead costs for work-in-process. For example, a simple calculation is based on the lead time of the order. If an order will be one-quarter completed in a period, then 25% of the labor and overhead is applied to the order. Another more accurate calculation is based on the routing and back scheduling logic like that described in the shop floor control system. In this calculation, operation schedule dates are developed for each operation on each scheduled receipt, planned, and firm planned order. Using this information and the cost information in the routing, it is possible to calculate exactly where an order should be on any given date, and add the proper amount of labor and overhead based on the routing.

Two reports would typically display the present or projected inventory value. The present or projected inventory value should be totalled, and, in the case of the projected inventory value, displayed in a time-phased format.

The details of this projection should also be available to back up these totals. Examples of these reports are shown in Figures 30 and 31.

PROJECTED CASH FLOW CALCUALTIONS

The financial planning software should provide a method for projecting cash flow. Cash flow projections cover both cash disbursements and cash receipts. Cash disbursements can be calculated for the material, direct labor, and variable overhead expenses. These cash disbursements can be combined with other financial numbers to develop a complete cash flow projection for the company.

Figure 30
Projected Inventory Value
$(000)

Date	Manufactured Parts	Purchased Parts	Raw Mat'l	Work-in-Process	Finished Goods	Total
Current	1,952	581	175	666	190	3,564
1/02/88	1,621	514	159	969	200	3,463
1/30/88	1,495	472	158	854	195	3,174
2/27/88	1,427	448	154	831	190	3,050
3/26/88	1,413	439	149	820	189	3,010
4/23/88	1,397	401	135	798	185	2,916
5/21/88	1,395	400	135	797	180	2,907
6/18/88	1,350	375	140	766	179	2,810
7/16/88	1,314	365	136	746	176	2,737
8/13/88	1,279	355	132	726	173	2,665
9/10/88	1,243	345	128	706	170	2,592
10/8/88	1,190	335	124	686	165	2,500
11/5/88	1,156	325	120	667	160	2,428
12/3/88	1,139	316	117	648	156	2,376

Expenses for purchased material can be calculated by extending the purchasing schedule by the unit material costs. The purchasing schedule is the sum of the scheduled receipts, firm planned orders, and planned order receipts for purchased items. To develop a projection for purchased material, this purchasing schedule is adjusted by the payables cycle. For example, if the payables cycle is thirty days, then the purchase dollars is offset by thirty days to reflect the proper timing of the cash disbursements. Capacity Requirements Planning can be used to project the direct labor payroll expense, including overtime. Capacity planning contains the number of standard hours required to meet the master production schedule. These standard hours are converted to manhours using the work center efficiency and accounting for breaks and lunch. The manhours are summarized by labor grade and extended by the labor rate to project payroll expense. Projected over-

Figure 31
Projected Inventory Value Details

DETAIL FOR PERIOD 1/16

Item Number	Description	Stockroom Inventory			Finished Goods	W-I-P
		Manufactured	Purchased	Raw Mat'l.		
B357	Rotor	100				10,000
B491			5,050			
B558				6,330		
C243		4,950				
D270		3,880				750
F222					750	4,750

time expense is calculated by taking the labor hours above the normal work center capacity, summarizing them by labor grade and extending them by the overtime labor rates.

Capacity Requirements Planning can also be used to calculate variable overhead expense. Variable overhead expenses are those overhead expenses that vary directly with levels of production. For example, the cost of electricity to run the automatic screw machines is a variable overhead expense; it varies based on the number of hours the screw machines run. The cost of the natural gas required to run a paint line is another variable overhead expense.

To calculate variable overhead expense, it is necessary to have some rates like the cost of electricity per hour on the automatic screw machines, the cost of natural gas per hour on the paint line, etc. These rates would then be extended by the capacity requirements for the work center to give the projected variable overhead costs.

Cash receipts can be projected using the master scheduling system. In a make-to-order company, the master production schedule is the schedule of shipments. Scheduled completions are extended by the selling price, or interplant transfer price, to give the projected billings. In a make-to-stock business, completions in the master production schedule represent transfers to stock, not shipments. In general, the sales forecast is the projection of shipments. An exception is where the master production schedule doesn't satisfy the forecast. (There is a negative projected on-hand balance in the master schedule report.) In other words, the projected shipments for a make-to-stock business are sales forecasts whenever the projected on-hand balance is not negative. Projected shipments are extended by the selling price to give projected billings. The dates of these billings can be adjusted by the receivables cycle to get a cash receipts projection.

Figure 32 shows the cash disbursements and cash receipts extracted from MRP II.

ALLOCATION OF FIXED OVERHEAD EXPENSE CALCULATIONS

In many companies, overhead expense must be allocated in an approximate and sometimes quite arbitrary way. While some types of expense, like general

Figure 32
Cash Flow Information from MRPII $(000)

Period of	Purchased Material	Cash Disbursements Direct Labor Normal	Overtime	Variable Overhead	Cash Receipts
1/02	3,300	900	200	30	6,200
2/06	3,140	750	150	22	5,990
3/06	3,140	875	125	30	6,500
4/03	3,010	875	100	33	6,310
5/01	2,915	875	40	28	6,358

administrative expense and general plant expense, can be allocated this way, there are other expenses that can and should be traced back to the items that caused them. For example, the cost of a highly specialized machining center and the engineers that support it should be traced back to the items produced on the machines. The cost of a paced assembly line should be divided among the assemblies built on the line. And the cost of a special powder paint area should be allocated to the items painted in the area.

Unless fixed overhead expenses are allocated to the items that caused them, there are a number of problems, including product costs and inaccurate make/buy decisions. This in turn may lead to improperly priced products and inaccurate financial projections.

MRP II provides a way to avoid these problems by computing the allocation of fixed overhead more accurately. This can be done by prorating the fixed overhead expense based on the capacity requirements plan of a machining center, work center, department, etc. By extracting the capacity requirements from the Capacity Requirements Planning system and summarizing them by item, it is possible to determine the overhead being absorbed by each item.

The capacity requirements plan includes the items, operation numbers, and hours required in the machining center, work center, department, etc. It also includes the total labor or machine hours required by machine center, work center, department, etc. By totalling the hours for each item and operation, and then dividing by the total labor or machine hours, it is possible to see the percentage of the fixed overhead absorbed (by operation) for each item going through the area.

The allocation of fixed overhead costs can be expressed in a number of different ways depending upon the type of costing system being used and the preferences of people in the accounting department. For example, one way is to express it as a percentage by item and operation. Another way is to express it as a dollar value by item and operation, or as a dollar value by item. Still another way is to express fixed overhead costs as a standard overhead rate for the area. How the allocation of fixed overhead costs is expressed is not tremendously important. What is important is that the fixed overhead is traced back to specific items that caused it.

In the examples that follow, the allocation of fixed overhead is shown as a dollar amount by item and operation number. This is a method that is sometimes used in standard process costing systems. In this method, the dollar value of the fixed overhead is assigned to the departments or work centers where the overhead applies. For example, the cost of the machines, the salaries of the engineers who support the machines, the foreman's salary, and the cost of expendable tooling is assigned to each area. In addition, a fraction of the general administrative and plant expenses would be applied to the machining center. This would give a total fixed overhead cost to be allocated among the items using the machinery. Then the fixed overhead costs are allocated to the specific items and operations. If an operation used 3% of the machining time, then it would get 3% of the fixed overhead cost for the area. If an item went through the same machining center several times or through several departments or work centers, then the fixed overhead expense is calculated for each operation and summarized to develop the total overhead expense for the item. By dividing the total overhead expense for the item by the number of pieces produced, the overhead expense per piece is computed.

An example of showing fixed overhead this way is shown in Figure 33. In this example, the fixed overhead expense for the NC machine group is $300,000. Item number K392 uses 44.9% of the work center capacity (4000 of the 8900 required machining hours). Consequently, item number K392 absorbs $134,700 of fixed overhead. Since 25,000 K392's are produced in the work center, each K392 absorbs $5.39 of overhead expense.

Once the fixed overhead costs have been allocated, people can use the information for financial decision making. For example, this information can be used in simulating the financial effects of making or buying an item. In a standard process costing system where overhead allocation has been expressed in the manner described above, this could be done in several steps. First, overhead is allocated assuming that the item in question is manufactured. This process was described above.

Next, total manufacturing costs are computed. These total costs are calculated by adding up the total labor, material, and overhead costs for each item. Total labor, material, and overhead cost for each item can be developed by extending the scheduled receipts and planned orders for each item by the unit material, labor, and overhead costs.

Next, fixed overhead is reallocated assuming that the item is purchased. The new manufacturing costs are recomputed using the new unit overhead costs, and the changed material and labor costs for the item in qestion. This new total cost is compared to the old total cost; any difference is the financial effect of purchasing the item.

A simplified example of this process is shown in Figures 33, 34, 35, and 36. In this example, a vendor has quoted a price of $29.80 per piece for item number L320 versus an in-house cost of $33.13 per piece for the item (Figure 34). While this appears to represent a significant savings ($3.33 times 10,000 pieces), Figures 33, 34, 35, and 36 illustrate how a financial simulation is done to check. Figure 33 shows, by item, the fixed overhead absorbed in the L320 is manufactured in-house: item number L320—$9.78, item number K392—$5.39, and item number X426—$4.21. These numbers were developed using the overhead allocation process described above. Using this same process, but assuming that the L320 will be purchased instead of manufactured, yields the overhead allocation

Figure 33
NC Machine Group
Allocated Fixed OH Costs: $300,000

Item	Hours	Pieces	%	Fixed OH Per Piece
K392	4000	25,000	44.9	5.39
X426	2000	16,000	22.5	4.21
L320	2900	10,000	32.6	9.78
	8900		100.0	

numbers shown in Figure 35: item number K392 jumps to $8.00 fixed overhead per piece (an increase of $2.61 per piece). From these numbers the comparison in Figure 36 shows how the savings from buying the L320 compares to the increased overhead expenses. Savings on the L320 is $33,300 ($3.33 per piece savings times 10,000 pieces). Increased costs on the K392 are $65,250 ($2.61 added overhead times 25,000 pieces); increased costs on the X426 are $32,640 ($2.04 added overhead times 16,000 pieces). Consequently, this comparison shows that purchasing the L320 would cause costs to increase by $64,590. In this example, it is better to continue to manufacture the L320 in-house.

Figure 34
L320 Costs

Material	$12.90
Labor	9.60
Fixed OH	9.78
Variable OH	.85
Total	$33.13
Outside cost	$29.80

Figure 35
NC Machine Group
Allocated Fixed OH Costs: $300,000

Item	Hours	Pieces	%	Fixed OH Per Piece
K392	4000	25,000	66.7	8.00
X426	2000	16,000	33.3	6.25
	6000		100.0	

Figure 36
Comparison

Savings			Increased Overhead		
L320		K392		X426	
Savings	$3.33	Added OH	$2.61	Added OH	$2.04
Pieces	× 10,000	Pieces	× 25,000	Pieces	× 16,000
	$33,300		$65,250		$32,640

$97,890

Chapter 24
Simulation

An MRP II system is a detailed and highly accurate model of a manufacturing business. As a result, it becomes possible to simulate changes to any events being planned using MRP II. For example, changes to sales and operations plans, master production schedules, routings, bills of material, new sources, etc. can be simulated. Since these kinds of changes may affect a number of other areas like material, capacity, finance, etc., a major change in any of these areas would normally be simulated and checked to see that the change is realistic before the change is implemented.

MRP II is one of the several possible ways to simulate a manufacturing business. These different approaches fall into two categories of simulation: detailed and macro.

MRP II is a detailed simulation. Every item, order, work center, tool, etc. is simulated in a high degree of detail using MRP II. Individual material plans and capacity plans are developed for each item, work center, and tool and for a planning horizon that stretches out well into the future. This detailed data can then be summarized to show the overall effect on different areas of the company and to use in evaluating the effects of a change. For example, in MRP, a projected on-hand balance is calculated for each item a year or more in the future. These projected on-hand balances can be costed and summarized to give the projected inventory value for each period. If this projection shows a potential problem, the detail exists in the system to identify which items make up the inventory so that someone can develop alternatives and propose solutions.

In addition, there are significant advantages in having the same people, logic, and reports used for both simulation and day-to-day planning. Planning and implementation are more effective. In addition, the accountability is more clear-cut since the same people accountable for evaluating a change will be accountable for implementing the change.

Finally, a detailed simulation using MRP II works well in all types of manufacturing businesses. MRP II does not make any assumptions about the type of business or business conditions at the time. Consequently, it also works well during periods when the business is changing. This is a significant advantage since the time that most companies need simulation most is when the business is changing.

The alternative to an MRP II simulation is some type of macro simulation. This type of simulation is generally a mathematical model of the business. In this type of simulation there is no attempt to predict what will happen for each different item, work center, tool, etc. The effects of change are predicted in aggregate without any supporting details.

One of the problems with the macro approach to simulation is that the model falls apart when needed most. These models are typically developed using historical data and are consequently based on the current business situation. When the business situation changes significantly, it is critical to have accurate data and projections. Yet this is exactly when the macro approach is least effective because the model is no longer valid.

The other problem with macro approaches is the lack of supporting detail. If a simulation shows a problem with inventory, material cost, etc., the details are necessary to do something about the problem. What makes up the excessive inventory? What makes up the abnormal costs? Without these answers, preventive action is limited and the simulation is only effective in the situation where there are no problems.

For these reasons, we recommend the detailed simulation approach rather than the macro simulation approach.

SIMULATION TRANSACTIONS

The simulation capabilities of MRP II provide a way to evaluate proposed changes to the sales and operations plan, master production schedule, bills of material, sources of supply, routings, etc. and see their impact on:

1. The Rough-Cut Capacity Plan.

2. The Material Requirements Plan.

3. The Capacity Requirements Plan.

4. The Financial Plan.

The first objective in a simulation is to present information in a form that can be analyzed effectively. In some situations, the amount of information that has to be analyzed is easy to manage. For example, if a company has 100 work centers, and simulates a change to the production plan, it is not unreasonable to ask a capacity planner to review every work center.

Generally no special logic is necessary to simulate and present information on the rough-cut capacity plan, the capacity requirements plan, and the financial plan. Either normal net change logic or normal regenerative logic can be used for these types of simulations. There are only a few key resources, work centers, or product families, so that a master scheduler or planner can review the output reports (resource requirements plan, capacity requirements plan, cash flow projection, etc.) on each facility or family. The volume of reports and data that have to be analyzed is manageable for Resource Requirements Planning, Capacity Requirements Planning, and financial planning.

On the other hand, the volume of information coming out of the material requirements planning system may be unmanageable. For example, if a change affects ten thousand different items, then it is unreasonable to expect a planner or group of planners to review each of these items. Here, having some type of logic that reduces the amount of information that has to be analyzed would be a significant advantage. In fact, this could also be true in the resource requirements planning or capacity requirements planning systems if there are large volumes of data that have to be interpreted and analyzed.

In these situations, there are two ways to handle the problem of large amounts of changed date to be analyzed. One is net change logic, like net change MRP logic. Net change logic processes only the items that have changed, and reports the exceptions. The other way to handle the volume of information is logic to compare the old plan to the new plan. For example, a regeneration can be done, and the exceptions from the simulation compared with the exceptions from the last regeneration. Only the differences are then reported.

The second objective of a simulation is to allow people to evaluate the simulation at the same time as people are working to meet the current plan. Generally, this means that the simulation will be done in a work area or on a work copy of the data base. This way, the normal logic of the system is used to process the changes against a copy of the active files and data bases, producing the normal output reports for analysis and review. Once a change is authorized, the work files are removed from the system and the change made to the active files.

It is also possible to develop specific simulation logic that uses a combination of the live files and a work area. All the changes are stored in the work area. The live files are unchanged.

Chapter 25

Performance Measurements

A key question once MRP on the air is, "How well are we doing?" Most people implementing and operating MRP II take a great deal of pride in their system, their progress in using the tools of MRP II, and their own professionalism. Like other professionals, they want an objective measurement of how well they are doing so they can measure themselves and be compared to other companies. In addition, a CEO needs a formal measurement system to know how effectively the system is being used, or whether there are problems that need to be corrected. There are a number of excellent reasons for instituting a formal performance measurement program, both before and after MRP II is operating:

1. To establish formal, objective measurements, rather than informal guesses or feelings.

2. To develop a standard that can be compared to other companies.

3. To establish goals and to take pride in achieving them.

4. To identify problems, to assist in prioritizing problems so they can be solved, and to provide a scorecard for monitoring improvement.

The ABCD checklist (1988: Oliver Wight Limited Publications, Inc.) is a detailed measurement system for MRP II. While there are other measures of how well a company is using the tools of MRP II, the ABCD checklist is well-known, has been proven effective in measuring MRP II performance, and is generally accepted among companies already operating MRP II systems. Consequently, the performance measurement system described in this topic is based on the ABCD checklist.

The ABCD checklist first appeared in Oliver Wight, Inc.'s 1977 Newsletter as a standard method of classifying MRP II users. While a complete explanation of the four classifications from the ABCD checklist appears in the checklist itself, a brief description of the classes of MRP II users is:

1. Class A: companies getting nearly the full benefits from MRP II. These companies use MRP II for scheduling, ordering, and financial planning.

2. Class B: companies getting much of the benefit from MRP II, but who could be getting significantly more benefits from the system. These companies use MRP II mainly for scheduling and ordering.

3. Class C: companies getting some benefits from MRP II, but falling far short of their potential. These companies use MRP for ordering material.

4. Class D: companies where there has been little, if any, improvement from implementing MRP.

The ABCD checklist was designed to be taken formally by the CEO and his staff every few months or at least once a year. This way a company can review its overall performance with MRP II frequently enough to catch any problems while they are minor. A company doing an excellent job with MRP II can use the ABCD checklist to help keep its performance at Class A levels. A company who is not Class A yet but who wants to do a better job with MRP II can measure its performance, develop an action plan, and start work on improving performance.

Some of the measurements in the ABCD checklist are objective (inventory record accuracy 95% or better); others are quite subjective (management really uses MRP to manage). The performance measurements described in this topic are those objective measurements that can or would typically be measured using a computer program. However, succeeding or failing with MRP doesn't hinge on how the measurements are taken. These measurements could be taken manually and, in fact, are taken manually in many Class A companies. In other Class A companies, computer programs are used for some measurements while others are taken manually. In still other Class A MRP II companies, all measurements are taken using computer programs. Using a computer program to take these measurements generally cuts the amount of clerical effort required and could make a great deal of sense for some companies. On the other hand, many companies don't object to the amount of clerical effort needed to develop the performance measurements and may prefer to take the measurements manually. This is fine. The issue is not how much clerical effort is required or how the measurements are taken, the important thing is that the measurements are taken.

The subjective measurements (for example, "Management really uses MRP to manage"), and other measurements that are difficult or impractical to measure using a computer (like bill of material accuracy and routing accuracy) are not covered in this topic. The subjective measurements can be developed by having a number of people from different departments meet and reach a consensus. The measurements that are difficult to measure with a computer program can be taken manually. For example, bill of material accuracy can be measured by choosing 100 bills of material at random and auditing them. Several knowledgeable foremen and engineers could do this audit.

The performance measures from the ABCD checklist and the recommended objectives are based on the experience of operating MRP II systems. For example, 98% bill of material accuracy and 95% inventory record accuracy seem to be about the minimum accuracy needed to operate an effective MRP II system. Master schedule performance of 95% is the accepted standard for companies getting the full benefits from MRP II.

Each measurement requires a sample (sometimes defined by a period of time) and a tolerance. The samples are taken differently depending upon the specific measurement. In some cases, the sample used for performance measurement could be based on random selection. For example, when measuring inventory record accuracy, the sample could be 100 items selected at random. In other cases, the sample could be based on the activities occurring during a specific period of time. An example of this would be when measuring master schedule performance. The sample could be all the orders completed during a week.

The performance measurement system described in this topic also assumes that there are reasonable tolerances. Tolerances recognize that certain activities may not occur exactly because of limitations in equipment, in system capabilities, or in human ability. For example, the inventory record for an item that is scale counted may not be exactly what's on-hand. In some companies, if it's within 3 to 5% of the actual on-hand balance, it would be considered accurate. The 3 to 5% tolerance defines the limitation in counting an item by weight. In this performance measurement program, like most others, the question is not whether there should be tolerances, but what reasonable tolerances there would be.

Tolerances can be established using rules of thumb to start the system. Later, more accurate tolerances can be used. The important thing is to start with tolerances that are reasonable and get on with the job of measuring performance, and not get caught up in a massive program to establish tolerances.

Tolerances should be changed only when they have been proven unreasonable. Some companies are tempted to change tolerances as a way to improve their performance. For example, one way to "improve" master schedule performance is to change the tolerance from five days to fifteen days. Unfortunately, changing the tolerance like this does not improve performance at all. Instead it masks a problem that someone needs to be aware of. The way to deal with a performance problem is to find and eliminate the causes of the problem, not to change the tolerance.

The measurements of delivery performance (master schedule, manufacturing, and vendor delivery) in this topic measure the percentage of orders completed on time. This can be done in several ways. One way is to measure the number of orders completed versus the number of orders scheduled. In this method, the percentage of orders completed on time is the number of orders completed divided by the number of orders due. Another way to measure delivery performance is to measure the number of orders received on time versus the number of orders received. This measurement is based on comparing the actual delivery of each order to the due date of the order. For example, vendor delivery performance can be measured as the percentage of orders delivered within tolerance to the due date. The tolerance could be a few days or it could be zero.

Either of these measurements of delivery performance works well in practice. While the two different methods of measuring performance may generate different numbers in a given week, over a long period of time they work out to be equivalent ways to measure delivery performance. Both are simple approaches to developing a scorecard on delivery performance.

However, in some circumstances there could be some problems in either approach. For example, sometimes people are concerned that a vendor will avoid a bad performance measurement by calling and rescheduling orders to later dates. This way, a vendor who calls and reschedules frequently could end up with the same performance measure as a vendor who delivers reliably without rescheduling.

If this is a problem, one simple solution is to record the number of vendor-requested reschedules. This way the vendor can be measured two ways, one way for delivery to the due date, the other for the number of reschedules that he requested.

Another solution to this problem is to measure delivery performance by comparing the actual delivery date to the need date of an order. In this method, a second date, the need date, is stored for each order. This need date is a snapshot of the schedule, changing only when the planning department requested the reschedule. It does not change if the vendor (in the case of a purchase order) or the shop (in the case of a shop order or master schedule order) requested the change. The delivery date is compared to this need date for performance measurement. This way a more accurate measurement of delivery performance against need dates will be shown, regardless of whether the vendor reschedules frequently.

MEASURING INVENTORY RECORD ACCURACY

The minimum inventory accuracy needed for effectively operating Class A MRP II is 95%. This means that 95% of the items in stock must be accurate to within their counting tolerances. If 100 items are selected at random and counted, a maximum of five items will have actual counts different from the on-hand balance in the computer by more than the counting tolerance.

A good rule of thumb for the counting tolerance for inventory accuracy is zero, one, or two pieces for hand counted items, and 3% to 5% of the on-hand balance for scale counted items. Sometimes items have different characteristics that make these simple tolerances inappropriate. For example, some items can be difficult to get while other items can be relatively easy to get and many people wish to use this fact when determining counting tolerances. The best way to handle these situations is to establish a counting tolerance on each item and use this tolerance until there is an obvious reason to change it.

For example, an item may be counted using a scale, but the weight per item is not uniform. For this reason, a scale count is not as accurate for this item as it would be for other items. If this is the case for some items, then it may be necessary to change the counting tolerance. On the other hand, if changing the tolerance could create a scheduling problem, this would not be the proper solution. The proper solution would be to use a different counting method.

The logical place to measure inventory record accuracy is in the cycle counting system; however, there are some exceptions. For example, in a company doing process control cycle counting, the inventory accuracy is developed from a small random sample. This random sample is probably counted once a month. In this situation, a small number of items is counted infrequently. Consequently, most companies do not have an automated system for calculating inventory record accuracy; the computer reports provide the basic data to make the calculations manually.

A company doing cycle counting based on a random sample or ABC classifications will probably measure inventory accuracy from the cycle counting system. One way to do this is to measure inventory record accuracy as the inventory adjustments are entered in the system. As each inventory adjustment transaction is entered, the system can compare the count to the computer on-hand balance plus or minus the tolerance. Inventory records that differ from the actual counts by less than the tolerance are accurate; those that differ by more than the tolerance are inaccurate. In a process control cycle counting system, the inventory adjustment program can accumulate the number of inaccurate items and the cycle counter can enter the total number sampled. In other types of cycle counting systems, the inventory adjustment program can accumulate both the number of items counted and the number of accurate inventory records. In either case, the total number of accurate records and the total number of items counted can be determined. Inventory record accuracy can then be calculated by dividing the number of accurate records by the total number of items counted. In addition, the number of accurate records and the total counts for the day can be added to accumulators for the week, month, or other time period that makes sense. This way, inventory accuracy for the period can be calculated at any time. Inventory record accuracy can be displayed periodically, often as frequently as daily.

MEASURING MASTER PRODUCTION SCHEDULE PERFORMANCE

The master schedule performance needed for a Class A MRP II system is 95%. Ninety-five percent of all master schedule orders produced during a time period must be delivered on time. In most cases, the tolerance used in determining whether an order is on time ranges from zero to several days.

Most companies measure master schedule performance on a weekly basis. The sample consists of all the orders completed in the prior week.

One way to measure master schedule performance is when each order is received. In this method, the program that records master schedule completions includes some additional logic. This logic compares the current date to the order due date plus or minus the tolerance for each order. Orders within the tolerance are on time; orders outside the tolerance are not. The number of orders delivered during the period and the number of orders on time can be accumulated for the period and stored in the system. Periodically, say once a week, these statistics can be printed for review and used with the ABCD checklist.

MEASURING MANUFACTURING PERFORMANCE

The shop delivery performance needed in an MRP II system is 95%. Ninety-five percent of all manufacturing orders should be delivered on time. As in the case of master schedule delivery performance, different companies may use different tolerances for measuring on-time performance. However, most companies use tolerances between zero and several days.

Shop delivery performance is normally measured based on all the shop orders delivered to stock in a week. An easy way to measure shop delivery performance is when each order is received. The current date is compared to the due date plus or minus a tolerance. Orders inside the tolerance are on time; orders outside the tolerance are not. The total number of deliveries and the number of on-time deliveries can be accumulated by period (in this case, in a week) and stored in the system. The on-time shop delivery performance is the number of on-time deliveries divided by the number of deliveries. This delivery performance can be printed periodically for use in the ABCD checklist.

MEASURING VENDOR PERFORMANCE

Vendor delivery performance is similar to shop delivery performance. The objective in a Class A MRP II company is to achieve at least 95% of all purchase orders delivered on time.

One way to measure vendor delivery performance is when each order is received. The current date can be compared to the due date plus or minus a tolerance. This tolerance typically ranges between zero and several days.

Orders inside the tolerance are on time; orders outside the tolerance are not. Statistics on the total number of deliveries and the number of on-time deliveries can be accumulated by time period and stored in the system. The on-time vendor delivery performance is the number of on-time deliveries divided by the number of deliveries. This delivery performance can be printed periodically for the ABCD checklist.

Many companies use the vendor delivery performance along with statistics on quality performance to develop a vendor scorecard. This vendor scorecard can be reviewed periodically with the vendor. Most vendors perform better if they are being measured.

The vendor scorecard does not have to be complicated. An example of a simple vendor evaluation would be to measure the number of orders received from a vendor each month, the number late, the number more than two weeks early, and the number rejected. This information can be extracted from the receiving and inspection transactions and listed by month for each vendor. The buyer dealing with the vendor can then review the results with the vendor.

PART IX

Design Aids and General Specifications

Chapter 26

Master Production Scheduling Module

The master production scheduling module is a simple, comprehensive set of calculations designed to achieve the following objectives:

1. Provide a point of interface between the material requirements planning system and the demand management software.

2. Provide a method for comparing demands to the master production schedule for the purpose of generating exception messages. This mechanism is regenerative, recomputing the exception messages for all items each time the mechanism is run.

3. Provide a method for computing the quantities that need to be added to the master production schedule to satisfy demands.

4. Provide a method for displaying the master production schedule.

5. Provide logic to support two-level master scheduling.

6. Provide a method for computing rough-cut capacity requirements and displaying them.

7. Provide a lead time picture.

The master production scheduling module was designed to handle items that are stocked as finished products or finished to order. In addition, the module includes logic to handle products assembled to order from a large number of options.

1. The maintenance of the master schedule orders forms the main interface between the master scheduling module and MRP. When master schedule orders are changed, the new master schedule orders are passed back to the master production scheduling system as firm planned orders. The firm planned order subsystem maintains these records. Component gross requirements are updated either through the firm planned order subsystem or through the explosion logic of MRP, depending upon the architecture of the system.

In a net change system, the generation of component requirements will mark the component items for replanning. In a regenerative MRP system, all the components will be replanned because gross requirements exist. In either case, when the next MRP run is made, these items will be replanned.

The advantage of using the firm planned order maintenance programs and normal system architecture for updating component requirements is that there is a simple interface between the master scheduling module and MRP.

The functions, files, and displays specified in the demand management module are required to develop the master production scheduling system. The master scheduling system requires functions like the available to promise computations that are part of demand management in order to properly function.

The interface of MRP to the master scheduling system requires the following additional modification:

A. Mark each of the items being master scheduled with a code in the item master record used in MRP. One of the existing codes in the item master record (such as item type for example) could be used for this purpose or a new code could be created.

The purpose of this code is to mark master schedule items so they are ignored by MRP. If firm planned orders are not exploded in MRP, modify the Requirements Planning program so master schedule items are ignored in MRP. When an item is read from the trigger files or the level chains (or whatever mechanism is used for entering items into replanning), each item should be checked to see if it is a master schedule item. If so, it should be deleted from the trigger file or level chain and bypassed. This would prevent any master schedule items from being planned in MRP.

However, if the architecture of the system is such that firm planned orders are exploded in MRP, modify the order planning logic to bypass master schedule items.

The master scheduling system uses files from the demand management system, as well as a load profile file, exception message file, planning bill of material file, and a production forecast file. Files needed include:

1. Calendar.

    A. Calendar date.

    B. Day of the week (S, M, T, W, etc.)

    C. Work day (Y, N).

    D. Fiscal month start (Y, N).

    E. Fiscal month number (1-13).

    F. Shop calendar date.

2. Master schedule item file.

   A. Item number.

   B. Product line or subgroup.

   C. Trapping Factor for identifying a single abnormal customer order (percentage of one week's forecast quantity).

   D. On-hand balance.

   E. Description.

   F. Lot size.

   G. Lead time.

   H. Safety stock.

   I. Shrinkage factor.

   J. Type of product for two-level master scheduling code (Y/N).

3. Abnormal demand mask file.

   A. Item number.

   B. Relative week number.

   C. Cumulative low factor (cumulative customer orders for period from current date through this week less than this percentage of cumulative sales forecast).

   D. Cumulative high factor (cumulative customer orders for period from current date through this week exceed this percentage of cumulative sales forecast).

   E. Period low factor (customer orders for period less than this percentage).

   F. Period high factor (customer orders for period exceed this percentage of total sales forecast).

4. Forecast file (sequenced by date within item number).

   A. Item number.

   B. Date.

   C. Quantity.

   D. Quantity already promised against this forecast.

5. Shipments history file (sequenced by date within item number).

   A. Item number.

   B. Date.

   C. Quantity shipped.

   D. Customer order number.

    E. Customer number.

    F. Date requested.

    G. Abnormal demand flag.

6. Customer order file (sequenced by date within item number).

    A. Item number.

    B. Promised date.

    C. Requested date.

    D. Quantity.

    E. Customer order number.

    F. Customer number.

    G. Abnormal demand code (A = abnormal, other values = normal).

7. Dependent demand file (sequenced by date within item number).

    A. Item number.

    B. Required date.

    C. Quantity.

    D. Parent item number.

    E. Parent order number.

    F. Status (A = allocation; other values = gross requirement).

8. Distribution requirements and interplant orders file (sequenced by date within item number).

    A. Item number.

    B. Required date.

    C. Quantity.

    D. Receiving location.

    E. Distribution order number.

    F. Status (A = allocation; other values = gross requirement).

9. Production forecast file (sequenced by date within item number),

    A. Item number.

    B. Required date.

    C. Quantity.

    D. Parent item number.

    E. Parent order number.

10. Master schedule orders file (sequenced by date within item number).

    A. Item number.

    B. Receipt date.

    C. Start date.

    D. Quantity.

    E. Status code (F = firm planned order, S = scheduled receipt).

    F. Order number.

11. Available-to-promise file (sequenced by date within item number).

    A. Item number.

    B. Date.

    C. Quantity.

12. Exception messages file.

    A. Item number.

    B. Exception code (RI, RO, CN, PD, RL, NA, AO).

    C. Order number.

    D. Due date.

    E. Need date.

    F. Quantity.

13. Planning bill of material file.

    A. Item number.

    B. Component item number.

    C. Quantity per.

    D. Percentage popularity.

    E. Effectivity start date.

    F. Effectivity due date.

14. Load profile file.

    A. Item number.

    B. Resource number.

    C. Quantity of the resource required for each item.

    D. Lead time offset in weeks.

The production forecast file contains the production forecasts for any options being master scheduled at two levels. This file is updated using a program explained below.

The exception message file contains all the master scheduling exceptions for each item, as well as the recommended dates for orders that are needed at earlier or later dates. For orders that should be added to the master production schedule, the quantity is also shown.

The load profile file contains a representative routing for each master schedule item. The item number is the master schedule item that uses the resource. The resource number could be a number or it could be a short description of the resource since there are typically only a few resources. The quantity of the resource required can be stated in terms of hours per item, hours per 100 items, or whatever measurement makes sense. Resource requirements planning can also be used to handle dollars or tons and so the quantity does not have to refer to hours. The lead time offset in weeks is the approximate time between the date the resource is used and the date of the item in the master production schedule. If the machining operations are done eight or so weeks before the final assembly date, the lead time offset for machining would be eight weeks.

2. Write a program to explode the available to promise for types of products. The basic logic of the available-to-promise explosion program is as follows:

A. Select a master schedule item for processing. Read the master schedule item file and find any items coded "type of product."

B. Set up a 482 element array in memory. This array, the available-to-promise array, will contain the individual available to promise quantities for the past, 480 individual days in the future, and any additional future available-to-promise quantities.

C. Read the available-to-promise records stored in the available-to-promise file. These records were created in a program that is part of the demand management module. Load the available-to-promise quantities into the appropriate elements of the array.

D. Retrieve the planning bill of material and explode the available-to-promise quantities into production forecasts for the components (options).

For each planning bill of material record, multiply each non-zero available-to-promise quantity by the quantity per. Then multiply the result by the percentage popularity. Offset each available-to-promise date by the lead time to compute the required date. Compare the required date to the effectivity dates and for those that are effective, generate a production forecast record. Write the production forecast record to the production forecast file.

3. Write a master schedule exception program. This program processes the master schedule data base through a netting, exception checking, and order planning

calculation, generates master schedule exception messages, and adds the exception messages to the exception file.

The following exceptions are generated:

Reschedule in to an earlier date.

Reschedule out to a later date.

Cancel order.

Past due master schedule order.

Release master schedule order.

Add an order to the master production schedule.

The basic logic of the master schedule exception program is as follows:

A. Select a master schedule item for processing.

B. Set up a 482 element array in memory. This array, the day buckets array, will contain the individual requirements for the past, 480 individual days in the future, and any additional future requirements.

C. Read the requirements files and load the day bucket array. Each requirement file, including the sales forecast file, customer order file, production forecast file, dependent demand file, branch warehouse and interplant orders file, should be read, in turn, and the records loaded to the appropriate day bucket.

For example, read the sales forecast file for the item. For each record, convert the due date to a shop date. Locate the corresponding element in the day bucket array, and add the requirement quantity to it. Repeat this process until all requirement records for the item have been loaded to the day bucket array.

D. Compute the beginning available balance for the item. Available balance = on hand less safety stock.

E. Apply the beginning available balance to the requirements. Read the day bucket array, one element at a time, and reduce each daily requirement by the available balance until it has been consumed.

F. Increase the remaining requirements by the shrinkage factor: read the day bucket array, one element at a time, and multiply each element by one plus the shrinkage factor to compute the unsatisfied requirements.

G. Read a master schedule order and apply it to the unsatisfied requirements.

Add the master schedule quantity to the available to balance. Convert the due date and the start date of the master schedule order to shop dates. If the due date is past due, generate a past due master schedule order exception message by writing a record to the exception message file. If the start date is within a week of the current date, and the master schedule order is a firm planned order, generate a master schedule order due for release exception message.

Locate the first non-zero element in the day bucket array and compare the shop date of the master schedule order to the shop date of the requirement. If different, generate an exception message to reschedule the order to an earlier or later date.

Read the day bucket array, one element at a time forward from the first non-zero requirement, and reduce each daily requirement by the available balance until it has been consumed.

If no unsatisfied requirement exists, generate a cancel exception message.

H. Repeat step (G) for all master schedule orders.

I. Create exception messages for orders that need to be added to the master schedule. If unsatisfied requirements exist after all master schedule orders have been processed, perform one of the following lot sizing routines:

1. Lot-for-lot: Read each non-zero element in the day bucket array and create an exception message for the date and unsatisfied requirement. Write the exception message to the exception message file.

2. Fixed: Read the first non-zero element in the day bucket array, and create an exception message for that date and the fixed order quantity. If the quantity in the day bucket exceeds the fixed order quantity, create an exception message for the date and a multiple of the fixed order quantity.

Apply the fixed order quantity to the requirements to determine the next unsatisfied requirement. Add the fixed order quantity to the available balance. Read the day bucket array, one element at a time forward from the first non-zero requirement, and reduce each daily requirement by the available balance until it has been consumed.

Repeat the fixed order quantity logic above until the entire array has been processed.

4. Write a display of exception messages by item. This on-line display should list the text of an exception message and any information about the exception.
The master scheduler should be able to specify a starting item number and be able to scroll forward (or backward) from that item.

5. Write a master schedule report program. This program displays the descriptive information for the MPS item and the time phased data.

Exception messages, pegging, and supporting details to scheduled receipts and firm planned orders may be shown on the report, or they can be displayed on-line.

A sample master schedule report is shown in Appendix 12 in Figure 44. In this example, the branch warehouse demands and interplant orders are all combined into a single line labeled EXPLODED DEMAND. Also the scheduled receipts and master schedule orders are combined into the master production schedule line. The pegging information is used to determine the source of the dependent demands and the order details are used to distinguish the scheduled receipts and master schedule orders.

The available to promise shown in the master schedule report can be computed when the report is run, or read directly from the available-to-promise file. The simplest method is to retrieve existing available to promise records and print them, rather than recomputing them.

Totals should be included in the master schedule report. The lines of information in the master schedule report should be accumulated into totals corresponding to the periods used for sales and operations planning and displayed by product line. If a product line has subgroups, subtotals should be displayed for each subgroup.

The format of the master schedule totals is exactly the same as the format of the master schedule report shown in Figure 44. The only differences are that the descriptive information about the item is missing and the numbers in the report are totals by sales and operations planning period.

The pegging information and the order detail information can be displayed in the master schedule report as shown in Figure 44. This information is stored in the master schedule data base and can be displayed when the report is printed.

The exceptions are also shown in Figure 44. This does not have to be done. It would also be workable to have only the on-line exception display. However, many people prefer to see all the information on a single report.

6. Provide transactions to add, change, delete, and display the load profiles by item.

7. Write a resource requirements generation program. This program processes the master schedule data base reading the master schedule order records. The master schedule orders are extended by the resource records in the resource file creating resource requirements. The process is exactly the same as the generation of capacity requirements by extending the planned orders by the routing. These resource requirements are written to a detailed resource requirements work file.

8. Sort the detailed resource requirements by resource number and date.

9. Write a program to print a summarized resource requirements planning report. This program would bucket the resource requirements in biweekly or weekly buckets and display the total requirements.

10. Write a program to print the pegging information to the summarized resource requirements. This pegging information is the detailed resource requirements in the resource requirements planning work file. The program is a simple listing of the detailed resource requirements by resource and date.

11. Develop a program to produce a lead time picture for the items being master scheduled. A lead time picture can be developed by modifying the program which produces the multi-level bills of material. The modification is to add logic to

accumulate the lead times as the multi-level explosion takes place and to display the accumulated lead times on the multi-level bill of material.

When a bill of material is exploded to produce a multi-level bill of material, the program has to suspend processing of one bill of material to explode another. When this is done the program has to store some information to tell itself where it left off. This information includes the item numbers of the items that were in the process of being exploded. These item numbers are loaded to a table to keep multiple levels in the correct sequence.

The modification is to expand this information which is stored as the multi-level explosion takes place. The table should be expanded to include the accumulated lead time as well as the item numbers that are stored now. The accumulated lead time for an item is the lead time of the item plus the accumulated lead time up to that point.

Once this accumulated lead time logic has been included into the multi-level explosion, the accumulated lead times can be displayed on the multi-level bills of material. The illustration below is an example of such a lead time picture:

Master Schedule Item—Accumulated Lead Time Listing

		Lead Time	Accumulated Lead Time
. 1	Sub assembly	5	5
. . 2	brace	6	11
. . . 3	steel	5	16
. . 2	bracket	5	10
. 1	bottom plate	12	12
. . 2	casting	20	32

This report is easy for the master scheduler to use as a way to check materials without doing a master schedule simulation. If the master scheduler is concerned with a change to the master production schedule fifteen weeks in the future, he only has to look at the accumulated lead time column for lead times greater than fifteen weeks. In this case, he only has to worry about the steel and the casting.

Chapter 27

Demand Management Module

The demand management module is a simple, comprehensive set of calculations designed to achieve a number of different objectives:

1. Provide a point of interface between the sales planning/master production scheduling system and the forecasting process.

2. Provide a method for comparing existing customer orders to the forecast for the purpose of identifying demands that may be abnormal. This mechanism handles both individual customer orders that may be abnormal, as well as a group of customer orders that represent abnormal demand.

3. Provide a way to specify demands that are known to be abnormal.

4. Provide forecast consumption logic that includes the following functions:

   A. A method for handling customer orders that do not match the forecast week-by-week, but which may be a good approximation of the demand forecast over longer periods.

   B. A method for handling past due forecasts and past due customer orders.

   C. Forecast consumption based on customer request dates, not order due dates.

5. Provide a method for computing total demand, including forecasts, normal customer orders, abnormal customer demands, dependent demands, distribution requirements, and interplant orders for each master schedule item.

6. Provide a method for computing demand and shipment information by product family for use in sales and operations planning.

7. Provide an available-to-promise calculation and report to show, by item, the quantities available to promise to customers.

   The demand management module could be developed and operated on a micro-computer separate from the main business computer.

1. Create demand management/master production scheduling files which will contain the following information:

A. Calendar.

    1. Calendar date.

    2. Day of the week (S, M, T, W, etc.)

    3. Work day (Y, N).

    4. Fiscal month start (Y, N).

    5. Fiscal month number (1-13).

    6. Shop calendar date.

B. Master schedule item file.

    1. Item number.

    2. Product line or subgroup.

    3. Trapping factor for identifying a single abnormal customer order (percentage of one period's forecast quantity).

    4. On-hand balance.

    5. Description.

    6. Lot size.

    7. Lead time.

    8. Safety stock.

    9. Shrinkage factor.

    10. Type of product for two-level master scheduling code (Y/N).

C. Abnormal demand mask file.

    1. Item number.

    2. Relative week number.

    3. Cumulative low factor (cumulative customer orders for period from current date through this week less than this % of cumulative sales forecast).

    4. Cumulative high factor (cumulative customer orders for period from current date through this week exceed this % of cumulative sales forecast).

    5. Period low factor (customer orders for period less than this %).

    6. Period high factor (customer orders for period exceed this % of total sales forecast).

D. Forecast file (sequenced by date within item number).

    1. Item number.

    2. Date.

    3. Quantity.

    4. Quantity already promised against this forecast.

E. Shipments history file (sequenced by date within item number).

    1. Item number.

    2. Date.

    3. Quantity shipped.

    4. Customer order number.

    5. Customer number.

    6. Date requested.

    7. Abnormal demand flag.

F. Customer order file (sequenced by date within item number).

    1. Item number.

    2. Promised date.

    3. Requested date.

    4. Quantity.

    5. Customer order number.

    6. Customer number.

    7. Abnormal demand code (A = abnormal; other values = normal).

G. Dependent demand file (sequenced by date within item number).

    1. Item number.

    2. Required date.

    3. Quantity.

    4. Parent item number.

    5. Parent order number.

    6. Status (A = allocation; other values = gross requirement).

H. Distribution requirements and interplant orders file (sequenced by date within item number).

    1. Item number.

    2. Required date.

    3. Quantity.

    4. Receiving location.

     5. Distribution order number.

     6. Status (A = allocation; other values = gross requirement).

  I. Master schedule orders file (sequenced by date within item number).

     1. Item number.

     2. Receipt date.

     3. Start date.

     4. Quantity.

     5. Status code (F = firm planned order; S = scheduled receipt).

     6. Order number.

  J. Available-to-promise file (sequenced by date within item number).

     1. Item number.

     2. Date.

     3. Quantity.

2. The calendar file contains the shop calendar and a way to identify fiscal month start dates.

The master schedule item file contains the item number, product line or subgroup identifier, and the factor for abnormal demand identification. The product line is used to sequence the printing of the demand management reports and also for accumulating totals by product line. A subgroup is used to accumulate subtotals within a product line. The factor for identifying an abnormal customer order is a percentage of the forecast quantity in a week: if a customer order exceeds the forecast in a week by more than this percentage, then it will be flagged as potentially abnormal.

The abnormal demand mask file contains factors for computing high and low forecast ranges and measuring groups of customer orders against these ranges. Each record contains a week number, low factor for this period, high factor for this period, low factor for the cumulative forecast, and a high factor for the cumulative forecast.

The sales forecast file is used to pass the sales forecast from the forecasting system to the demand management logic. It is also used as a primary input to developing the demands for master scheduling. The quantity sold against the forecast is provided as a way to store the amount that has been consumed by customer orders in the demand management logic.

The shipments file contains records for shipments made in the prior period. These records are necessary to consume the forecast in past periods (or if orders are shipped early), so that demand does not increase simply because the product was shipped. Each shipment record contains the date and quantity of the shipment, as well as the customer requested date taken from the original customer order.

The customer order file is used to store the customer orders and present them to the forecast consumption logic. The promised date is the date the customer can expect shipment. The requested date is the date the customer requested shipment, and it is the date used in the forecast consumption logic. The customer number is stored only for the information of the master scheduler and order promising people.

The dependent demand file and the distribution requirements and interplant orders files are used to store demands from material requirements planning or DRP. Each record contains the required date and quantity, as well as source information (parent item number or receiving location) and status.

The master schedule orders are the statement of production and these have been used to state the master production schedule. The receipt date is the date the master schedule order is due to be completed and available for shipment to customers. The start date is the date the component parts are needed for assembly.

The available-to-promise file contains the computed available to promise for display on-line and in the master schedule displays and reports.

3. Maintain the different records in the demand management/master schedule data base. Some of the files should be purged and replaced each time the demand management module is run; others should be maintained in the master schedule data base until the forecast is updated. Others are maintained only for the purposes of being passed back to update files in the master scheduling system.

A. Create transactions to add, change, and delete records from the calendar file.

B. Create programs and transactions to add, delete, and change master schedule items.

1. Write a program that extracts master schedule items from the master production scheduling system and writes them to a work file. This work file should contain the item number and any product group/subgroup identifier. This program will be used to load the master schedule item file and maintain it once the demand management system is in use.

2. Write a program that loads the master schedule item file from the work file of master schedule items. This program would load one record for each item number in the work file and would be run only one time when the demand management system is started. An alternative to writing this program would be to manually load the master schedule item file.

3. Write a program that matches the master schedule item work file from the master production scheduling system with the master schedule item file used for demand management. Records not contained in the master schedule item file used in demand management, but now part of the master production scheduling system should be added to the master schedule item file. Records contained in the master schedule item file but not part of the master production scheduling system should be purged from the master schedule item file and the abnormal demand mask file.

4. Create transactions to add, change, and delete records from the master schedule item file. These transactions should maintain the descriptive information and demand factors in the file.

C. Create transactions to add, change, and delete records from the abnormal demand mask file.

D. Write a program that reads any existing forecasting files and generates sales forecast records. This program has the following parts:

1. Purge the old sales forecast file. All forecast records should be deleted from the file. An audit report listing all items with unconsumed forecast records with past due dates should be printed.

2. Create new sales forecast records. Existing forecast quantities would be split into a weekly quantities (if necessary) and written as individual records to the file.

E. Write a program that clears the quantity promised field in each forecast record.

F. Write a series of programs to extract shipment information from the master production scheduling/material requirements planning system and write it to the demand management module.

1. Write a program that extracts shipments from the prior week, and writes them to a work file. This work file should contain the item number, quantity, date shipped, customer order number, customer number, and the date the shipment was requested. The date the shipment was requested can be found in the master scheduling system customer order file.

2. Write a program that purges the shipments file in the demand management module.

3. Write a program that loads the shipments file from the shipments work file.

G. Write a series of programs to recreate customer orders from the information currently in the master production scheduling system. These programs should also provide some method of updating the abnormal demand code in both the demand management and the master scheduling systems.

1. Write a program that extracts customer orders from the master production scheduling system, and writes them to a work file for demand management. This work file should contain the item number, quantity, date promised, customer order number, customer number, abnormal demand code, and the request date.

2. Write a program that purges the customer orders file from the demand management system.

3. Write a program that loads the customer orders file to the demand management logic from the customer orders work file.

4. Provide a method of updating abnormal demand codes. Add an abnormal demand code field to the unused space at the end of the customer order

record in the master scheduling system. Then provide maintenance using either of the following methods:

    a. METHOD 1: Create a master scheduling system transaction, and a demand management system customer order change transaction to manually maintain the abnormal demand code.

    b. METHOD 2: Create a transaction to manually maintain the abnormal demand code. Write a program to extract customer orders from the demand management customer order file and write them to a work file in the master scheduling system. This work file must contain the item number, customer order number, and the abnormal demand code. Write a program to update the master scheduling system customer order file from the work file.

H. Write a series of programs to extract dependent demand, distribution requirements, and interplant orders from the master scheduling system and write them to the demand management module.

    1. Write a program that extracts these requirements and writes them to a work files.

    2. Write a program that purges the dependent demand file and the distribution requirements and interplant orders file in the demand management system.

    3. Write a program that loads the dependent demand file and the distribution requirements and interplant orders file in the demand management module from the work files.

I. Write a series of programs to extract master production schedule information from the master scheduling system and write it to the demand management module.

    1. Write a program that extracts scheduled receipts and planned master schedule orders from the master production scheduling system, and writes them to a work file in the demand management system.

    2. Write a program that purges the master production schedule file from the demand management system.

    3. Write a program that loads the master production schedule file in the demand management system from the work file.

J. Provide on-line inquiry programs to each of the demand management module files.

4. Write a program to reduce forecasts by shipments. In this logic, each shipment record is processed, one at a time, against the sales forecast file.

This program reads shipment records, locates the corresponding sales forecast record and physically reduces the forecast quantity by the shipment quantity. The logic first reduces the forecast quantity in the period the shipment was requested, then if necessary, finds and reduces earlier forecasts and finally, if necessary, finds and reduces later forecasts. Abnormal demands are bypassed.

5. Write a program to identify past due customer orders, and mark them "abnormal demands." This prevents forecasts in later periods from being consumed by customer orders that have past due requested dates when the past due forecast has been dropped.

This program simply reads the customer order file and compares the requested date of each customer order to the current date. Orders where the requested date is earlier than the current date are marked abnormal.

6. Write a program to identify individual orders that are potentially abnormal. The program reads each normal customer order and finds the corresponding sales forecast record (sales forecast date = or less than customer request date). The sales forecast quantity is multiplied by the trapping factor to get a maximum customer order size. The customer order quantity is compared to the maximum customer order size and those orders that exceed the maximum are listed on an audit report for manual review.

7. Create the necessary files and programs to identify groups of customer orders that are potentially abnormal. In this logic, a series of arrays are set up to accumulate the sales forecast and the customer orders. The cumulative sales forecast array is multiplied by cumulative high factor and the cumulative low factor to compute two arrays (cumulative high quantity array, cumulative low quantity array), and multiplied by the period high factor and period low factor to compute two arrays (period high quantity array, period low quantity array). The cumulative customer order array contains the total of customer orders promised through each period.

Cumulative customer orders for each period are compared to the cumulative high quantity and the cumulative low quantity for the same period. If outside the range (high or low) there may be demand problems that need to be assessed and an exception message is generated on an audit report for manual review.

Customer orders for each period are compared to the period high quantity and the period low quantity for the same period. In this case as well, if the customer orders are outside the range, there may be demand problems that need to be assessed and an exception message is generated on an audit report for manual review.

8. Write a program to reduce forecasts by normal customer orders. In this logic, each customer order record is processed, one at a time, against the sales forecast file.

This program reads customer orders records, locates the corresponding sales forecast record and updates the quantity promised field stored in each forecast record. The logic first updates the promised quantity in the period the order was requested. Once the promised quantity in a period is equal to the forecast, the program finds and updates earlier forecast records and finally, if necessary, finds and reduces later forecasts. Abnormal demands are bypassed.

9. Write a program that calculates both total independent demand and total demand, prints a report showing demand by item, updates the demand interface file for the master scheduling system, and summarizes demand by product family. Total independent demand for each period is the sum of the unconsumed forecast (original forecast less quantity promised), normal customer orders, and abnormal demands. Total demand is the sum of the total independent demand for the period plus any dependent demands, distribution requirements, or interplant orders. The demand information on the printed report should show:

Item number: xxxxxxxx

Date	xx/xx/xx	xx/xx/xx	xx/xx/xx . . .
Sales Forecast			
Customer Orders (By Request Date)			
Abnormal Demands (By Request Date)			
Consumer Forecast			
Customer Orders (By Due Date)			
Abnormal Demands (By Due Date)			
Total Independent Demand			
Dependent demand (if non-zero)			
Distribution requirements (if non-zero)			
Interplant orders (if non-zero)			
Total Demand			

The total independent demand should be moved to the demand interface file from the master scheduling system and passed back to the MPS module of the system.

In addition, the total demand for each product family should be accumulated as each item is processed. After all the demand information for items within the family is printed, the total weekly demand for the family should be totalled into fiscal periods for two years and displayed.

10. Provide an available-to-promise calculation and report to show, by item, the quantities available to promise to customers.

11. Set up job streams for monthly, weekly, and daily processing.

A. Monthly:

Run the program that extracts master schedule items from the master scheduling system and writes them to a work file.

Run the program that matches the master schedule item work file with the master schedule item file in the demand management module and adds or deletes records as required.

Purge sales forecast records from the demand management module.

Read the forecasting files and generate sales forecast records for the demand management module.

Purge customer orders from the demand management module.

Extract customer orders from the master scheduling system and write them to a work file in the demand management system.

Load customer orders in the demand management module from the customer order work file.

Purge dependent demands, distribution requirements, and interplant orders from the demand management module.

Extract dependent demands from MRP and write them to a work file in the demand management module.

Extract distribution requirements from the master scheduling system and write them to a work file in the demand management module.

Extract interplant orders from MRP and write them to a work file in the demand management module.

Load the dependent demand, distribution requirements, and interplant orders files in the demand management module.

Purge the master production schedule file from the demand management system.

Extract scheduled receipts and planned master schedule orders from the master production scheduling system, and write them to a work file in the demand management system.

Load the master production schedule file in the demand management system from the work file.

Run the program that identifies past due customer orders and marks them as abnormal demands.

Run the program that identifies individual orders that are potentially abnormal.

Run the program that identifies groups of customer orders that are potentially abnormal.

B. Monthly (second batch run):

Run the program that consumes the forecast with customer orders.

Run the program that computes total demands.

C. Weekly or daily:

Run the program that extracts master schedule items from the master scheduling system and writes them to a work file.

Run the program that matches the master schedule item work file with the master schedule item file in the demand management module and adds or deletes records as required.

Purge shipments records from the demand management module.

Read the shipments files and generate shipments records for the demand management module.

Clear the quantity promised field in each forecast record.

Reduce the forecast in the demand management module by shipments.

Purge customer orders from the demand management module.

Extract customer orders from the master scheduling system and write them to a work file in the demand management system.

Load customer orders in the demand management module from the customer order work file.

Purge dependent demands, distribution requirements, and interplant orders from the demand management module.

Extract dependent demands from MRP and write them to a work file in the demand management module.

Extract distribution requirements from the master scheduling system and write them to a work file in the demand management module.

Extract interplant orders from MRP and write them to a work file in the demand management module.

Load the dependent demand, distribution requirements, and interplant orders files in the demand management module.

Purge the master production schedule file from the demand management system.

Extract scheduled receipts and planned master schedule orders from the master production scheduling system, and write them to a work file in the demand management system.

Load the master production schedule file in the demand management system from the work file.

Run the program that identifies individual orders that are potentially abnormal.

Run the program that identifies groups of customer orders that are potentially abnormal.

D. Weekly or daily (second batch run):

Run the program that consumes the forecast with customer orders.

Run the program that computes total demands.

Chapter 28

Material Requirements Planning

The material requirements planning module is a simple, comprehensive set of calculations designed to achieve the following objectives:

1. Provide a netting calculation that compares requirements to existing scheduled receipts and firm planned orders for the purpose of generating exception messages.

2. Provide an order planning calculation that generates planned orders to cover any unsatisfied requirements.

3. Provide an explosion calculation that explodes firm planned orders and planned orders into gross requirements for the components.

4. Provide a well-engineered set of reports that display the time-phased data, exception messages, pegging, and details to scheduled receipts and firm planned orders.

The material requirements planning calculations are regenerative with a two year planning horizon. The logic is fail-safe: all items are entered into the sequence for replanning.

1. The maintenance of the master schedule orders forms the main interface between the master scheduling module and MRP. When master schedule orders are changed, the new master schedule orders are passed back from the master production scheduling module as firm planned orders. The firm planned order subsystem maintains these records. Component gross requirements will be updated through the explosion logic of MRP. The advantage of using the firm planned order maintenance programs and the explosion logic of MRP for updating component requirements is that there is a simple interface between the master scheduling module and MRP.

The interface of MRP to the master scheduling system requires the following additional modification:

A. Mark each of the items being master scheduled with a code in the item master record used in MRP. One of the existing codes in the item master record (like item type for example) could be used for this purpose or a new code could be created.

The purpose of this code is to mark master schedule items so they are ignored by MRP. The Requirements Planning program will bypass master schedule items that are ignored in MRP, except for the explosion of firm planned orders into component requirements.

2. The material requirements planning module requires several files, some of which are the same as those used in the demand management and master production scheduling systems. In cases where the files are the same as those modules, no explanation of the maintenance routines is provided. For information on these routines, refer to the chapters explaining the demand management and master production scheduling modules.

Files used for material requirements planning include:

A. Calendar.

1. Calendar date.

2. Day of the week (S, M, T, W, etc.).

3. Work day (Y, N).

4. Fiscal month start (Y, N).

5. Fiscal month number (1-13).

6. Shop calendar date.

B. Item master file (sequenced by item number).

1. Item number.

2. On-hand balance.

3. Description.

4. Lot size.

5. Lead time.

6. Safety stock.

7. Shrinkage factor.

8. Master schedule code (Y/N).

9. Low-level code.

C. Forecast file (sequenced by date within item number).

    1. Item number.

    2. Date.

    3. Quantity.

    4. Quantity already promised against this forecast.

D. Shipments history file (sequenced by date within item number).

    1. Item number.

    2. Date.

    3. Quantity shipped.

    4. Customer order number.

    5. Customer number.

    6. Date requested.

    7. Abnormal demand flag.

E. Customer order file (sequenced by date within item number).

    1. Item number.

    2. Promised date.

    3. Requested date.

    4. Quantity.

    5. Customer order number.

    6. Customer number.

    7. Abnormal demand code (A = abnormal; other values = normal).

F. Dependent demand file (sequenced by date within item number).

    1. Item number.

    2. Required date.

    3. Quantity.

    4. Parent item number.

    5. Parent order number.

    6. Status (A = allocation, other values = gross requirement).

G. Distribution requirements and interplant orders file (sequenced by date within item number).

    1. Item number.

    2. Required date.

    3. Quantity.

4. Receiving location.

5. Distribution order number.

6. Status (A = allocation, other values = gross requirement).

H. Production forecast file (sequenced by date within item number).

1. Item number.

2. Required date.

3. Quantity.

4. Parent item number.

5. Parent order number.

I. Scheduled receipts and firm planned orders file (sequenced by date within status [scheduled receipts before firm planned orders] within item number).

1. Item number.

2. Due date.

3. Start date.

4. Quantity.

5. Status code (F = firm planned order, S = scheduled receipt).

6. Order number.

J. Exception messages file.

1. Item number.

2. Exception code (RI, RO, CN, PD, RL, NA, AO).

3. Order number.

4. Due date.

5. Need date.

6. Quantity.

K. Bill of material file.

1. Item number.

2. Component item number.

3. Quantity per.

4. Scrap factor.

5. Effectivity start date.

6. Effectivity due date.

L. Planned orders file (sequenced by date within item number).

1. Item number.

2. Due date.

3. Start date.

4. Quantity.

M. Trigger file (sequenced by item within low-level code).

1. Low-level code.

2. Item number.

3. Write a program to clear the files created by the material requirements planning process. These files can be deleted and recreated without any data, or the individual records contained in the files can be deleted.

The following files should be cleared:

A. Trigger file. The simplest method is to delete the file and recreate it.

B. Exception file. If the exception file is also used for master schedule exceptions, then the best method is to delete the exception records for any items that are not master scheduled. If the exception file is not used for master schedule exceptions, then the simplest method is to delete the file and recreate it.

C. Dependent demand file. If the dependent demand file contains time-phased allocations, then the best method is to delete the gross requirement records individually, bypassing the allocations.

D. Planned order file. The simplest method is to delete and recreate it.

4. Write a program to select items for replanning. The basic logic of the program is as follows:

A. Read the item master file sequentially.

B. For each item, write a trigger record.

5. Write a material requirements planning program. This program processes each non-master schedule item through a netting, exception checking, and order planning calculation, generates exception messages, and adds the exception messages to the exception file. In addition, the program computes new planned orders for non-master schedule items and explodes firm planned and planned orders into gross requirements.

The following exceptions are generated:

Reschedule in to an earlier date.

Reschedule out to a later date.

Cancel order.

Past due scheduled receipt.

Release planned or firm planned order.

The basic logic of the material requirements planning program is as follows:

A. Select an item for processing. The trigger file, already sequenced by low-level code and item number, is read sequentially. For each trigger record, the item master record is retrieved.

B. Set up a 482 element array in memory. This array, the day buckets array, will contain the individual requirements for the past, 480 individual days in the future, and any additional future requirements.

C. Set up a second 482 element array in memory. This array, the planned order array, will create individual planned order quantities by date for the entire planning horizon. By setting up an array of planned orders, it is possible to make the explosion logic in the system as efficient as possible.

D. If the item is master scheduled, read all firm planned orders and load the firm planned order quantities into the appropriate elements of the planned order array. The firm planned orders should be loaded into the array based on their start dates. Bypass the exception and order planning logic by skipping forward to step (1).

E. Read the requirements files and load the day bucket array. Each requirement file, including the sales forecast file, customer order file, production forecast file, dependent demand file, branch warehouse and interplant orders file, should be read, in turn, and the records loaded to the appropriate day bucket.

For example, read the sales forecast file for the item. For each record, convert the due date to a shop date. Locate the corresponding element in the day bucket array, and add the requirement quantity to it. Repeat this process until all requirement records for the item have been loaded to the day bucket array.

F. Compute the beginning available balance for the item. Available balance = on hand less safety stock.

G. Apply the beginning available balance to the requirements. Read the day bucket array, one element at a time, and reduce each daily requirement by the available balance until it has been consumed.

H. Increase the remaining requirements by the shrinkage factor: read the day bucket array, one element at a time, and multiply each element by one plus the shrinkage factor to compute the unsatisfied requirements.

I. Read a scheduled receipt or firm planned order and apply it to the unsatisfied requirements.

If a firm planned order, add the order quantity to the appropriate element of the planned order array based on the start date of the firm planned order.

Add the order quantity to the available-to-balance. Convert the due date and the start date of the order to shop dates. If the due date is past due and the order is a scheduled receipt, generate a past due scheduled receipt exception message by writing a record to the exception message file. If the start date is within a week of the current date and the order is a firm planned order, generate a planned order due for release exception message.

Locate the first non-zero element in the day bucket array, and compare the shop date of the order to the shop date of the requirement. If different, generate an exception message to reschedule the order to an earlier or later date.

Read the day bucket array, one element at a time forward from the first non-zero requirement, and reduce each daily requirement by the available balance until it has been consumed.

If no unsatisfied requirement exists, generate a cancel exception message.

J. Repeat step (I) for all scheduled receipts and firm planned orders.

K. Create planned orders to satisfy remaining requirements.

If unsatisfied requirements exist after all scheduled receipts and firm planned orders have been processed, perform one of the following lot sizing routines:

1. Lot-for-lot: Read each non-zero element in the day bucket array and create a planned order for the date and the quantity of each unsatisfied requirement. Offset the due date by the lead time to compute the planned order start date.

   Write the planned order to the planned order file. Add the planned order quantity into the appropriate element of the planned order array, based on the start date of the planned order.

2. Fixed: Read the first non-zero element in the day bucket array and create a planned order for the date and the fixed order quantity. If the quantity in the day bucket exceeds the fixed order quantity, create a planned order for the date and a multiple of the fixed order quantity. Offset the due date by the lead time to calculate the planned order start date.

   Write the planned order to the planned order file. Add the planned order quantity into the appropriate element of the planned order array, based on the start date of the planned order.

   Apply the fixed order quantity to the requirements to determine the next unsatisfied requirement. Add the fixed order quantity to the available balance. Read the day bucket array, one element at a time forward from the first non-zero requirement and reduce each daily requirement by the available balance until it has been consumed.

   Repeat the fixed order quantity logic above until the entire array has been processed.

L. Explode the planned and firm planned orders into component requirements using the bill of material.

For each bill of material record, multiply each non-zero element of the planned order array quantity by the quantity per. Then increase the result by any expected scrap (multiply the result by one plus the bill of material scrap factor). Compare the date of the array element to the effectivity dates stored in the bill of material and for those that are effective generate a gross requirement record. Write the gross requirement record record to the dependent demand file.

M. Loop back to step (A).

6. Write a report or on-line display of exception messages by item. This display should list the text of an exception message and any information about the exception.

In the case of an on-line display, a planner should be able to specify a starting item number and be able to scroll forward (or backward) from that item.

7. Write an MRP report program. This program displays the descriptive information and the time-phased data for each item. Exception messages, pegging, and supporting details to scheduled receipts and firm planned orders may be shown on the report, or they can be displayed on-line.

Provide a way to print by exception, or by a specified range of items.

A sample time phased MRP is shown in Appendix 12 in Figure 43. In this example, all demands have been combined into a single line labeled GROSS REQUIREMENTS. Also the scheduled receipts and firm planned orders are combined into the SCHED RECEIPTS line. The pegging information is used to determine the source of the demands and the order details are used to distinguish the scheduled receipts and master schedule orders.

The pegging information and the order detail information can be displayed in the MRP report as shown in Figure 43. This information is stored in the data base and can be displayed when the report is printed.

The exceptions are also shown in Figure 43. This does not have to be done. It would also be workable to have only the on-line exception display. However, many people prefer to see all the information on a single report.

Chapter 29

Shop Scheduling and Dispatching Module

The shop scheduling and dispatching module is a simple, comprehensive set of calculations designed to achieve the following objectives:

1. Provide logic to create and maintain open order detail records for each scheduled receipt and firm planned order.

2. Provide a basic transaction system to record the movement of material and the completion of operations in the shop.

3. Provide a back scheduling calculation to compute operation schedule dates for scheduled receipts and firm planned orders.

4. Provide a daily dispatch list to show the shop schedule.

5. Provide an open order status report to show the status of each operation on a scheduled receipt or firm planned order.

The shop scheduling and dispatching module requires several files, some of which are the same as those used in the MRP system. In those cases, no explanation of the required maintenance transactions and programs is provided.

Files used for shop scheduling and dispatching include:

1. Calendar.

    A. Calendar date.

    B. Day of the week (S, M, T, W, etc.).

    C. Work day (Y, N).

    D. Fiscal month start (Y, N).

    E. Fiscal month number (1-13).

    F. Shop calendar date.

2. Item master file.

    A. Item number.

    B. On-hand balance.

    C. Description.

    D. Lot size.

    E. Lead time.

    F. Safety stock.

    G. Shrinkage factor.

    H. Master schedule code (Y/N).

    I. Low-level code.

3. Scheduled receipt and firm planned orders file.

    A. Order number.

    B. Item number.

    C. Due date.

    D. Start date.

    E. Quantity.

    F. Order status.

4. Work center file.

    A. Work center number.

    B. Description.

    C. Number of men or machines.

    D. Number of hours for shift 1.

    E. Number of hours for shift 2.

    F. Number of hours for shift 3.

    G. Work center queue.

5. Routing file.

    A. Item number.

    B. Operation number.

    C. Operation description.

    D. Work center number.

    E. Setup time standard.

    F. Run time standard.

/ MRP II Standard System

G. Time basis code.

H. Scheduling time.

I. Number of men or machines.

J. Efficiency.

K. Outside processing operation identifier (Y/N).

L. Outside processing time.

M. Teardown time.

6. Open order detail file.

A. Order number.

B. Item number.

C. Operation number.

D. Operation description.

E. Work center number.

F. Standard setup hours.

G. Standard run hours.

H. Time basis code.

I. Scheduling time.

J. Number of men or machines.

K. Efficiency.

L. Operation start date.

M. Operation due date.

N. Operation status.

O. Outside processing operation identifier (Y/N).

P. Outside processing time.

Q. Teardown time.

7. Dispatch list work file.

A. Item number.

B. Operation number.

C. Operation description.

D. Work center number.

E. Standard setup hours.

F. Standard run hours.

G. Time basis code.

H. Scheduling time.

I. Number of men or machines.

J. Efficiency.

K. Outside processing operation identifier (Y/N).

L. Outside processing time.

M. Teardown time.

N. Operation start date.

O. Operation due date.

P. Operation status.

Q. Order due date.

R. Next operation.

S. Next work center.

T. Prior operation.

U. Prior work center.

The time basis code determines whether the run time is per piece, per ten pieces, per hundred pieces, per thousand pieces, etc. Programs that compute total run time must include logic that multiplies the run time by the order quantity and a time basis code adjustment factor. For example, if the time basis code is "per thousand," then total run time is run time multiplied by order quantity divided by one thousand.

1. The programs that add and delete shop orders provide the main interface between the shop scheduling and dispatching module and the scheduled receipts and firm planned order subsystems.

When scheduled receipts and firm planned orders are created, open order detail records should be created in the shop scheduling and dispatching module. When scheduled receipts and firm planned orders are deleted, open order detail records should be deleted.

The interface of shop scheduling and dispatching to the scheduled receipts and firm planned order subsystems requires the following modifications:

A. Add logic to the programs that create scheduled receipts and firm planned orders. As each record is created, copy the operation records from the item's routing, and attach them to the record as open order detail records.

B. Add logic to the programs that delete scheduled receipts and firm planned orders and removes them from the scheduled receipt and firm planned order file. As each record is deleted, delete any attached open order detail records.

Once open order detail records have been created, some method must be provided to maintain them. Write a program to add, change, and delete operation detail records.

2. Write a program to update the operation status codes based on transactions from the factory. This program processes move transactions, operation completion transactions, and transactions reporting a simultaneous completion and movement. The operation status code must be updated based on the shop movement.

3. Write a program to compute operation schedule dates. Operation schedule dates are calculated each night prior to producing the daily dispatch list. No attempt is made to keep these dates current as changes are made to orders or as operations are added, changed, or deleted.

This program does a back scheduling calculation by processing the open order detail records through two successive forward scheduling computations. In the first forward scheduling calculation, the system accumulates the lead time for the order. The due date is offset by this lead time to calculate the order start date. In the second forward scheduling calculation, the system computes the actual operation schedule dates from the computed order start date.

The basic logic of the program is as follows:

A. Read the scheduled receipts and firm planned orders file sequentially to identify any orders that have not been closed. Clear the lead time accumulator field.

B. For each scheduled receipt or firm planned order, read an open order detail record and perform the following calculations:

1. If the open order detail record is the first operation, set the paperwork preparation and parts issue time. This is an arbitrary number usually 1-3 days. Add this to the lead time accumulator.

2. Calculate the time required for the operation.

If the operation is an outside processing operation, then compute total elapsed time as:

Elapsed time = outside processing time.

If the operation is not an outside processing operation, then:

Elapsed time = [Standard setup hours + Standard run hours / (number of men or machines x efficiency)] / (Shift 1 hours + Shift 2 hours + Shift 3)

where

Setup time = setup time from the routing.

Standard run hours = (Run time x order quantity x time basis code adjustment factor).

Number of men or machines is taken from the routing if the field is non-zero. Otherwise, the number of men or machines is taken from the work center record.

Add elapsed time to the lead time accumulator.

3. Compute time between operations.

Add scheduling time plus work center queue to the lead time accumulator.

C. Repeat step b for next operation record. Once all operations have been processed, convert the order due date to a shop date. Subtract the lead time accumulator from the shop date to compute an order start date.

D. For each scheduled receipt, read an open order detail record and perform the following calculations:

1. Calculate the operation start date. If the open order detail record is the first operation, set the operation start date equal to the order start date plus paperwork preparation and parts issue time.

If the open order detail record is not the first operation, set the operation start date equal to the prior operation due date plus time between operations. Time between operations equals scheduling time plus work center queue.

2. Calculate the operation due date based on the time required for the operation.

Operation due date = operation start date + elapsed time.

If the operation is an outside processing operation, compute total elapsed time as:

Elapsed time = outside processing time.

If the operation is not an outside processing operation, then:

Elapsed time = [Standard setup hours + Standard run hours / (number of men or machines x efficiency)] / (Shift 1 hours + Shift 2 hours + Shift 3)

where

Standard setup hours = setup time from the routing.

Standard run hours = (Run time x order quantity x time basis code adjustment factor).

Number of men or machines is taken from the routing if the field is non-zero. Otherwise, number of men or machines is taken from the work center record.

4. Write a series of programs to produce a daily dispatch list. This has several parts:

Write a program to extract open order detail records and create dispatch list work records.

A. Read the scheduled receipts and firm planned order file sequentially and process scheduled receipts whose status is not closed or cancelled.

B. For each, read the open order detail file. Test each operation for the following:

Running in the work center.

Present in the work center.

Scheduled to start in the work center within a few, say 3-5, days.

In each case, write a record to the dispatch list work file.

Write a sort for the dispatch list work file. Sort by work center number, operation status, operation start or due date, order due date.

Write a dispatch list report program. This is a simple listing of the sorted dispatch list work file.

5. Write an open order status display program. This program displays the status of an order and all the operations on-line. The display is a simple listing of the information in the scheduled receipts and firm planned order file and the open order detail file.

Chapter 30

Capacity Requirements Planning

The design of this system is as simple as possible and has three basic steps. These are:

1. Extract capacity requirements from the shop scheduling and dispatching system.

2. Generate capacity requirements from planned and firm planned orders.

3. Provide a reporting function that includes the summary and detail capacity requirements planning displays.

The capacity requirements planning module requires several files, some of which are the same as those used in the MRP and shop scheduling and dispatching systems. In those cases, no explanation of the required maintenance transactions and programs is provided.

Files used for capacity requirements planning include:

1. Calendar.

    A. Calendar date.

    B. Day of the week (S, M, T, W, etc.).

    C. Work day (Y, N).

    D. Fiscal month start (Y, N).

    E. Fiscal month number (1-13).

    F. Shop calendar date.

2. Item master file (sequenced by item number).

    A. Item number.

    B. On-hand balance.

    C. Description.

     D. Lot size.

     E. Lead time.

     F. Safety stock.

     G. Shrinkage factor.

     H. Master schedule code (Y/N).

     I. Low-level code.

3. Scheduled receipt and firm planned orders.

     A. Order number.

     B. Item number.

     C. Due date.

     D. Start date.

     E. Quantity.

     F. Order status.

4. Planned order file.

     A. Item number.

     B. Due date.

     C. Start date.

     D. Quantity.

5. Work center file.

     A. Work center number.

     B. Description.

     C. Number of men or machines.

     D. Number of hours for shift 1.

     E. Number of hours for shift 2.

     F. Number of hours for shift 3.

     G. Work center queue.

6. Routing file.

     A. Item number.

     B. Operation number.

     C. Operation description.

     D. Work center number.

    E. Setup time standard.

    F. Run time standard.

    G. Time basis code.

    H. Scheduling time.

    I. Number of men or machines.

    J. Efficiency.

    K. Outside processing operation identifier (Y/N).

    L. Outside processing time.

    M. Teardown time.

7. Open order detail file.

    A. Order number.

    B. Item number.

    C. Operation number.

    D. Operation description.

    E. Work center number.

    F. Standard setup hours.

    G. Standard run hours.

    H. Time basis code.

    I. Scheduling time.

    J. Number of men or machines.

    K. Efficiency.

    L. Operation start date.

    M. Operation due date.

    N. Operation status.

    O. Outside processing operation identifier (Y/N).

    P. Outside processing time.

    Q. Teardown time.

8. Capacity planning work file.

    A. Item number.

    B. Operation number.

    C. Operation description.

D. Work center number.

E. Standard setup hours.

F. Standard run hours.

G. Tear down time.

H. Operation start date.

I. Operation due date.

J. Operation status.

K. Order due date.

The time basis code determines whether the run time is per piece, per ten pieces, per hundred pieces, per thousand pieces, etc. Programs that compute total run time must include logic that multiplies the run time by the order quantity and a time basis code adjustment factor. For example, if the time basis code is ''per thousand'', then total run time is run time multiplied by order quantity divided by one thousand.

1. Extract the capacity requirements for scheduled receipts and firm planned orders from the shop scheduling and dispatching data base.

The basic logic of the program is as follows:

A. Read the scheduled receipts and firm planned orders file sequentially to identify scheduled receipts and firm planned orders whose status is not closed or completed.

B. For each scheduled receipt or firm planned order, read an open operation record and check its status. For operations that are not closed or completed, write a record to the capacity planning work file.

C. Repeat step (b) for all operations attached to an order.

D. Repeat starting at step (a) until all orders are processed.

2. Schedule the planned orders. This requires several steps, similar to those performed in the shop scheduling and dispatching module for calculating operation schedule dates for scheduled receipts and firm planned orders. The simplest method of developing these programs is to modify the back scheduling programs for scheduled receipts.

Write a program to back schedule each planned order through its routing, compute opertion schedule dates for each operation, and write a record to the capacity planning work file. This program does a back scheduling calculation by processing the routing through two successive forward scheduling computations. In the first forward scheduling calculation, the system accumulates the lead time for the order. The due date is offset by this lead time to calculate the order start date. In the second forward scheduling calculation, the system computes the actual operation schedule dates from the computed order start date.

The basic logic of the program is as follows:

A. Read the planned order file sequentially to identify planned orders. Clear the lead time accumulator field.

B. For each planned order, read an operation record from the routing file and perform the following calculations:

1. If the operation record is the first operation, set the paperwork preparation and parts issue time. This is an arbitrary number usually 1-3 days. Add this to the lead time accumulator.

2. Calculate the time required for the operation.

   If the operation is an outside processing operation, then compute total elapsed time as:

   Elapsed time = outside processing time.

   If the operation is not an outside processing operation, then:

   Elapsed time = [Standard setup hours + Standard run hours / (number of men or machines x efficiency)] / (Shift 1 hours + Shift 2 hours + Shift 3)

   where

   Setup time = setup time from the routing.

   Standard run hours = (run time × order quantity × time basis code adjustment factor).

   Number of men or machines is taken from the routing if the field is nonzero. Otherwise, number of men or machines is taken from the work center record.

   Add elapsed time to the lead time accumulator.

3. Compute time between operations.

   Add scheduling time plus work center queue to the lead time accumulator.

C. Repeat step (b) for next operation record. Once all operations have been processed, convert the order due date to a shop date. Subtract the lead time accumulator from the shop date to compute an order start date.

D. For each planned order, read each record in the routing a second time and perform the following calculations:

1. Calculate the operation start date. If the operation record is the first operation, set the operation start date equal to the order start date plus paperwork preparation and parts issue time.

   If the operation record is not the first operation, set the operation start date equal to the prior operation due date plus time between operations.

2. Calculate the operation due date based on the time required for the operation.

Operation due date = operation start date + elapsed time.

If the operation is an outside processing operation, compute total elapsed time as:

Elapsed time = outside processing time.

If the operation is not an outside processing operation, then:

Elapsed time = [Standard setup hours + Standard run hours / (number of men or machines x efficiency)] / (Shift 1 hours + Shift 2 hours + Shift 3)

where

Standard setup hours = setup time from the routing.

Standard run hours = (Run time x order quantity x time basis code adjustment factor).

Number of men or machines is taken from the routing if the field is non-zero. Otherwise, the number of men or machines is taken from the work center record.

3. Compute time between operations.

Scheduling time plus work center queue time is time between operations.

4. Write a record to the capacity planning work file.

3. Provide capacity requirements planning reports. This has several parts:

A. Sort the capacity requirements from the capacity planning work file into sequence by work center and date.

B. Write a program to process the sorted capacity planning work file and summarize the capacity requirements. This program would summarize the capacity requirements by week for each work center and print a report similar to the example shown in Figure 57. In this program some decision is required about how the capacity requirements are prorated across the time between the operation start date and the operation due date. One method is to add the entire capacity requirement at the operation start date. Another method is to spread the capacity requirement over the entire duration of the operation.

C. Write an on-line inquiry program to display the detail capacity requirements for a work center. This program would access the capacity planning detail file by work center and show at least the following information on each capacity requirement:

1. Operation start date.

2. Item number.

3. Setup hours.

4. Run hours.

5. Teardown time.

6. Order number.

7. Operation number.

Chapter 31

Input/Output Control

This chapter explains the systems work and programming needed to provide an input/output control system. The design of this system has two basic steps. These are:

1. Maintain the input/output control information.

2. Provide an input/output control report.

1. There are several steps in maintaining the input/output control information:

A. Create an input/output control file, or expand the work center file to include input/output control data. In either case, the file stores the following information:

　1. Work center number.

　2. Work center description.

　3. Work center queue.

　4. Work center desired queue.

　5. Input tolerance in standard hours.

　6. Output tolerance in standard hours.

　7. Queue tolerance in standard hours.

　8. Planned input (eight weekly buckets).

　9. Actual input (eight weekly buckets).

　10. Planned output (eight weekly buckets).

　11. Actual output (eight weekly buckets).

　12. Planned queue (eight weekly buckets).

13. Actual queue (eight weekly buckets).

The number of buckets, in this case eight, is really somewhat arbitrary. Nearly any number of buckets greater than four and less than thirty or forty would do. The objective is to have several weeks of history, one current week, and several weeks of future information. If eight buckets are used, four could be history, the fifth would be the current week, and the remaining three would be the future.

B. Maintain the work center descriptive information, planned input, and planned output with transactions. A simple transaction system must be created to update these different pieces of information.

The planned input for current and future periods is a number developed and entered by a capacity planner. The capacity requirements over the first four weeks is often averaged by the capacity planner to give the planned input to a work center.

The planned output for current and future periods is also developed and entered manually. The shop people decide what they will be able to produce as output from the work center and this is entered as the planned output for the work center.

C. Maintain the actual input, the actual output, and the work center queue. This information is extracted from the shop scheduling and dispatching system by modifying some of the shop movement transactions and programs. These programs and modifications are listed below:

The actual input comes from move transactions. When a job is moved to a work center, the standard hours for the operation is added to the actual input bucket for the current week.

The actual output comes from the operation complete transaction. When an operation is completed, the standard hours for the operation is added to the actual output bucket for the current week.

The work center queue can be calculated during the program which prints the daily dispatch list. The additional logic would accumulate the hours for all the jobs that are physically present at a work center and store this as the work center queue. The status code in the operation record would be used to determine which jobs are physically present at a work center. Any orders with status codes indicating the job has been moved to the work center or that labor has been reported are present at the work center can be used to calculate the queue.

D. Write a program to calculate planned queue for the current and future periods. Planned queue at the end of the current period is the work center queue plus planned input less actual input less planned output plus actual output. For future periods, the planned queue at the end of the period is the planned queue at the end of the prior period plus planned input less planned output.

E. Write a program to roll the buckets once a week. In this program the first bucket is dropped from the system, each bucket is shifted, and a new bucket is added to the end. The simplest way to do this is to move the contents of the second bucket into the first, the third into the second, and so on. Then the last bucket can be zeroed.

2. Provide an input/output control report. This is a simple report listing the information in the input/output control data base. An example of this report appears in Appendix 12 in Figure 60.

Chapter 32

Vendor Scheduling and Negotiation

This chapter explains the systems and programming work needed to develop a vendor scheduling and negotiation module. The design of this system has five basic steps. These are:

1. Maintain sourcing information for each item.

2. Extract open and firm planned purchase orders from the scheduled receipts and firm planned orders file.

3. Project vendor requirements from planned orders.

4. Provide a reporting function that shows the vendor schedule for each vendor.

5. Provide a reporting function that shows negotiation information by commodity code.

The vendor scheduling and negotiation module requires several files, some of which are the same as those used in the MRP system. Files needed include:

1. Calendar.

   A. Calendar date.

   B. Day of the week (S, M, T, W, etc.).

   C. Work day (Y, N).

   D. Fiscal month start (Y, N).

   E. Fiscal month number (1-13).

   F. Shop calendar date.

2. Item master file (sequenced by item number).

   A. Item number.

   B. On-hand balance.

    C. Description.

    D. Lot size.

    E. Lead time.

    F. Safety stock.

    G. Shrinkage factor.

    H. Master schedule code (Y/N).

    I. Low-level code.

    J. Commodity code.

    K. Standard cost.

    L. Current cost.

3. Scheduled receipts and firm planned orders.

    A. Order number.

    B. Item number.

    C. Due date.

    D. Start date.

    E. Quantity.

    F. Status.

    G. Vendor number.

4. Planned order file.

    A. Item number.

    B. Due date.

    C. Start date.

    D. Quantity.

5. Vendor file.

    A. Vendor number.

    B. Vendor name.

    C. Address.

6. Item sourcing file.

    A. Item number.

    B. Vendor number.

    C. Percentage of total volume.

D. Manufacturer's part number.

7. Vendor scheduling and negotiation work file.

A. Item number.

B. Vendor number.

C. Order due date.

D. Quantity.

E. Percentage of total volume.

F. Order number.

G. Order status (scheduled receipt, firm planned, planned).

H. Commodity code.

I. Standard cost.

J. Current cost.

1. Write a simple transaction system to maintain the vendor file and the item sourcing file. The transaction system should include transactions to add, change, and delete information from the files.

2. Extract the data for scheduled receipts and firm planned orders from the scheduled receipts and firm planned order file and write it to the vendor scheduling and negotiation work file.
   The basic logic of the program is as follows:

A. Read the scheduled receipts and firm planned orders file sequentially to identify scheduled receipts and firm planned orders whose status is not closed or completed.

B. For each scheduled receipt or firm planned order, write a record to the vendor scheduling and negotiation work file.

C. Repeat starting at (a) until all orders are processed.

2. Extract the data for planned orders. This requires several steps:

A. Read the planned order file sequentially to identify planned purchase orders. Retrieve the item information for each item with a planned purchase order.

B. For each planned order, read an item sourcing record from the item sourcing file. For each item sourcing record, write a record to the vendor scheduling and negotiation work file.

C. Repeat step (b) until all sources have been processed.

D. Repeat starting at step (a) until all planned orders have been processed.

3. Provide vendor scheduling and negotiation reports. This has several parts:

   A. Sort the records from the vendor scheduling and negotiation work file into sequence by vendor number, item number, and date.

   B. Write a program to process the sorted work file, summarize the vendor schedules into weekly periods, and print a vendor scheduling report. This program would summarize the schedule by week for each vendor and item and print a report similar to the example shown in Appendix 12 in Figure 61.

   In this program some decision is required about how the planned orders should be shown. One method is to show the full planned order quantity to each vendor that can source the item. In this method, the percentage of volume data should be displayed. Another method is to multiply the planned order quantity by the percentage of volume information and display the anticipated planned order release.

   Most companies prefer to display the full planned order quantity and the percentage of volume data.

   C. Sort the records from the vendor scheduling and negotiation work file into sequence by commodity code and item number.

   D. Write a program to process the sorted work file, summarize planned orders by item, and print a vendor negotiation report. This program should produce a report like that shown in Appendix 12 in Figure 62.

Two-Level Master Production Scheduling

Two-level master production scheduling is the method for assisting a master scheduler in coordinating related master production schedules. For example, in master scheduling automobiles, the master production schedule for engines must be coordinated with the master production schedule for bodies, accessory options, etc. The right number of 4-cylinder, V-6, and V-8 engines need to be scheduled at the right time to support the production of cars. And changes in the production of cars, as well as changes in the mix of options being selected on customer orders, need to be reflected in the master production schedules for the options.

The Standard System explains a simple and effective method for passing information from the master production schedule for a type of product (say automobiles) to the master production schedules for the product options (in this case, engines, trim package options, etc.) The information that is passed from one master production schedule to a group of related master production schedules is called the production forecast. In the method explained in the Standard System, the production forecasts are computed using the uncommited portion of the master production schedule for the type of product and a planning bill of material.

The method for developing production forecasts explained in the Standard System works well for many companies. However, some companies use a somewhat different calculation. The purpose of this appendix is to explain both the normal calculation and a somewhat more complicated alternate calculation. This alternate calculation has proven effective in some situations.

NORMAL METHOD FOR DEVELOPING PRODUCTION FORECASTS

The normal method for developing production forecasts uses the available-to-promise quantity for the type of product. In this calculation, the available-to-promise quantity for the type of product is recomputed as the customer orders are promised. New production forecast quantities for all the options are generated based on the new available to promise. In effect, the production forecasts are recalculated each time a customer preference reveals itself. The master scheduler is immediately alerted to trends in customer orders that he may need to be aware of, and which might also cause a change to the master production schedule for the product options. For example, if customer orders were running at a higher than predicted rate for V-8 engines, this calculation would detect it. The master scheduler would be notified so he can review the situation. He can decide whether or not it makes sense to change the master production schedule.

Figure 37 is an example to the master production schedule report for a product being master scheduled at two levels using this method. This example shows the extension of the available-to-promise quantity by the planning bills of material. In the sample reports, the master schedule options (V-8 and V-6 engines) each have a quantity per assembly in the planning bill of material of 50%. And in the sample report, the V-8 engine is selling at a higher than predicted rate.

The assumption in this method of calculating the production forecasts is that the percentages specified in the planning bill of material will hold for future customer orders. It's like flipping a coin. The outcome of the next flip is 50/50,

Figure 37
Master Production Schedule Reports

TYPE OF PRODUCT

	Period							
	1/09	1/16	1/23	1/30	2/06	2/13	2/20	2/27
Forecast					6	4	10	10
Customer Orders		20		14		6		
Master Schedule		20		20		20		20
Projected Available	0	0	0	6	0	10	0	10
Available To Promise		0		6		14		20

PLANNING BILL OF MATERIAL = 50%
MODULE BEING MASTER SCHEDULED

	Period							
	1/09	1/16	1/23	1/30	2/06	2/13	2/20	2/27
Production Forecast		0		3		7		10
Customer Orders		12		7		5		
Master Schedule		12		12		10		10
Projected Available	0	0	0	2	2	0	0	0
Available To Promise		0		5		5		10

regardless of the outcome of the earlier flips. Even if heads have come up the last ten times, the likelihood of the next flip being heads is 50%. In this approach to developing production forecasts, the system assumes that the likelihood of the next customer order specifying a certain module will not be affected by earlier customer orders. If this is true (the chance that the next customer order will specify a V-8 engine is still 50% regardless of how many are already sold), then the available-to-promise method should be used to develop the production forecasts. The only problem in this assumption could occur when sales of an option seem to be more than the production forecast, but end up being close to the original forecast, or when there are very small lots (like three or four units) in the master production schedule. When the available to promise is exploded to create production forecasts, the master scheduling system recalculates the production forecasts for all the options each time an option is sold. When the production forecasts are recalculated for all the options, the master scheduling system may recommend that some options be rescheduled to earlier dates (options selling more than forecast) and others be rescheduled to later dates (options selling less than forecast). If sales of the options eventually end up close to what was originally forecast, the master scheduler may have had to review a number of exception messages that were of little real value. Note that the master scheduler is not forced to take action or change the master production schedule in any way. All that is required is that the master scheduler review the situation to see if the master schedule needs to be changed. When this happens a lot, and the exception messages aren't of any real value, some companies choose to use a different calculation of the production forecasts.

ALTERNATE METHOD FOR COMPUTING PRODUCTION FORECASTS

The other way to develop production forecasts is to explode the entire master schedule quantity and ignore customer orders until an option is actually oversold. In this method, the total demand on the product options remains the same until one of the options is oversold. The only time that the production forecasts are recomputed for all the related options is when the forecast on one of them has been proven wrong (the option is oversold).

In this method, customer orders reduce the production forecast on the options. When an option is oversold, the system reduces the production forecast to zero and switches to using the customer orders for that option as the demand in the master production schedule. In addition, the production forecasts are recomputed for the related options. In this logic the system would reduce the production forecasts for the related options. This recalculation is necessary because the total of the production forecasts and customer orders for the options must be in line with the master production schedule for the type of product. For example, unless this logic exists, it would be possible to show 150 4-cylinder, V-6, and V-8 engine options required to support production of 100 automobiles. Overselling the V-8 engine option in a period means that the 4-cylinder and V-6 engine options must be undersold for the same period. Consequently, the production forecasts for these options should be reduced by the amount oversold on the V-8. The logic to calculate production forecasts using this method has three main parts:

1. Reducing the production forecast and checking for an oversold option.

2. Recalculating the production forecasts for the options that were not selected if an option is oversold.

3. Recomputing the future production forecasts for all the options.

The first section of logic reduces the production forecast for a module by the amount of the customer order. If the new production forecast quantity is greater than zero, the option is not oversold. In this case, no further processing is required. On the other hand, if the new production forecast is less than zero, the option has been oversold. In this case, the production forecasts for any other related options need to be reduced by the amount the option was oversold. In addition, in order to keep the total forecast correct, the system would reach ahead to adjust the production forecasts in later periods. For the product options that were not oversold, this means that the production forecasts in later periods would be increased. For the product option that was oversold, the production forecasts in later time periods would be reduced by the amount the option was oversold. By reaching ahead and recalculating the production forecasts in this way, the system would attempt to keep the total demand on the options the same as the original forecast. This method seems to work well anytime the original production forecast for a period is reasonably accurate.

The production forecasts for the options are not changed until an option is oversold; there are no recalculations until the forecast is proven wrong. And even in the situation where the production forecast is wrong for one period, the system assumes that over the horizon the forecast will be correct. This logic reduces the number of reschedule in and reschedule out exception messages produced by the system. Consequently, it may also reduce some clerical effort associated with reviewing master schedule items with exception messages.

Figure 38 is an example of a master production schedule report for a product being master production scheduled at two levels using this method. This example shows the reduction of the production forecasts because of customer orders that have been promised. In these sample reports, as in the earlier example, the V-8 engine has a quantity per assembly in the planning bill of material of 50%, and the V-6 engine has a quantity per of 50%. The V-8 engine option is selling at a rate higher than predicted by the planning bill of material. In effect, this method of generating production forecasts is like forecasting the type of ball that you'll pull out of a barrel of fifty black and fifty white balls. When you start to pull balls out of the barrel, the likelihood that you'll pull a black ball is 50%. After you pull fifty balls and forty have been black, the chances of pulling a black ball on the next try is no longer 50%, it's 20%. On average the chance of pulling a black ball is 50%; at any point during the process of reaching into the barrel the probability changes. It may be higher or lower depending on what's already been pulled.

In practice this calculation seems to work best for the situations described above: products with low volumes, like four or five units per week, or whenever the

Figure 38
Master Production Schedule Reports

TYPE OF PRODUCT

	Period							
	1/09	1/16	1/23	1/30	2/06	2/13	2/20	2/27
Forecast					6	4	10	10
Customer Orders		20		14		6		
Master Schedule		20		20		20		20
Projected Available	0	0	0	6	0	10	0	10
Available To Promise		0		6		14		20

PLANNING BILL OF MATERIAL = 50%
MODULE BEING MASTER SCHEDULED

	Period							
	1/09	1/16	1/23	1/30	2/06	2/13	2/20	2/27
Production Forecast		0		3		5		10
Customer Orders		12		7		5		
Master Schedule		12		12		10		10
Projected Available	0	0	0	2	2	2	2	2
Available To Promise		0		3		5		10

options chosen on customer orders eventually come out close to the forecast percentages in the planning bills of material. It makes sense in any situation where the total forecast is close to being right, even though one option may be selling more or less than expected right now.

The major drawback to this method is the complexity of the calculations. It's difficult to look at the production forecast for an option and see how it was developed. The method is not as transparent as the method of exploding the available to promise. In addition, this method is not as effective in identifying trends in customer preferences.

Consequently, many companies may be be unsure of the best way to develop production forecasts. Without any evidence for or against either method, most companies should probably start by using the method which develops production forecasts by exploding the available to promise. The method for exploding the available to promise is superior for picking up trends in customer preferences. And the master scheduler does not have to change the master production schedule when an exception message is produced. The system is only providing information that it may make sense to review the master production schedule and decide if there is a trend. If exploding the available to promise proves to generate too many unnecessary exception messages, or in some way proves ineffective for displaying the demands for the product options, then it might make sense to change to the other method of developing production forecasts.

Bucketless and Bucketed Systems

The differences between bucketed and bucketless systems and the inherent problems in a bucketed system are summarized in this appendix.

The terms ''bucketed'' and ''bucketless'' refer to the way gross requirements, scheduled receipts, and planned orders are stored in the system. In a bucketed system, a fixed number of accumulators are set up within the system. There are a certain number of gross requirements accumulators, scheduled receipts accumulators, and planned order accumulators. All accumulators have a date and a quantity. The quantity is the real accumulator and the date is just a piece of descriptive information.

Bucketless systems are distinguished by the lack of a fixed number of accumulators. An unlimited number of gross requirements, scheduled receipts, and planned orders are available as needed. Each has its own record containing information such as the due date, quantity, order number, parent item number, and other descriptive information. Records are created for these gross requirements, scheduled receipts, and planned orders only as needed and no fixed number of gross requirements, scheduled receipts, and planned orders are required.

A bucketless system solves a number of problems that exist in a bucketed system. These problems are the following:

PROBLEM #1—THE PLANNING HORIZON

In a bucketed system, the number of gross requirements buckets and the time span of these buckets defines the planning horizon. For example, fifty two weekly buckets define a one-year planning horizon. Any requirements beyond the last bucket cannot be accommodated in the system and they are lost. Consequently the planning horizon is more or less frozen. The number of buckets is a technical systems parameter. Changing it generally requires a fair sized systems and programming effort.

In a bucketless system, an unlimited number of storage areas exist, and the planning horizon can be varied at will by the users of the system. In a bucketless system, it is possible to have one planning horizon on some products and another planning horizon for other products.

PROBLEM #2—A LIMITED NUMBER OF BUCKETS

In a bucketed system, there is no requirement to completely cover the planning horizon with certain types of buckets. In the case of scheduled receipts and planned orders, the system could, for example, have fifty two weekly gross requirements buckets and twenty scheduled receipts buckets.

The obvious problem occurs on an item with twenty one scheduled receipts. As far as the system is concerned, the twenty-first order does not exist. The result is a serious error since the system fails to give a valid simulation of reality for that item, as well as those items below it in the product structure. The best solution to this problem is to completely cover the planning horizon with all the different types of buckets, regardless of the amount of disk storage required.

A bucketless system has a virtually unlimited number of scheduled receipts and planned orders. As a result, there is no problem in covering the planning horizon.

PROBLEM #3—EXCEPTION CHECKING AND LEAD TIME DISTORTION

In a bucketed system, all dates are in terms of the gross requirement bucket dates. Any differences in timing between gross requirements and scheduled receipts in the same bucket are ignored. In a system with weekly buckets, a gross requirement due the first day of the bucket and a scheduled receipt due the last day of the bucket is not recognized as a problem. Actually, there is a problem since the parts are needed four days before they are scheduled to be completed.

In a bucketless system, all netting, exception checking, and order planning are done in days. Therefore, a gross requirement due the first day of the week and a scheduled receipt due the last day of the week will be considered a problem and an exception message will be generated.

People with bucketed systems generally establish some rules for assigning due dates because of this problem. Rather than having orders due anytime during the week, scheduled receipts are generally due on one specific day of the week. For example, one rule is to make all scheduled receipts due in the middle of the week. However, even with this rule, the problem still exists: the requirements could be needed early in the week or late in the week, and the system is unable to recognize this. On the other hand, the shop has some rules for completing orders and, if the orders are due in the middle of the week, the due date of the scheduled receipts and the date of the gross requirements can only be off by one or two days and not as much as four days.

In a bucketed system, planned orders are offset by a number of buckets before they are exploded and posted as gross requirements. Because of this, the lead times are effectively rounded up to multiples of the bucket length. For example, in a system with weekly buckets, a lead time of less than one week is rounded up to one week, and a lead time of six days is rounded up to two weeks. This distortion of lead time can be a problem when several levels are accumulated, resulting in one or more weeks of distortion. This could happen, for example, in a manufacturing process where the lead times are two to three days. A bucketed system with weekly buckets will round these lead times up to one week. If the product structure is four levels deep, the date the raw materials are needed could be in error by two weeks or so.

In a bucketless system, order planning is done by date. The lead time in days is used to offset and explode the planned orders. No distortion of lead time occurs.

PROBLEM #4—DETAILS TO SUMMARY INFORMATION

A bucket is an accumulator and as such does not retain the details of what went into its total. A separate system must exist to either preserve this detail or to recreate it when the planner needs to know what makes up a bucketed total. Pegging and open order details are examples of this type of detail information.

In a bucketless system, each gross requirement, scheduled receipt, or planned order is stored in detail form. When needed for display or reporting, these details can be summarized, but the detail information is always there.

A note of perspective on bucketed and bucketless systems is appropriate here. Both types of systems will work. A bucketless system solves a number of problems that exist in a bucketed system. These problems are significant, but they are not usually critical to the success or failure of the system.

Material Planning Logic That Does Not Make the Rescheduling Assumption

This appendix explains the problems that exist in netting logic that does not make the rescheduling assumption. This type of logic plans a new order for dates earlier than an existing scheduled receipt. It does not assume the existing order will be rescheduled to an earlier date.

Planning a new order that is due to be completed before an existing order goes against the good sense of a planner or buyer. A shop order that is on the floor and is being worked on has the best chance of any order to be completed by a date earlier than the current due date. Releasing a new order to the shop floor to be completed before an existing order doesn't make sense. Taken to its extreme, this logic would order material not based on the number of end items to manufactured, but based on the number of times the schedule has been changed.

Logic that does not make the rescheduling assumption will cause items to be planned incorrectly. However, this is only part of the problem. Once a new order has been planned, gross requirements are generated and posted to the component parts. These requirements are incorrect because their origin is an incorrect planned order. The effect is a progression of errors through the system, and the number of errors grows geometrically with each level of the product structure. Gross requirements, planned orders, and exception messages soon become meaningless. The system fails because it is no longer a simulation of reality.

Given the problem of an order needed sooner than its due date, a computer, with the limited ability to solve problems, can only make the most reasonable assumption. The computer must assume that the order can be rescheduled and point out the situation to the planner and let him take care of any problems.

Automatic Rescheduling

Automatic rescheduling is a misnomer. Nothing is automatic about rescheduling since decisions must be made by people about what can and cannot be done. The question is really one of how accountability will be maintained as rescheduling decisions are made.

Two groups of people need to evaluate whether or not an order can or should be rescheduled. Both planners and shop people participate in the process of rescheduling orders.

Planners are responsible for evaluating the reschedule to make sure that it is valid and was not caused by a negative on-hand balance or an incorrect or unrealistic gross requirement. The planner is also required to look for alternate ways to solve the problem in cases where a significant reschedule is requested. For example, one or two pieces of scrap may cause an order to be needed ten weeks earlier. In such a case, the planner may be able to avoid this reschedule by changing the quantity of the parent order. Maybe the order was a normal lot size that could be reduced by a few pieces and not cause any problems. In such a case, the planner should recognize these types of situations and solve the problem without forcing the shop to jump through loops just to satisfy some arbitrary ordering rule. Finally, the planner is responsible for bypassing the trivial or impractical reschedules. Trivial reschedules are reschedules of a day or so on a purchase order which are not worth calling the vendor and forcing him to review the order and respond on a new delivery date.

Shop people are responsible for agreeing to the rescheduled due date on an order or changing the date. They must review whether or not the new due date can be met and what problems are likely to result in the process of meeting it. The shop people should not be forced to review each of the reschedules, but they should review where there could be a question about whether the new due date can be met. The shop people will be held accountable for meeting the new date.

In a system where the due dates of the orders are not changed automatically by the computer, the planner is responsible for evaluating the reschedule and also talking with the shop people about any reschedules that could cause a problem in the shop. The shop people are responsible for reviewing the requested reschedule dates and either agreeing to the new date or refusing the new date with a reason.

Only when the shop people have agreed that they can meet the new date will the due date of the order be changed. Using this method, the responsibility requirements are clear and straightforward. The planner reviews the exception messages, he reviews the reschedules with the shop people, and the shop people agree to the ones they feel can be made. People are responsible for developing the plan and they will be held accountable for meeting the plan.

In a situation where the computer is allowed to change the due date of the order before the planner or shop people look at the change, the responsibility is still there. The planners and shop people must review all changed due dates and they must reverse any that are not correct. An incorrect reschedule could be caused, for example, by a negative on-hand balance. The shop people must also review the changed due dates to make sure that they actually can meet the new due date on the order. If either the planners or the shop people find a reschedule to be unrealistic or otherwise incorrect, they must make the change to put an attainable due date on the order. The responsibilities of people in this method are not as clean and easy to administer. Instead of having people review and agree to a plan, a plan is being made and they are responsible for catching any problems and reversing them.

Most working MRP systems today are of the type where the exception messages are generated and the planner and shop people are responsible for evaluating the reschedule before the due date of the order is changed. This method defines the responsibility requirements more clearly and seems to be the most effective kind of system to administer. However, there are some systems that do work where the due dates of the manufacturing orders are changed by the computer.

A typical misconception that leads people to conclude that the computer should change the order due dates is that rescheduling occurs at many levels in the product structure and rescheduling manually would consume too much time to accurately reflect the correct priorities. This argument assumes that rescheduling an order will affect the component requirements and require rescheduling of the component orders. The resultant chain reaction of reschedules, the argument goes, can only be reflected to the next lower level when the plan is run again showing the new requirements to the lower levels. In a regenerative system, the plan is run weekly and, so the argument goes, five weeks would be required to pass new priorities down five levels.

This assumption is incorrect and no chain reaction of reschedules is created. Rescheduling a scheduled receipt at one level does not typically affect the requirements for the component parts. In most cases, the component parts have been issued and are sitting on the shop floor waiting to be worked on. Rescheduling the due date of the order in this situation cannot possibly cause any rescheduling of component scheduled receipts.

Safety Stock and Safety Time

Both safety stock and safety time are ways to change the date an item is needed in MRP. They are different methods for doing the same thing. Safety stock is a quantity that is planned to be kept on hand at all times. By planning to keep this quantity on hand, it will be available for exceptional situations, for example, a policy to keep 500 pieces of an item on hand at all times could be stared using a 500 piece safety stock.

Safety time is a way to ask for delivery or completion of an item before it is needed. For example, asking for delivery two weeks before the item is needed is safety time. Safety time has the effect of keeping a minimum quantity on hand at all times. The quantity is the sum of the gross requirements over the safety time (in this case the requirements over two weeks). There are a number of things to keep in mind when using either safety stock or safety time. These are:

1. It should be simple.

2. It should be easy to understand.

3. It should be easy to update.

4. Safety stock and safety time should only be used in certain situations.

5. Safety stock and safety time distort priorities.

IT SHOULD BE SIMPLE

In the past, safety stock has been calculated using some fairly complicated mathematical formulas. It would also be possible to do the same type of thing with safety time, although it is not done as frequently. Yet, all the precise and involved mathematical calculations of safety stock hide the fact that these are just guesses.

Formulas for safety stock calculations assume two things. One is that the future will be like the past—that the statistical deviations which have occurred in the past will happen the same way in the future. In many cases this isn't remotely true; in others it is a bad guess but better than nothing. The other assumption is that the lead time is known and fixed. In practice lead times vary depending on how badly an item is needed, and so a fixed lead time is a poor approximation. So, as long as its necessary to guess, it makes little sense to hide behind the illusion of mathematical precision. Its better to be honest about it and have someone decide on, for example, two weeks safety time or a safety stock of 400 instead of spending a great deal of time and effort to calculate a precise safety stock of 537.

IT SHOULD BE EASY TO UNDERSTAND

MRP is a people system and it depends on people understanding what is going on in the system. Using a safety stock of 300, or safety time of two weeks is easy to understand. Someone has evaluated the situation and decided on a quantity of safety stock or a safety time. This is much easier to understand than the explanation of how the safety stock formulas are developed and used.

IT SHOULD BE EASY TO UPDATE

Safety time is generally easier to update. To use one or two weeks of safety time means that the planner can set it and forget it. If the demand for the item increases, for example, two weeks of safety time will mean that more is on hand. This compensates for the change in demand. Using safety stock, the planner will have to periodically recalculate and update the safety stocks. Safety time also handles temporary changes in demand, like promotions, easily. A large change in demand due to the promotion will cause the safety time (two weeks for example) to result in more on hand during the promotion, and then drop to the normal quantity after the promotion is over.

SAFETY STOCK AND SAFETY TIME SHOULD ONLY BE USED IN CERTAIN SITUATIONS

Safety stock and safety time are used differently in MRP than in conventional inventory management. It used to be that safety stock was considered good for every item. In MRP the situation is different. The strength of MRP is that it tells the truth about when items are needed. Safety stock or safety time ask for items when they are not needed. Therefore safety stock or safety time should only be used where something is quite likely to happen and there is no other way to identify it to MRP. These are situations where there is an uncertainty of demand, or an uncertainty of supply.

Uncertainty of demand can exist for a number of different types of items. Basically these are independent demand items and dependent demand items.

Independent demand items are items like master schedule items, spare parts items, end items in branch warehouses (the method for handling these items is explained in the Distribution Resource Planning topic), or end items that are not significant enough to master schedule (these items are explained in the master production scheduling topic).

The items that are handled in MRP (spare parts, end items in branch warehouses, and end items that are not significant enough to master schedule) all have a legitimate uncertainty of demand. The forecasted demand will be wrong in most weeks. Sometimes the forecast will be too low and other times too high. The weeks where the demand is above forecast are the reason for either safety stock or safety time.

Master schedule items have an uncertainty of demand, but that should be handled in the master schedule. The master scheduler may choose to plan more in the master production schedule than is forecasted to sell. Then as the date becomes nearer, he can either promise that extra quantity to sales which have exceeded the forecast, or remove it from the master production schedule. This is sometimes called a marketing hedge.

There are a couple of things to keep in mind about a marketing hedge. First of all, a marketing hedge is a part of the master production schedule and so you must be able to actually produce it if necessary. If the marketing hedge is used as a way to load up the master production schedule just to play it safe, then MRP is no longer a simulation of reality. The capacity requirements and gross requirements are false since they are larger than what is really needed. Another thing to keep in mind when using a marketing hedge is to decide when to remove it from the master production schedule if it has not been sold. The closer the marketing hedge comes to the current date, the more components are being made or purchased, and the more labor is being expended on these items.

Dependent demand items may have an uncertainty of demand, but normally only in unusual situations. These happen most often when the bill of material quantity is variable. An example of this would be in the manufacture of a milk product. The milk which is used as an ingredient varies from lot to lot. Sometimes it is high in sugar (or some other quality), and other times it is low. As a result, the amount of sugar that has to be added to the product varies. There is no way to know for sure how much sugar will be required until the milk arrives and can be tested. The bill of material for the product includes sugar and uses an average quantity as the quantity per assembly. However, significant variations around this average can occur. This would be a legitimate example of an uncertainty of demand for sugar, and so safety stock or safety time would make sense.

The other use safety stock or safety time would be where there is an uncertainty of supply. An uncertainty of supply does not mean that on occasion the vendor fails to deliver on time. Uncertainty of supply means that there is some special situation or persistent problem which requires that extraordinary measures be taken. Typically, the reliability of delivery and the impact of a shortage determine whether or not safety stock or safety time are needed. An example would be bearings that are shipped from overseas. Because of the great distance, the different freight carriers involved, customs, etc. the delivery reliability is poor. In addition, these bearings are used in most of the products this company produces and so any shortage will just about shut the plant down. This is an example where safety stock or safety time make sense.

SAFETY STOCK AND SAFETY TIME DISTORT PRIORITIES

Whether an item is an independent demand item or a dependent demand item, safety stock or safety time distorts priorities. MRP doesn't truly tell when the items are needed. So, unless there is an uncertainty of supply or an uncertainty of demand, safety stock or safety time should not be used. In those situations where safety stock or safety time does apply, the planner should still be able to see the actual need date for the order. This is the date, ignoring safety stock or safety time, when a shortage is projected to occur.

Dynamic Order Quantities

Dynamic order quantities are recalculated by the computer each time MRP is run in an attempt to balance the ordering and carrying cost. Dynamic order quantities are appealing because they seem to offer the capability to always order the most economical quantity. In practice, however, these dynamic ordering policies have some problems.

1. In a dynamic ordering calculation, numbers of doubtful accuracy are operated on with great precision. The ordering cost is a guess and the carrying cost is an estimate. Any order quantities derived using these numbers are subject to large degrees of error, generally somewhere in the area of plus or minus 50%.

2. The balancing of ordering and carrying costs is a relatively insensitive function. A large change in the order quantity makes a relatively small difference in dollars over the course of a year. Halving or doubling the order quantity only changes the total carrying cost by around 25%.

3. There are other factors besides the ordering and carrying cost that must be considered when deciding on an order quantity. These are things like a practical quantity on the shop floor, adequate skids or baskets, any limited lifetime or deterioration in the item, and extended running times on key pieces of equipment. Also to be considered are the restraints on setups and order picking. A deluge of work or a lack of work for the order pickers or setup people are also reasons to tread carefully in using order quantities which are determined solely by the balancing of ordering and carrying costs. These other factors could easily erase any anticipated savings, especially when the relationship between the order quantity and the total ordering and carrying cost is so insensitive.

4. Dynamic ordering policies continue to change the order quantity even after the component supply schedules have been firmed up. The recalculation of the order quantity will continue to cause changing gross requirements for the component parts. These changing requirements can cause rescheduling and ordering to satisfy a different order quantity. This ordering and rescheduling is not necessary to meet

the assembly schedule but is only needed to meet the newest calculation of the optimum order quantity. The confusion and the wasted time and effort far exceed any savings from using the optimum order quantity.

5. The most serious problem with the dynamic ordering policies is one of accountability. The calculation of the order quantity is removed from the planner's control. The order quantity is determined by a calculation and not by a planner. Yet the order quantity is the type of thing that a planner should review and be held accountable for. The different factors and elements in determining the order quantity are the types of things that a person must evaluate. A person needs to determine with the shop people what is a workable quantity to have on the shop floor at one time, or what is a reasonable order quantity considering a limited lifetime for the item. By removing the order quantity from the control of the planner, he or she can no longer be held accountable for any problems that are caused by an incorrect order quantity. For example, if the order quantity calculation produced an order quantity which left several thousand pieces to be scrapped, or ordered a quantity that would not fit in the receiving dock or the paint department, who is accountable? How can the planner realistically be held accountable for this type of thing? The only way to maintain this accountability is to use simple ordering policies like fixed and lot-for-lot, and have the planner review the order quantity.

Offset Gross Requirements Dates

The feature to give gross requirements a different date than the start date of the planned order is meant for components that enter the assembly at a significantly different time than the start date of the order. If component parts enter the assembly a week or so later than the start date of the order, the priorities on the components will be significantly in error if the gross requirements have the start date of the order. The gross requirements should show the date the component parts are needed in the assembly. If a component enters the assembly less than a week from the start date of the order, the option to give the gross requirements a different date could still be used, but in general would not be. Most companies do not want to have several parts issued for components which are used within several days of each other. So for all practical purposes, these components are treated as though they are assembled at the same time.

Offsetting the gross requirement dates is done in the planned order explosion logic. A lead time offset is stored in the product structure file. This lead time offset is zero for those components that are being asked for on the start date of the planned order. On those components that are needed in assembly after the start date of the planned order, the lead time offset would be the time after the start date that the parts are needed. For example, if some components are needed in assembly two weeks after the start date of the order, the lead time offset would be two weeks. As the planned order is exploded, the product structure record is used to generate the gross requirements, and the lead time offset is applied to the planned order start date to give the gross requirements date.

When this feature is used, some supporting systems must be available as well. If all the components are not going to be called for on the start date of the planned order, a system must exist to notify the planner and the stockroom people when it is time to pick these other items. There will be several stockroom picks for the same assembly, and this must be provided for in the component availability check, the component allocation logic, and the picking list.

The component availability check logic bypasses the components that are not due to be picked. Component availability checking takes place only on items due to be issued. The system also includes a reminder to signal the planner when it is time to check the availability and produce a picking list for the remaining components.

The allocation logic bypasses the components which are not ready to be picked. In some systems this is done by creating a special class of allocations. These special allocations are treated like gross requirements and are not treated as though they are needed right away.

The picking list logic prints only the items that are due to be picked. Components that will be picked later are bypassed and listed later in another pick list.

Many times people are tempted to use lead time offsets to avoid restructuring the bills of material. This happens most often when a subassembly exists but is not shown in the bills of material. If a subassembly exists, the bills should be restructured to show this. Attempting to use the lead time offset to avoid restructuring does not solve the problem. If the product contains a subassembly and the bills of material do not reflect the way the product is built, then MRP is in error and is no longer a simulation of what happens.

Sequencing Items for Replanning

Most systems use one of three different mechanisms for recording, in low level code sequence, those items scheduled for replanning. These mechanisms are:

1. Level chains.

2. Trigger files.

3. Work files.

Level chains link all items at the same level of the bill of material together. A special record, the level table, stores the address of the first item scheduled for replanning at each level. The item master record for each item stores the address of the next item scheduled for replanning, which in turn points to the next, etc. The last item does not point to an item, but contains a message like the term END. In this way, items are "chained" together by low-level code.

Items can be inserted into the level chains by "pushing down" the low-level chain: the record containing the start of the level chain is read, the starting address moved to the item master record for the item being inserted into the chain, and a new starting address created using the address of the item being inserted.

MRP processing logic selects the first level to be replanned by reading the level table record and finding the address of the first item. After each item is replanned, the system reads the next item in the low-level chain (the address stored in the item master file for the last item replanned). Once the system reaches the end of a low-level, the level table is reread for the first item at the next low-level code.

The selection process continues until all items that require replanning have been processed. Using this mechanism, the system can start at the top of the bill of material (low-level code 0), and work its way to the bottom.

A trigger file is another way to mark items for replanning. In this method, a record containing the item number and low-level code is created for each item scheduled for replanning. The trigger file is sorted into low-level code sequence before any items are replanned.

MRP processing logic selects the first level to be replanned by reading the sorted trigger file sequentially. After each item is replanned, the system removes the trigger record and selects the next item for processing. Once the system has replanned a level, the trigger file is sorted again into low-level code sequence since replanning at one level may cause lower levels to be entered into planning.

The sorting and selection process continues until all items that require replanning have been processed. Just as in the other methods, processing starts at the top of the product structure and works its way to the bottom.

The third mechanism for marking and sequencing items for replanning is by using work files containing the gross requirements. A record for each gross requirement, allocation, forecast requirement, and safety stock requirement is written to the work file. Each gross requirement record stores the item number, low-level code, date and quantity. Typically the initialization process also writes a record to the work file for any items with a scheduled receipt or firm planned order: in these cases, the gross requirement quantity is zero.

Writing records to the gross requirement work file includes an item into the planning process. The gross requirements work file is the list of items to process for each low level. At the beginning of the replanning process, the work file is sorted by low-level code. After a level has been processed, the work file is resorted.

As in the method using a trigger file, the sorting and selection process continues until all items that require replanning have been processed. Processing starts at the top of the bill of material and works its way to the bottom.

Firm Planned Orders

There are a number of situations where the firm planned order is used to allow MRP to truly be a simulation of reality. These are exceptions to the normal ordering rules; situations where the planner needs to be able to override the normal ordering rules. Some of the most common of these situations are listed below with the solution using firm planned orders:

PROBLEM   A component part will be late. However, it is possible to make up the lost time during fabrication and assembly of the parent parts. Several orders will start later than the planned order dates in MRP. How does the planner show the correct component need dates to the other components?

SOLUTION   The planner can enter firm planned orders for any fabrication or assembly orders that will be starting late. The start date of the firm planned orders is the date the planner expects the orders to actually start. This causes the component gross requirements to be generated for the right dates. If the system allows both a start date and a due date or a due date and a lead time for firm planned orders (some systems allow both a start date and a due date, others allow only a due date), the due date of the late component order is the start date of the order for the parent item.

PROBLEM   A component part cannot be supplied in a quantity large enough to satisfy the gross requirements. However, the gross requirements are coming from a planned order which is in the quantity of normal lot size for the item. This lot size can be split in an emergency. How does the planner show that a short lot will be produced (this affects the timing of the remaining planned orders) and show the correct gross requirement quantities to the components?

SOLUTION   The planner can enter a firm planned order with a quantity equal to the quantity of the short lot. This firm planned order will be used in the netting calculation in MRP and timing of the remaining planned orders will be based on the short lot. The firm planned order will also show the correct gross requirements quantities to the component parts.

PROBLEM   A capacity overload exists in the future, but there is available capacity during some earlier time periods. How does the planner move work up to an earlier date and make sure the components or raw material will be available?

SOLUTION   The planner can identify some of the jobs from the overloaded time periods and move them up using firm planned orders. The firm planned orders for these items are entered for the time periods when available capacity exists. These firm planned orders appear in the capacity planning reports during the time periods where available capacity exists. The firm planned orders would create gross requirements for components or raw material at the earlier dates when capacity is available.

PROBLEM   A vendor is likely to go on strike, a department is going to be shut down for maintenance, or, for any reason, the planner wants to schedule items to be completed at a date different from the need date in MRP.

SOLUTION   The planner can enter firm planned orders to schedule production whenever he wants. If he wants to schedule purchase order releases, or manufacturing production at a time when planned orders are normally be created, he can do it using firm planned orders.

Appendix 10
Full Pegging

Full pegging is an extension to single-level pegging and traces the gross requirements all the way up to the master production schedule. Single-level pegging forms a link for the planner and shows him the parent items causing the gross requirements for a component. If the planner is interested in tracing the requirements up to the master production schedule, he must do so one level at a time. This is done by using single-level pegging to find the parent item number causing particular gross requirements. The planner would then use the time phased MRP report for the parent item to analyze the situation and if necessary use single-level pegging to find the source of the gross requirements for the parent. Single level pegging at each level will show the planner the parent item, and he can trace it all the way up the product structure. Full pegging does this process automatically. The computer goes through the same steps the planner would go through to trace the requirements to the master production schedule.

The reason that full pegging is not included as part of the Standard System is that it makes it easy to do the wrong thing. It makes it easy to go to the master production schedule and change it every time there is a problem with scrap, vendor deliveries, or production delays. This is not the way the planner should be working and in most cases it is not necessary.

The objective is to meet the master production schedule. If the plan truly cannot be made, then the master production schedule must be changed; but it should not be changed until all means to meet the schedule have been exhausted. There is no way to make sure that all methods have been exhausted unless the planner looks at and analyzes each item as he traces his way up the product structure. Many times lead times for higher level items can be compressed as a way to make up lost time due to vendor or production delays. The normal lot sizes for items can many times be split to make up for scrap or delays at the lower levels.

Single-level pegging forces the planner to step his way up the product structure one level at a time. At each level it forces the planner to look at and analyze the situation. This is the way the planner should be working and so any more automatic way to do it, like full pegging, is no advantage and only presents the opportunity for not doing the job right.

Vertical Versus Horizontal MRP Displays

Figure 21 is an example of a horizontal format. It is the most popular type of display and is seen most frequently among users of the system and also in the literature of the field. Time is divided into a series of blocks. One of the advantages in this type of display is the linear presentation of the future. The planner's eye can measure distance along the page and translate it into time without going through any calculations or conversions. The planner learns that anything on the second tier of blocks is so many weeks in the future, or that a request to move a scheduled receipt by three buckets is a request to move it three weeks.

In a vertical format only the dates that have activity are listed. Figure 40 is a vertical display listing the same information shown in Figure 39. When more than one event (gross requirement, scheduled receipt, planned order, etc.) occurs on a date, the date has as many lines as there are events. Time is no longer linear; it is disjointed and the planner will have to do some calculations to determine how far in the future the events are occurring and how much time spans any two events.

Although the presentation of time is the most significant difference between the two displays, the ability to show the details of the manufacturing events is important to a planner working with the report. A horizontal display is a summary. It gives the summary information depicting the manufacturing events in the future. By its nature it is not well suited to presenting the details. These details are typically given below the horizontal presentation or in another report. This inability to show the details is both a weakness and a strength. The summary remains uncluttered but creates the need for two displays, one for the summary and one for the details. A vertical display is ideally suited for showing the details since it lists them individually. In doing so, however, the report is crowded and sometimes hard to interpret.

The horizontal display consumes paper voraciously. The details must be listed as well as the summary information. A vertical display lists only the details and so it uses less paper. In addition, a vertical display seems to be better suited to a CRT display.

On the other hand, in a horizontal format it is almost impossible to mistake a gross requirement for a scheduled receipt, or a scheduled receipt for a planned order. Each is listed in a separate line which is labeled. In many vertical formats,

Figure 39
Horizontal MRP Display

PART NUMBER	G39056		LEAD TIME	25 DAYS
DESCRIPTION	BASE ASSEMBLY		ON HAND BALANCE	145
UNIT OF MEASURE	EACH		ALLOCATED	30
ORDER POLICY	FIXED		SAFETY STOCK	0
ORDER QUANTITY	300			

Week	Past Due	11/16/87	1/23/88	1/30/88	2/06/88
Gross Reqt		20		130	
Sched Rect					300
On Hand	115	95	95	−35	265
Planned Order		300			300

Week	2/13/88	2/20/88	2/27/88	3/05/88	3/12/88
Gross Reqt	15	400		100	300
Sched Rect					
On Hand	250	150	150	50	50
Planned Order					

Week	3/19/88	3/26/88	4/02/88	4/09/88	Totals
Gross Reqt			20		985
Sched Rect					300
On Hand	50	50	30	30	
Planned Order					600

this not the case. In many cases, the different types of orders and requirements are not separated at all. Instead, codes are used to distinguish the different types of orders and demands. The orders and demands are jammed together and resemble one another in these displays and so it is easier to confuse them.

It is possible to design a vertical format that separates the different types of orders and demands. This is the case in the example shown in Figure 40. In this report, separate columns are used to present the gross requirements, scheduled receipts, planned orders, and projected on-hand balance.

Even though there are some differences in format for the two different types of displays, both are workable and usable. Each has some advantages and disadvantages but these are mostly minor items that do not affect the use of the display.

Figure 40
Vertical MRP Display

PART NUMBER   G39056
DESCRIPTION   BASE ASSEMBLY
UNIT OF MEASURE   EACH
ORDER POLICY   FIXED
ORDER QUANTITY   300
LEAD TIME   25 DAYS
ON-HAND BALANCE   145
ALLOCATED   30
SAFETY STOCK   0

Date	Gross Reqmt	Sched Recpt	Projected on Hand	Planned Order (Due)	Details
1/16/88			115		Beginning available
1/16/88	20		95		Parent H49123
1/30/88	130		−35		Parent K30071
2/06/88		300	265		Order#39267
2/13/88	15		250		Parent I11390
2/20/88	400				Parent L34562
			150	300	Release date 1/12/84
3/05/88	100		50		Parent G11302
3/12/88	300				Parent Z42356
			50	300	Release date 2/02/84
4/02/88	20		30		Parent L11326

Report Summary

This appendix is a listing of the reports which are functional requirements in the standard system. A complete software package will have many more reports than the ones listed in this appendix. Audit listings are an example of some of these additional reports. Audit listings should be produced whenever any information in the computer files is changed. The listings should be conveniently organized and should show the information before and after the change. The reports in this appendix are the key reports. They would typically be used in the day-to-day operation of the system.

This appendix also includes report formats for the key reports. In some cases, these sample reports are fairly representative of formats found in working MRP II systems. Examples of reports with generally accepted formats are:

1. Sales and Operations Planning

2. MRP report(s).

3. Master Production Schedule report(s).

4. Daily Dispatch List.

5. Capacity Requirements Planning report(s).

6. Input/Output Control report.

7. Vendor Schedule.

Other reports included in this appendix are meant only as samples of what could be displayed. These reports (for example, the projected inventory value details and the forecast report) could be provided in any of a number of different formats showing a number of different pieces of information.

The reports are listed by the functional areas which correspond to the topics in the Standard System.

SALES AND OPERATIONS PLANNING

1. Sales and Operations Planning (Figures 41 and 42).

2. Rough-Cut Capacity Planning (Figure 46).

MASTER PRODUCTION SCHEDULING

1. MPS Report (Figure 44).

2. Rough-Cut Capacity Planning (Figure 46).

3. Lead Time Picture (Figure 47).

THE LOGIC OF MRP

1. MRP report or reports, in either a horizontal (Figure 43) or vertical format, listing the following categories of information:

   A. Time-phased picture on the item.

   B. Exception messages.

   C. Supporting details to any summary information. This includes the pegging and the details to the scheduled receipts.

2. Master schedule report (Figure 44) or reports listing the following categories of information:

   A. Time-phased master schedule picture for an item.

   B. Exception messages.

   C. Supporting details to any summary information. This includes the customer order details, the pegging if any dependent demands exist, details to any scheduled receipts, and any master schedule order details.

   D. Master schedule totals by product group (Figure 45).

3. Rough-Cut Capacity Planning report (Figure 46).

4. Lead Time Picture (Figure 47).

BILL OF MATERIAL SUBSYSTEM

1. Single-Level Bill of Material (Figure 48).

2. Multi-Level Bill of Material (Figure 49).

3. Single-Level Where-Used Listing (Figure 50).

INVENTORY TRANSACTION SUBSYSTEM

1. Cycle Count Listing (Figure 51).

2. Transaction History (Figure 52).

SCHEDULED RECEIPTS SUBSYSTEM

1. Component Availability Check (Figure 53).

2. Scheduled Receipts Status Report (Figure 54).

SHOP FLOOR CONTROL

1. Daily Dispatch List (Figure 55).

2. Manufacturing Orders Status Report (Figure 56).

CAPACITY REQUIREMENTS PLANNING

1. Summary Capacity Requirements (Figure 57).

2. Detailed Capacity Requirements (Figure 58).

3. Display by Manufacturing Family (Figure 59).

INPUT/OUTPUT CONTROL

1. Input/Output Control Report (Figure 60).

PURCHASING

1. Vendor Scheduling Report (Figure 61).

2. Vendor Negotiation Report (Figure 62).

3. Inspection Dispatch List (Figure 63).

DISTRIBUTION REQUIREMENTS PLANNING

1. Transportation Planning Report (Figure 64).

FINANCIAL PLANNING INTERFACE

1. Inventory Valuations (Figure 65).

2. Cash Flow Projections (Figure 66).

PERFORMANCE MEASUREMENT

1. Performance Measurement Report (Figure 67).

Figure 41
Production Planning Report-Make to Stock Products
Push Lawn Mowers

PRODUCT FAMILY: M350
UNIT OF MEASURE: UNITS
CURRENT INVENTORY: 435

CURRENT DATE:
1/2/88

SALES PLAN

Date	9/11/87	10/10/87	11/07/87	12/05/87	1/02//88	1/30/88	2/27/88	3/26/88	4/23/88
Planned Demand	420	450	480	500	550	550	550	550	550
Actual Demand	455	495	500	550					
Deviation	+35	+45	+20	+50					
Cum Deviation	35	80	100	150					
Customer Orders by Due Date	455	495	500	550					
Actual Shipments	455	495	500	550					

PRODUCTION PLAN

Date	9/11/87	10/10/87	11/07/87	12/05/87	1/02//88	1/30/88	2/27/88	3/26/88	4/23/88
Planned Production	500	500	500	500	550	550	550	550	550
Actual Production	450	450	460	470					
Deviation	−50	−50	−40	−30					
Cum Deviation	−50	−100	−140	−170					

INVENTORY PLAN

Date	9/11/87	10/10/87	11/07/87	12/05/87	1/02//88	1/30/88	2/27/88	3/26/88	4/23/88
Planned Inventory	685	735	755	755	435	435	435	435	435
Actual Inventory	600	555	515	435					
Deviation	−85	−180	−240	−320					

Figure 42
Production Planning Report—Make to Order Products

PRODUCT FAMILY: 0138 LIFT TRUCKS
UNIT OF MEASURE: UNITS
CURRENT BACKLOG: 448

CURRENT DATE:
1/2/88

SALES PLAN   Current

Date	9/11/87	10/10/87	11/07/87	12/05/87	1/02//88	1/30/88	2/27/88	3/26/88	4/23/88
Planned Bookings	300	300	300	300	300	300	300	300	300
Actual Bookings	300	290	305	303					
Deviation	0	−10	+5	+3					
Cum Deviation	0	−10	−5	−2					
Customer Orders by Due Date	300	300	300	300	300	148			
Actual Shipments	300	300	300	300					

PRODUCTION PLAN

Date	9/11/87	10/10/87	11/07/87	12/05/87	1/02//88	1/30/88	2/27/88	3/26/88	4/23/88
Planned Production	300	300	300	300	150	150	150	150	150
Actual Production	300	300	300	300					
Deviation	0	0	0	0					
Cum Deviation	0	0	0	0					

BACKLOG PLAN

Date	9/11/87	10/10/87	11/07/87	12/05/87	1/02//88	1/30/88	2/27/88	3/26/88	4/23/88
Planned Backlog	450	450	450	450	598	748	898	1048	1198
Actual Backlog	450	440	445	448					
Deviation	0	−10	−5	−2					

Figure 43
Time Phased MRP Display Showing Exceptions,
Pegging, and Supporting Details

ITEM NUMBER: X201   ORDER POLICY: FIXED
DESCRIPTION: THROTTLE PLATE   ORDER QUANTITY: 150
UNIT OF MEASURE: EACH   LEAD TIME: 5 DAYS
ON-HAND BALANCE; 200   SCRAP FACTOR: 0
ALLOCATED: 0
SAFETY STOCK: 0

	Past	1/02	1/09	1/16	1/23	1/30
Gross Requirements		200	100	50	50	50
Sched Receipts		150				
Projected OH	200	150	50	0	100	50
Planned Orders				150		

Pegging			
Date	Quantity	Parent	Type
1/02	100	N1222	GR.REQ.
1/02	100	M1515	GR.REQ.
1/09	100	N1222	GR.REQ.
1/16	50	L3664	GR.REQ.
1/23	50	M1222	GR.REQ.
1/30	50	L3664	GR.REQ.

Order Details			
Date	Quantity	Type	Order#
1/02	150	Sched. Rec.	10595

Exceptions			
Message	Order#	From Date	To Date
Reschedule Out	10595	1/02	1/09

Figure 44
Master Production Schedule

ITEM: M472312 22 INCH ROTARY MOWER
PRODUCT GROUP: M12 SELF PROPELLED MOWERS
ON HAND: 200

	Past	1/02	1/09	1/16	1/23	1/30	2/06	2/13	2/20	2/27
Sales Forecast		30	50	50	50	50	50	50	50	50
Customer Orders		20								
Exploded Demand				340		200				
Master Schedule				500			500			
Projected Available	200	150	100	210	160	−90	360	310	260	210
Available to Promise		140		0			500			

Pegging			
Date	Quantity	Type	Order#/ Location
1/02	5	Cust. Ord.	29362
1/02	15	Cust. Ord.	29349
1/16	200	Br. Whse.	San Fran.
1/16	140	Interplant	Dallas
1/30	200	Br. Whse.	New York

Order Details			
Date	Quantity	Type	Order#
1/16	500	MPS	12957
2/06	500	MPS	13692

Exceptions			
Type	Order#	From Date	To Date
Reschedule In	13692	2/06	1/30

Figure 45
Master Schedule Totals by
Product Group

PRODUCT GROUP: M12 SELF PROPELLED MOWERS
ON HAND: 2200

	Past	1/02	1/09	1/16	1/23	1/30	2/06	2/13	2/20	2/27
Sales Forecast		330	550	550	550	550	550	550	550	550
Customer Orders		220								
Exploded Demand		240	120	340	300	310	200	150	0	90
Master Schedule		500	500	500	500	500	500	500	500	500
Projected Available	2200	1910	1740	1350	1000	640	390	190	140	0
Available to Promise		2240	380	160	200	190	300	350	500	410

Figure 46
Rough-Cut Capacity Requirements Plan

RESOURCE: 615 SUBASSEMBLY LABOR HOURS
NORMAL CAPACITY: 6000 STANDARD HOURS/MONTH

Date	1/02/88	1/30/88	2/27/88	3/26/88
Resource Requirements	5250	7800	4139	5043
Four Period Average	5558			

Date	4/23/88	5/21/88	6/18/88	7/16/88
Resource Requirements	3750	4240	5110	3800
Four Period Average	4225			

Date	8/13/88	9/10/88	10/8/88	11/5/88
Resource Requirements	3100	5100	2700	4200
Four Period Average	3775			

Date	12/3/88
Resource Requirements	5200
Four Period Average	

Figure 47
Lead Time Picture

PARENT ITEM: M472312 22-INCH ROTARY MOWER

Components	Lead Time	Accumulated Lead Time
. M42215	10	10
. M41173	5	5
. . D87151	6	11
. . . F11249	5	16
. . . G98711	7	18
. . . . H87879	6	24
. . E00011	7	12
. 071835	5	5
. Q20591	8	8
. R97232	5	5

Figure 48

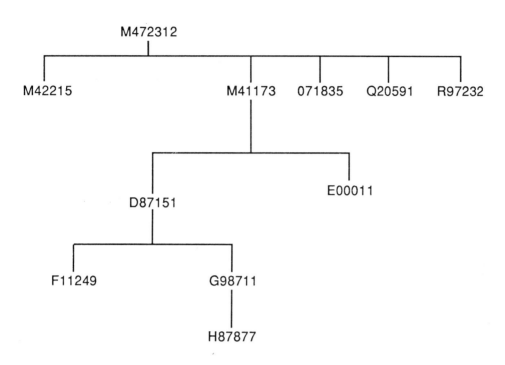

SINGLE LEVEL BILL OF MATERIAL

PARENT ITEM NUMBER: **M472312**   UNIT OF MEASURE: EACH

Components	Quantity Per	Unit of Measure	Effectivity Dates From	To
. M42215	1.000	Each		
. M41173	2.000	Each	3/15/87	3/15/88
. 071835	2.000	Each	3/16/88	
. Q20591	1.000	Each		
. R97232	1.000	Each		

Figure 49
Multi-Level Bill of Material

PARENT PART: M472312
UNIT OF MEASURE: EACH

Components	Quantity Per Assembly	Unit of Measure
. M42215	1.0000	Each
. M41173	2.0000	Each
. . D87151	1.0000	Each
. . . F11249	1.0000	Each
. . . G98711	4.0000	Each
. . . . H87879	3.2000	Lbs
. . E00011	4.6000	Yards
. 071835	2.0000	Each
. Q20591	1.0000	Each
. R97232	1.0000	Each

Figure 50
Single-Level Where-Used Listing

COMPONENT ITEM NUMBER: G98711
UNIT OF MEASURE: EACH

Parents	Quantity Per	Unit of Measure	Effectivity Dates From	To
D87151	4.0000	Each		
C19752	2.0000	Each		
C19668	4.0000	Each		
M11871	2.0000	Each		
M97837	2.0000	Each		

Figure 51
Cycle Count Listing

ITEMS TO BE COUNTED BY 1/06/88

Item Number	Description	Location		Count
M472312	22-inch rotary mower	2004-001	Finished goods	—
		2012-012	Finished goods	—
Q71855	22-inch blade	1001-111	Main stores	—
		1010-110	Main stores	—
R97232	Housing	1910-150	Main stores	—
		1890-110	Main stores	—
		1440-110	Main stores	—

Figure 52
Transaction History

Item Number	Transaction	Date/Time	Quantity	Location	Location Bal. Before	After	On Hand Before	After
071835	22-inch blade							
	Planned receipt (complete) —P.O.1595	12/19/87:8.01	600	1010-110	1000	1600	1000	1600
	Planned issue (partial) —M.O.16420	12/19/87:10.52	300	1010-110	1600	1300	1600	1300
	Unplanned issue —M.O.15400	12/20/87:9.30	100	1010-110	1300	1200	1300	1200
	Planned issue (complete) —M.O.16420	12/23/87:12.41	200	1010-110	1200	1000	1200	1000
	Planned receipt (partial) —P.O.1610	12/26/87:9.50	500	1001-111	0	500	1000	1500

Figure 53
Component Availability Check

ITEM NUMBER: M472312   22-INCH MOWER
ORDER DUE DATE: 1/16/88
ORDER QUANTITY: 500

Component	Description	Required	On Hand	Alloc	Avail	Message
M42215	Briggs & Stratton eng.	500	800	300	500	
M41173	Rear wheels	1000	1200	400	800	Short
071855	Front wheels	1000	1500	0	1500	
Q20591	22-inch blade	500	500	0	500	
R97232	Housing assy	500	875	215	600	

Figure 54
Scheduled Receipts Status Report

Item Number	Description	Order Number	Quantity Open	Ordered	Due Date	Order Status	Vendor/ Work Center
M75761	Blade assy	11850	720	750	1/16	Picked	WC:6033
N64582	Base assy	12860	169	526	1/18	Running	WC:9050
Q11759	Swivel	13910	0	500	1/16	Complete	
R19957	Shield	14810	50	50	1/17	Not started	Stock

Figure 55
Daily Dispatch List

WORK CENTER: 3001 PUNCH PRESS
TODAY'S DATE: 1/16/88
PRIORITY: OPERATION DUE DATE

Item #	Order #	Operation #	Operation Description	Operation Dates Start	Operation Dates Due	Order Due Date	Hours Set Up	Hours Run	Qty. REM	Prev Op #	Prev Op W/C	Next Op #	Next Op W/C

JOBS AT THIS WORK CENTER

L930	1326	10	Punch	1/11/88	1/13/88	1/30/88	.0	4.0	1500	—	—	20	4510
K421	2937	10	Punch	1/12/88	1/13/88	1/27/88	2.0	6.0	2000	—	—	20	4775
D430	2561	10	Punch	1/17/88	1/18/88	1/23/88	1.0	1.0	500	10	3000	20	4510
N862	3817	20	Punch	1/19/88	1/20/88	1/24/88	.5	3.5	1000	—	—	20	4000
G315	4123	10	Punch	1/26/88	1/27/88	2/15/88	.5	3.5	1200	—	—	15	4100

JOBS COMING TO THIS WORK CENTER IN THE NEXT 3 DAYS

| K319 | 2497 | 15 | Punch | 1/17/88 | 1/18/88 | 1/27/88 | 1.0 | 3.0 | 800 | | Stock | 20 | 4510 |
| B412 | 3515 | 20 | Punch | 1/17/88 | 1/20/88 | 2/08/88 | 2.0 | 20.0 | 10,000 | 10 | 3000 | 30 | 9500 |

Figure 56
Manufacturing Order Status Report

ITEM NUMBER: M472311   SELF-PROPELLED MOWER
ORDER NUMBER: 16940   STATUS: STARTED
DUE DATE: 1/12/88   QUANTITY: 50

Operation	Description	Work Center	Schedule Dates Start	Schedule Dates Due	Remaining Hours Setup	Remaining Hours Run	Quantity Complete	Status
10	Serialize	6337	1/07/88	1/08/88	1.00	.7	0	In queue
20	Assemble	6543	1/08/88	1/10/88	.50	13.1	0	
25	Balance	9500	1/09/88	1/11/88	.50	9.3	0	
30	Pack	9503	1/10/88	1/11/88	.00	3.4	0	

Figure 57
Capacity Requirements Plan

WORK CENTER: 3001 PUNCH PRESS
NORMAL CAPACITY: 37 STANDARD HOURS/WEEK

Week	Past Due	1/16/88	1/23/88	1/30/88	2/06/88
Capacity Requirements	12	32	26	30	16
Four Week Average		29			

Week	2/13/88	2/20/88	2/27/88	3/05/88	3/12/88
Capacity Requirements	9	50	25	16	60
Four Week Average	25				43

Week	3/19/88	3/26/88	4/02/88	4/09/88	4/16/88
Capacity Requirements	52	45	15	37	32
Four Week Average				32	

Week	4/23/88	4/30/88	5/7/88	5/14/88	5/21/88
Capacity Requirements	28	31	20	36	30
Four Week Average			29		

Week	5/28/88
Capacity Requirements	20
Four Week Average	

Figure 58
Capacity Requirements Planning Details

WORK CENTER: 3001 PUNCH PRESS
DEPARTMENT: 633

Week	Hours	Operation	Quantity	Item #
1/09/88	4	10	200	L930
1/09/88	8	10	400	K421
	12			
1/16/88	2	10	190	D430
1/16/88	4	20	300	N862
1/16/88	4	15	250	K319
1/16/88	22	20	1800	B412
	32			
1/23/88	14	10	900	C692
1/23/88	2	10	400	K361
1/23/88	4	10	500	G315
1/23/88	6	20	630	F410
	26			

Figure 59
Orders By Manufacturing Family

FAMILY: 015 LEGS & POSTS - EARLY FRANCIS

	Weeks								
Item Number	1/16	1/23	1/30	2/06	2/13	2/20	2/27	3/05	3/12
2416 Cherry Post		1000							
5639 Walnut Post								1200	
3931 Pine Post					2100				
8420 Oak Post									
6420 Cherry Leg								900	
2175 Walnut Leg		1600							
9806 Pine Leg		800							
1248 Oak Leg								1000	

Figure 60
Input/Output Control Report

WORK CENTER   3001 PUNCH PRESS   **PLANNED QUEUE**   28 HOURS
TOLERANCE   10 HOURS   **ACTUAL QUEUE**   28 HOURS

	← ——————————— Past			Current Week	Future ——————→	
Week	*12/20/87*	*12/27/87*	*1/02/88*	*1/09/88*	*1/16/88*	*1/23/88*
Planned Input	39	20	16	32	26	30
Actual Input	32	29	14			
Cumulative Deviation	−7	+2	0			

Planned Output	37	37	37	37	37	37
Actual Output	35	40	32			
Cumulative Deviation	−2	+1	−4			

Planned Queue	66	49	28	23	12	5
Actual Queue	57	46	28			
Deviation	−9	−3	0			

Figure 61
Vendor Schedule

VENDOR: 1540 ACME AND CO.
VENDOR SCHEDULER: A. GRAY
BUYER: A. FARRAGHER

SCHEDULING HORIZON INFORMATION:
FIRM ZONE — FIRST 4 WEEKS
MATERIAL COMMITMENT ZONE - NEXT 6 WEEKS

Item#/ Description	Order Detail	Past Due 1/16/88	Week of 1/23/88	Week of 1/30/88	Week of 2/06/88	Week of 2/13/88	Week of 2/20/88	Month of 2/27/88	Month of 3/26/88	Qtr of 4/23/88
F11249	Quantity: Order#:		100 Q1178				100	100	300	200
H87877	Quantity: Order#:	20 P1178	20 P1178	20 P1435	20 P1510	20	20	80	80	80
M42215	Quantity: Order#:		300 P1435		500 P1510			1100		3500
R97232	Quantity: Order#:			40 P1619			200			

Figure 62
Vendor Negotiation Report—Purchase Orders Due for Release in the Next 12 Weeks

4/2/88
NEGOTIATOR LANE

Part Number	Planned Order Quantity	Yearly Planned Order Total	Planned Order Release Date	Cost/100	Variance	Projected Yearly Purchases	Projected Yearly Variance
G391	3,000	30,000	4/29/88	$60.00	$9.00	$1,800,000	$270,000
K392	1,500	12,000	5/3/88	70.00	3.00	840,000	36,000
L138	10,000	100,000	4/7/88	8.00	.50	800,000	50,000

Figure 63
Inspection Dispatch List

WORK CENTER: 9890 INCOMING INSPECTION
TODAY'S DATE: 1/16/88
PRIORITY: OPERATION DUE DATE

Item #	Order #	Operation #	Operation Description	Operation Dates Start	Due	Order Due Date	Hours Set Up	Run	Qty. REM	Prev Op #	W/C	Next Op #	W/C
JOBS AT THIS WORK CENTER												
Q20591	15408	10	Inspect	1/15/88	1/16/88	1/16/88		4.0	1000	—	—		Stock
E00011	15408	10	Inspect	1/18/88	1/19/88	1/20/88		8.0	2000	—	—		Whse
M42215	17101	10	Inspect	1/17/88	1/20/88	1/23/88		17.0	5000	—	—		Whse
JOBS COMING TO THIS WORK CENTER IN THE NEXT 3 DAYS												
R97232	17101	10	Inspect	1/17/88	1/20/88	1/20/88		17.0	5000	—	—		Stock
H87877	19652	10	Inspect	1/18/88	1/23/88	1/23/88		18.0	6000	—	—		Stock

Figure 64
Transportation Planning Report

Week	Distribution Center	Number of Pallets	Weight	Cube
1/02	Atlanta	190	780,000	19,600
1/09	Atlanta	160	680,000	16,080
1/16	Atlanta	220	840,000	21,460
1/23	Atlanta	196	810,000	20,760
1/30	Atlanta	200	784,000	20,120

Figure 65
Projected Inventory Value
$(000)

Date	Manufactured Parts	Purchased Parts	Raw Mat'l	Work-in-Process	Finished Goods	Total
Current	1,952	581	175	666	190	3,564
1/02/88	1,621	514	159	969	200	3,463
1/30/88	1,495	472	158	854	195	3,174
2/27/88	1,427	448	154	831	190	3,050
3/26/88	1,413	439	149	820	189	3,010
4/23/88	1,397	401	135	798	185	2,916
5/21/88	1,395	400	135	797	180	2,907
6/18/88	1,350	375	140	766	179	2,810
7/16/88	1,314	365	136	746	176	2,737
8/13/88	1,279	355	132	726	173	2,665
9/10/88	1,243	345	128	706	170	2,592
10/8/88	1,190	335	124	686	165	2,500
11/5/88	1,156	325	120	667	160	2,428
12/3/88	1,139	316	117	648	156	2,376

Figure 66
Cash Flow Information from MRPII $(000)

Period of	Purchased Material	Cash Disbursements		Variable Overhead	Cash Receipts
		Direct Labor			
		Normal	Overtime		
1/02	3,300	900	200	30	6,200
2/06	3,140	750	150	22	5,990
3/06	3,140	875	125	30	6,500
4/03	3,010	875	100	33	6,310
5/01	2,915	875	40	28	6,358

Figure 67
Performance Measurement Report

MRP II performance
Period beginning 1/02/88   Ending 1/08/88

Inventory record accuracy

   Number of counts: 1500
   Number of counts within item tolerance: 1470
   Inventory record accuracy: 98%

Master production schedule delivery performance

   Number of MPS orders received: 17
   Number of orders received on time ($\pm$ X days): 16
   Master schedule delivery performance: 94.1%

Shop delivery performance

   Number of shop orders received: 140
   Number received on time ($\pm$ X days): 135
   Shop delivery performance: 96.4%

Purchase order delivery performance

   Number of purchase orders received: 620
   Number received on time ($\pm$ X days): 602
   Purchase order delivery performance: 97.1%

Modular Bills of Material

This appendix is a short explanation of some of the reasons for using modular bills of material rather than using a transaction like the same-as-except transaction. Extensive use of the same-as-except transaction means that a large number of bills of material are being constructed with similar characteristics. While it would be possible to continue to construct these bills of material this way, there are some advantages in using what are called modular bills of material.

Modular bills of material are a way to break a product down into logical groupings of items. For example, an automobile would be broken down into the basic car, the engine (of which several are available), the transmission (of which several are available), a number of accessories like an accessory trim package, a vinyl roof, a radio which could be AM only, AM/FM, or AM/FM/stereo with tape deck, etc. The objective here is to break the automobile down in the logical groupings rather than taking a bill of material and crossing items off and adding other items.

There are a number of advantages to this method but the most important are that modular bills of material allow much better forecasting, master production scheduling, and general planning and execution of the plan. In forecasting, it is much easier to forecast how many cars are likely to be sold and what percentages are likely to have V-8 engines, V-6 engines, automatic transmissions, manual transmissions, AM/FM radios, etc. It is nearly impossible to forecast the number of cars that will have a V-8 engine, an automatic transmission, an AM/FM radio, the accessory trim package, and white sidewall tires and then to forecast the number of cars that will have a V-6 engine, an automatic transmission, an AM radio, the special interior, etc. Forecasting these combinations of customer choices is nearly impossible. However, forecasting a percentage for each choice is a manageable task.

The same problems that make it hard to forecast these combinations of customer choices make it difficult to master schedule these combinations. It makes more sense to master schedule the options like engines, transmissions, radios, and trim packages. Then as customer orders come in, the engines, transmissions, etc. can be assigned to specific customer orders.

As a result of this improved ability to master schedule, the planning and execution of the plan will be much better. By planning the options that are likely to be sold and by adjusting the plan based on the actual sales, the ability to have the options that the customer wants are greatly improved. Instead of being constantly surprised by the customer orders, some problem solving can be done before the fact.

There are also a number of other reasons for using modular bills of material. One of these is that the task of maintaining the bills of material is much simpler using modular bills. The only bills that have to be maintained are the modules. There is no need to maintain enormous numbers of unique product configurations that are not likely to recur in the future.

Appendix 14
Low-Level Code Logic

This appendix is an explanation of why most low-level code logic will increase the low-level code for an item, but generally will not decrease the low-level code. For example, if an item has a low-level code which is three levels down from the top of the product structure, and a change is made so that the item is now four levels from the top; then low-level code logic will increase the low-level code from three to four. However, if the change were then reversed (either because the original change was an error, or the bills of material have been changed again) most systems would leave the low-level code at four and not reset it to three.

This logic does not create an error in MRP processing and it does simplify the computer logic for maintaining low-level codes. It does not create an error because it holds items out of MRP planning longer than needed. The purpose of low-level codes is to hold items out of MRP planning until all gross requirements have been posted to the item. Once all gross requirements have been posted, it doesn't make any difference when the item is planned. Holding the item out of planning longer than would be absolutely necessary does not create a problem since all gross requirements have been posted.

Disassembly, Sorting, and Chemical Processes

This appendix is an explanation of capabilities to assist in scheduling disassembly, refining, sorting and grading operations, and chemical production with by-products. All of these situations are somewhat different from the normal situation where one or more components come together to create a parent item. This is because in companies with these kinds of operations, producing one item creates several by-products, or as an item is torn down, it yields several other items. As a result, some additional capabilities are needed for planning and scheduling both material and capacity in a company with significant amounts of disassembly, refining, sorting, and chemical production with by-products.

In this explanation of disassembly, refining, sorting, and chemical processes, a number of different terms are used that need definition:

1. Core: an assembly that will be torn down to create several other item numbers.

2. Yielded items: the items that are created by disassembling a core, or taking an unsorted production lot of parts and grading them into a number of different items, or refining a raw material to result in various chemicals. In effect, the yielded items are the ones that result from pulling another item from stock and disassembling, grading, or refining it.

3. By-products: the different items that are created as a result of producing another item. These items are the ones created as a result of a production process like chemical production. By-products could also result from a fermentation process or some types of sorting and grading operations. In effect, by-products result from a production process rather than a disassembly process.

The remainder of this appendix is split into two parts, and covers the situations where:

1. A manually set and maintained schedule exists for pulling an item from stock and disassembling, grading, or refining it into a number of other items.

2. There is a primary item that is produced and scheduled using the normal logic

of MRP, and where the company is willing to accept all the by-products that result from the primary production.

The first method, where the schedule is manually set and maintained, could be used to support the scheduling of disassembly, refining, and (in some companies) sorting and grading operations. In this method, the scheduled receipts of yielded items would be based on pulling an item (in this case a core, unsorted item, or raw material) from stock and tearing it down, grading it, or "cracking" it into a number of other items. In effect, the scheduled receipts would be predicted from a separate disassembly schedule.

The second method, where there is a primary item that is produced and scheduled using the normal logic of MRP and where the company is willing to accept any by-products that result from the normal production, would typically handle chemical processes with by-products and some sorting and grading operations. In this method there would be a primary item, say a specific chemical or type of semiconductor chip, that is scheduled and where the by-products result from the production of the primary item. Since the planned orders for the primary item are a simulation of the future production of the primary item, in this method, the by-products would be predicted from any planned orders for the primary item.

METHOD 1: ITEMS YIELDED FROM DISASSEMBLY OPERATIONS

In a company with disassembly, refining, and some types of sorting operations, the disassembly, refining, or sorting schedule represents taking an item from stock and tearing it down, "cracking" it, or grading it into a number of different items. For example, in a disassembly operation, a core (a used copying machine, for example) is pulled from stock and disassembled into component parts. In a refining operation, a raw material (crude oil, for example), is cracked to yield gasoline, diesel fuel, etc. In some sorting operations, an unsorted or "neuter" item (an ungraded semiconductor, for example) is taken from stock and graded based on electronic characteristics. This grading process results in the item being relabeled into several other item numbers. In each of these cases, a material is purchased or produced, put into stock, then pulled from stock for the disassembly process.

An example of an MRP display for an item that is disassembled to yield a number of other items is shown in Figure 68. For the item which is disassembled, the scheduled receipts and planned orders in MRP are the additional quantities of the item that have to be purchased (or manufactured) and put into stock. The disassembly schedule for the item is different and represents the quantity that will be taken from stock for disassembly, refining or sorting.

For this reason, the disassembly or refining schedule is shown as a separate type of schedule in the system. Since it is a schedule of when things should be removed from stock, it would be treated as a type of requirement (it reduces the on-hand balance). This way the normal logic of MRP can compare the disassembly schedule with the purchasing schedule, manufacturing schedule, or anticipated returns for the item to generate exception messages and additional planned

Figure 68
Disassembly Scheduling

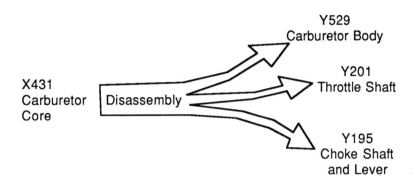

MRP DISPLAY
SHOWING DISASSEMBLY
SCHEDULE

ITEM NUMBER: X431   CARBURETOR CORE
ON HAND: 75

	Past	1/02	1/09	1/16	1/23	1/30
Disassembly Sched		150			150	
Sched Receipts			200		200	
Projected OH	75	−75	125	125	175	175
Planned Orders						

Exceptions			
Message	Order#	From Date	To Date
Reschedule In	12990	1/09	1/02

orders. These planned orders represent the additional quantities of the item that need to be purchased or produced to support disassembly.

In the example shown in Figure 68, the disassembly schedule for cores is shown as a separate type of requirement on the MRP display. The logic of MRP works in the normal way. The disassembly schedule is netted against the on-hand balance and scheduled receipts.

Exception messages are produced for scheduled receipts that need to be rescheduled to earlier or later dates. In addition, planned orders will be created to cover the additional cores that need to be purchased to support the disassembly schedule.

In a company with disassembly, refining, or sorting operations, the scheduled receipts for the yielded items also have to be shown in MRP. These yielded items are put back into stock as a result of the disassembly schedule (tearing down a core, refining a raw material, sorting and grading). Consequently, it's important to show the scheduled receipts for all of these items in MRP. Otherwise, MRP may ask for additional items to be purchased or manufactured, when these items are not really needed at all.

These scheduled receipts can be computed through some special explosion logic in the system. This logic explodes the disassembly schedule against the disassembly bill of material to compute scheduled receipt quantities for each yielded item. These scheduled receipts would be posted against the yielded items. Since the disassembly schedule is maintained manually, and not developed in the logic of MRP, the explosion of the disassembly schedule into scheduled receipts can be done outside of the normal MRP logic in the system. In most situations, the easiest way to do this would be to post the scheduled receipts prior to the netting and order planning logic of MRP.

Once the scheduled receipts have been posted, MRP would treat them just like normal scheduled receipts. Gross requirements coming from sales or the use of the item in higher level assemblies would be netted against the on-hand balance and scheduled receipts. Exception messages would be generated for scheduled receipts that should be rescheduled to earlier dates as well as for scheduled receipts that should be rescheduled to later dates. Planned orders would then be generated to cover any unsatisfied gross requirements.

In most cases, the scheduled receipts coming from disassembly would carry an identifier showing this. In the example shown in Figure 69, scheduled receipts for items yielded from the disassembly schedule are shown as normal scheduled receipts in the time-phased MRP display. However, in the section of the report displaying the details of scheduled receipts, these orders are identified as coming from disassembly.

For many companies it might also make sense to add some additional logic to process or consolidate certain rescheduling exception messages for scheduled receipts resulting from a disassembly schedule. In most situations, a planner would not change the disassembly schedule because of excess inventory on one of the yielded items. Yet if all the items had excess inventory, a planner might want to reschedule the disassembly operation to a later date. In other situations, like in cracking crude oil to yield gasoline, etc., it may be possible for the planner to change the process to yield different quantities of each product, provided the planner can identify the exceptions on all the yielded items. Finally, unless a method is provided to see all the exception messages on the related scheduled receipts, a planner could spend significant amount of effort pegging back to the disassembly schedule, checking each item number to see whether there are exception messages on related scheduled receipts, and determining whether it is possible to make the reschedule. For instance, in the simple example shown in Figure 70 (disassembly schedule for a carburetor core and three of the yielded items) a planner would have to check all four items to determine whether it is possible to

Figure 69
Disassembly Scheduling

MRP DISPLAY FOR YIELDED ITEM

ITEM NUMBER: Y529   CARBURETOR BODY
ON HAND: 200

	Past	1/02	1/09	1/16	1/23	1/30
Gross Requirements		200	100	50	50	50
Sched Receipts		150			150	
Projected OH	200	150	50	0	100	50
Planned Order						

Pegging			
Date	Quantity	Parent	Type
1/02	100	N1220	GR REQT
1/02	100	M1514	GR REQT
1/09	100	N1220	GR REQT
1/16	50	L3665	GR REQT
1/23	50	M1220	GR REQT
1/30	50	L3665	GR REQT

Order Details			
Date	Quantity	Type	Order#
1/02	150	From Disassy of Item X431	10590
1/23	150	From Disassy of Item 431	10600

Exceptions			
Message	Order#	From Date	To Date
Reschedule Out	10590	1/02	1/09

change the disassembly schedule because of excess inventory on the first yielded item.

Consequently, a good solution would be to create some special logic to sort and consolidate the exception messages for related scheduled receipts. In this logic, the exception messages would be listed twice: once grouped together for all the by-products and listed for each disassembly order, and once listed in the normal way for each by-products. An example of how these exceptions could be grouped by disassembly order is shown in Figure 71.

This way, a planner can review the time-phased display of the disassembly schedule and also see all exceptions on scheduled receipts for the yielded items. If need be, he can go to the time-phased display for each of these items and review the situation on each of them. This method provides visibility into the system and allows the planner to see the picture on both the disassembly schedule and the individual items that are yielded without having a major research project.

Figure 70
Disassembly Scheduling

MRP DISPLAY FOR CORE:

ITEM NUMBER: X431 CARBURETOR CORE
ON HAND: 75

	Past	1/02	1/09	1/16	1/23	1/30
Disassembly Sched		150			150	
Sched Receipts			200		200	
Projected OH	75	−75	125	125	175	175
Planned Orders						

Exceptions			
Message	Order#	From Date	To Date
Reschedule In	12990	1/09	1/02

MRP DISPLAYS FOR YIELDED ITEMS:

ITEM NUMBER: Y529 CARBURETOR BODY
ON HAND: 200

	Past	1/02	1/09	1/16	1/23	1/30
Gross Requirements		200	100	50	50	50
Sched Receipts		150			150	
Projected OH	200	150	50	0	100	50
Planned Orders						

Exceptions			
Message	Order#	From Date	To Date
Reschedule Out	10590-1	1/02	1/09

ITEM NUMBER: Y201   THROTTLE SHAFT
ON HAND: 125

	Past	1/02	1/09	1/16	1/23	1/30
Gross Requirements		100	50	50	50	150
Sched Receipts		150			150	
Projected OH	125	175	125	75	175	25
Planned Orders						

Exceptions			
Message	Order#	From Date	To Date
Reschedule Out	1059-2	1/02	1/09
Reschedule Out	1165-2	1/23	1/30

ITEM NUMBER: Y195 CHOKE SHAFT AND LEVER
ON HAND: 125

	Past	1/02	1/09	1/16	1/23	1/30
Gross Requirements		100	100	100	50	50
Sched Receipts		150			150	
Projected OH	125	175	75	−25	75	25
Planned Orders						

Exceptions			
Message	Order#	From Date	To Date
Reschedule Out	1059-3	1/02	1/09
Reschedule In	1065-3	1/23	1/16

Deleting Planned Orders at the Time of Order Release

The logical and technically correct thing to do when a planned order is released is to find and delete the planned order. In a bucketless system, the order might be found and the same physical record changed in status from planned to released.

While finding the planned order may be the correct thing to do, it is by no means necessary in certain situations. A regenerative system destroys all planned orders at the beginning of the next planning run. Finding and deleting planned orders at the time of order release provides little benefit since all the planned orders will be deleted anyway.

In a net change system, the planned orders are not erased before each replanning run. Therefore, it would appear that the planned orders must be found as they are released into scheduled receipts. Actually, this is not necessary. The new scheduled receipt could be entered into the files without finding or deleting the planned order. As a result of adding this order, the item will be entered into the planning sequence for net change replanning. The netting and order planning logic in the net change run will move any existing planned orders to the dates they are needed. The planned order which would have been released is therefore moved to the date of the next unsatisfied requirement (which in most cases will correspond to the date of the next planned order). In effect, the planned orders are rearranged based on the new scheduled receipt and the last planned order will probably be pushed off the end of the planning horizon and deleted. While this is workable, it is not the best thing to do. Letting the planned orders trade places like this loses any identity that may have been attached to each. In many systems this is not a problem since planned orders do not have an identity. However, some systems do have planned orders with identifying information like an order number, the fact that the planned order is using a special or substitute bill of material, or a special quantity. In these cases, the identity would become confused with the next order and could cause problems. Such systems must find and delete the planned orders as they are released.

In systems where planned orders are found, the gross requirements may require updating. The logical thing to do if a planned order is found and deleted is to find and update the component gross requirements. But this is not always necessary. In a regenerative system, all gross requirements are destroyed with each replanning run and it makes little difference whether they are updated or not. In a net change system the gross requirements are not deleted. The only time they are changed is when the planned orders are altered. Therefore in a net change system, the component gross requirements must be found and updated only if the planned orders are deleted. If the planned orders are not found and deleted, the component gross requirements do not have to be updated. This will be done as part of the next net change replanning run when the planned orders are rearranged.

Alternative Method for Final Assembly Scheduling

This appendix is an explanation of an alternate method for handling final assembly scheduling. Final assembly scheduling is the process of converting a customer order stated in terms of modules and other groupings of parts into a shop order for a specific product. In effect, a final assembly schedule order provides a way to build a product to the customer's specification.

Final assembly scheduling is the capability for handling scheduled receipts for products made-to-order from a number of options. These products (for example, automobiles) are made from a number of modules or options, some of which can be actual subassemblies, others of which are just logical groupings of parts. The logical groupings of parts can't physically be assembled, but instead must be put together with the components of other modules and options to create a number of different subassemblies. In this type of product, the modules that are subassemblies are often built in advance and stocked. The modules that are logical groupings of parts are not, and in some cases cannot be, assembled and stocked. Instead the master production schedule for this type of option is the way to get matched sets of component parts in stock, in anticipation of the final assembly process.

The main goal of final assembly scheduling is to put a shop order and a picking list onto the final assembly floor for use in building a specific product. In addition, there are some requirements for a type of bookkeeping logic to keep the numbers in the master production scheduling system in balance.

There are several ways to achieve these objectives:

1. Convert each customer order to a type of scheduled receipt.

2. Create a specific item number and bill of material for the final assembly and then create a scheduled receipt for this item.

Chapter 14 in the Standard System (Scheduled Receipt Subsystem) explains the final assembly scheduling method where each customer order is converted to a type of scheduled receipt. In this method, the customer order number is a unique identifier, and the line items on the customer order are a type of bill of material. At the time the final product is to be produced, the customer order goes through a process of component availability checking, authorization, and allocation of components. In effect, the customer order is converted to a scheduled receipt for the product, and allocations for the components. Shop paperwork, including a picking list showing all the components that need to be picked and a shop routing, is created. When this method is used, one final assembly order exists for each customer order.

Another way to handle final assembly scheduling is to create a specific item number and bill of material for the final assembly. At the time the final assembly schedule is created, the customer order would be converted to an item number and bill of material for the product. This new bill of material would list each line item on the customer order. Then a scheduled receipt can be created for the finished item number. In addition, when the scheduled receipt is created, the customer order would be changed over to the specific item number, and both the scheduled receipt and the customer order would exist in terms of the specific product, rather than in terms of the options.

In this approach to final assembly scheduling, the mechanics of releasing a final assembly schedule order has two parts:

1. Checking component availability using the customer order as the bill of material.

2. Creating a unique item and bill of material, releasing the order, and some bookkeeping to keep the customer orders (demands) offset by master schedule orders (production orders).

The first step in releasing the final assembly order is the component availability check. This logic is similar to the normal component check logic with one exception. In the component check logic prior to creating the final assembly order, the line items on the customer order would be used as the bill of material.

If all the components are available, or if the master scheduler chooses to override the component check, the final assembly order is ready for release. The process of releasing the order would be to create an item number (unique identifier) and bill of material matching the line items on the customer order. Then a scheduled receipt for the unique item would be created, components allocated, and the shop paperwork produced. Creating a scheduled receipt, allocating components, and producing shop paperwork would be done in the normal manner and along the lines of the explanation in the Standard System.

However, this method, like the method where the customer order is used as the final assembly order, requires some additional bookkeeping logic for the pseudo or phantom options. For these items, master schedule orders still exist in the system, and are being exploded into requirements as a way to schedule the correct components. Once the final assembly order is released, these same components are allocated to a scheduled receipt.

Consequently, continuing to explode the master schedule orders for the options into gross requirements for the components would create duplicate requirements. As a result, part of the logic in the order release process for final assembly orders would be to find the master schedule orders for the options and delete them.

Once these master schedule orders are deleted from the master scheduling system, the system must also delete the old customer order and the customer order line items from the master scheduling system. Otherwise, the customer order (demand) is not offset by a matching master schedule order (supply), causing a misleading picture on the options. Once the master scheduler authorizes the final assembly, customer order information and the product configuration only exist in the final assembly schedule. This information would not be part of the master scheduling system and would not be shown in the master production schedule report for the product options.

Updating Component Requirements in Firm Planned Order Maintenance

In most regenerative systems, the firm planned order maintenance system does not have to be concerned with the component gross requirements. It is enough to simply update the firm planned orders and not provide any maintenance to the component gross requirements. The gross requirements for firm planned orders and planned orders are destroyed at the beginning of each planning run. During the order planning and explosion logic, new component gross requirements are generated and exploded for both planned and firm planned orders.

In many net change systems, on the other hand, gross requirements are updated only when a planned order or firm planned order is changed. The gross requirements are not destroyed at the beginning of the planning run. The planned orders in a net change system are changed by the logic of MRP. The planned order explosion logic then finds and updates the component gross requirements.

Since firm planned orders are not changed in the logic of MRP, another method must be provided to update component gross requirements coming from firm planned orders. One way to do this would be to provide special explosion logic that finds and maintains these gross requirements. Another more common method is to update these gross requirements through the firm planned order maintenance system. The logic to update these gross requirements is exactly the same as the explosion logic in MRP. Adding a firm planned order is handled in the same way as creating a planned order, changing a firm planned order uses the same logic as changing a planned order, and deleting a firm planned order is like deleting a planned order.